GINTERMEDIATE Business

Linda Daniel, Julia Joslin, Karen McCafferty,
Linda Porter and Amanda Thomas

with contributions by
Alec Main and Christine Woodrow

Nelson

Thomas Nelson and Sons Ltd
Nelson House Mayfield Road
Walton-on-Thames Surrey
KT12 5PL UK

Thomas Nelson Australia
102 Dodds Street
South Melbourne
Victoria 3205 Australia

Nelson Canada
1120 Birchmount Road
Scarborough Ontario
M1K 5G4 Canada

© Linda Daniel, Julia Joslin, Karen McCafferty, Linda Porter,
Amanda Thomas 1996

First published by Thomas Nelson and Sons Ltd 1996
I(T)P Thomas Nelson is an International Thomson Publishing Company
I(T)P is used under licence

ISBN 0-17-490011-2
NPN 9 8 7 6 5 4 3 2 1

All rights reserved. No paragraph of this publication may be reproduced,
copied or transmitted save with written permission or in accordance with
the provisions of the Copyright, Design and Patents Act 1988, or under the
terms of any licence permitting limited copying issued by the Copyright
Licensing Agency, 90 Tottenham Court Road, London, W1P 9HE.

The publisher grants permission for copies of pages 3, 66–75, 91, 123, 168,
174 and 202 to be made without fee as follows:
Private purchasers may make copies for their own use or for use by their
own students; school purchasers may make copies for use within and by the
staff and students of the institution only.
This permission to copy does not extend to additional institutions or
branches of an institution, who should purchase a separate master copy of
the book for their own use.

For copying in any other circumstances prior permission must be obtained
in writing from Thomas Nelson and Sons Ltd.

Printed in Great Britain by Ebenezer Baylis & Son Ltd,
The Trinity Press, Worcester, and London

Acknowledgements:
Acquisitions: Sonia Clark
Administration: Jenny Goode
Editorial: Debbie Howard, Simon Bell
Marketing: Jane Lewis
Production: Liam Reardon
Staff Design: Maria Pritchard
Design/Typesetting: Pardoe Blacker Publishing
Illustrated by: Gary Andrews, Annabelle Brend, Dawn Brend,
Sophie Grillet, David Horwood, Jeremy Long, Nick Raven, Martin Shovel,
Rodney Sutton, Margaret Welbank, Ian West and Paul Weston

Contents

The Intermediate GNVQ Business Team	vi
About this book	vii
The structure of the book	vii
Toolkit	**1**
Introduction	1
General skills for GNVQ Business	1
Carrying out research	1
Activity: Let's get started	3
Presenting information	4
Managing your work	4
Carrying out assignments	5
Preparing for assessment	6
Communication	9
Taking part in discussions	9
Producing written material	12
Case study: Sunday opening	13
Using images	24
Application of Number and Information Technology	25
Rounding	25
Activity: Rounding up and down	26
Activity: Rounding money	27
Activity: Rounding decimals	29
Percentages	29
Activity: Using percentages	33
Ratios	33
Activity: Writing ratios	34
Activity: Using ratios	36
Measure	36
Paper	38
Shape	39
Activity: Using shape	40
Conversion	41
Activity: Converting measurements	42
Negative numbers	43
Activity: Using negative numbers	43
Drawing graphs and charts	44
Activity: Choosing a scale	45
Activity: Reading and drawing composite bar charts	49
Activity: Using pictograms	50
Activity: Using pie charts	54
Probability	55
Activity: Working out probability	55
The mean, the mode and the range	56
Activity: Mean, mode and range	58
Using information technology	59
Answers	64
Documents for you to photocopy	66
Unit 1 Business organisations and employment	**76**
The Elements	77
Explain the purposes and types of business organisations	77
Examine business location, environment, markets and products	77
Present results of investigation into employment	77
Purposes and types of business organisations	78
Developments in industrial sectors	78
Activity: Industrial sectors	80
Types of business organisation	81
Activity: Small, medium and large businesses	82
Case study: Linda Penn	84
Case study: Linda and Michelle	84
Case study: Linda and Michelle – private limited company?	85
Activity: Share performance	86
Case study: Linda's franchise alternative	87
Case study: Linda's co-operative alternative	87
Purposes of business organisations	88
Activity: Calculating Linda's profit	89
Case study: Linda's market share	89
Activity: Finding out more about customer service	90
Case study: From public to private – a change of purpose	90
Activity: Classifying business organisations	91
The operation of a business organisation	92
Case study: Steve Parker and Comp-U-Clic	92
Activity: The operation of Comp-U-Clic	93
Business location, environment, markets and products	94
Business location	94
Case study: Aromatherapy resources	95
Activity: Where were the customers?	95
Activity: Moving goods around	96
Case study: Barnaby' new department store	97
Activity: Locating a business	99
How does the business environment affect a business?	100
Activity: Meeting standards	100
Markets	101
Case study: Granada Group	102
Activity: Comp-U-Clic's market share	102
Activity: Chocolate bars and fizzy drinks	104
Case study: Mud Monsters	105
Activity: Market and demand	105
Activity: Needs and wants	105
Activity: Price rise	106
Activity: Buying vegetables	107
Products and customers	107
Activity: What type of product?	107
Activity: Comp-U-Clic's market, products and customers	109
Business activities	109
Case study: Comp-U-Clic's advertising	110
Activity: Spending Steve's budget	111
Investigating employment	111
Activity: Who is gaining employees?	111
Case study: Rover car plant	112
Activity: Technology and employment	112
Activity: Who is losing employees?	112
Analysing information about employment	113
Case study: Merseyside shipbuilding	113
Case study: Motorway services	113

iii

Activity: Seeing is believing	114
Looking at information for one region	115
Activity: Analysing employment in Wolverhampton	117
Comparing information for different regions	118
Activity: Vive la différence	122
Factors contributing to employment	124
Activity: Factors affecting your own region	124
Types of employment	125
Case study: The Comp-U-Clic payroll	125
Working conditions	126
Case study: Jean Herrault	126
Case study: Lawrence Wood	126
Activity: Jean and Lawrence	127
Summary questions	128
Assignment: Chamber of Commerce report	128
Assignment: In the market	130
Assignment: Research in action	131
Self-check questions	132

Unit 2 People in business organisations 134
The Elements	135
Examine and compare structures and working arrangements in organisations	135
Investigate employee and employer responsibilities and rights	135
Present results of investigation into job roles	135
Prepare for employment or self employment	135
Investigating structures, working arrangements and job roles in organisations	136
Job roles	136
Activity: Emergency!	139
Organisational structures	139
Activity: Span of control	141
Activity: Hierarchical structures	142
Activity: Looking at your own organisation	143
Working as a team	143
Departments within organisations	144
Activity: What needs to be bought?	146
Activity: Changes in administration	147
Activity: Delivering the goods	148
Working arrangements	149
Activity: Flexible working hours	150
Activity: Shift workers and flexi-time	150
Activity: Where are they based?	151
Reasons for changing work arrangements	151
Activity: The competitive edge	152
Employee and employer responsibilities and rights	153
Activity: Looking at health and safety	156
Activity: Sex discrimination?	157
The role of trade unions	159
Activity: Trade unions	159
Ways to resolve disagreements	159
Activity: Susan Edwards	160
Activity: Legal positions	161
Preparing for employment or self-employment	162
Types of employment and self-employment	162
Case study: Zoe Harris, secretary to a legal executive	162
Activity: Private and public sector employers	163
Activity: Voluntary sector	163
Case study: Les Spree	164
Activity: The Thomson Local	164
What opportunities are there?	164
Activity: Finding out about self-employment	166
Analysing skills needed	167
Activity: Developing skills	167
Activity: What skills do they have?	169
Summary questions	169
Assignment: Inside an organisation	170
Assignment: Employment booklet	171
Assignment: Just the job	172
Assignment: Your skills	174
Self-check questions	175

Unit 3 Consumers and customers 176
The Elements	177
Explain the importance of consumers and customers	177
Plan, design and produce promotional material	177
Provide customer service	177
Present proposals for improvements to customer service	177
The importance of consumers and customers	178
The effect of consumers on sales of goods and services	179
Activity: Consumers and change in demand	179
The buying habits of consumers	180
Activity: Designer trainers	181
Activity: Targeting advertising	181
Activity: Geographical buying habits	182
Trends in consumer demand	182
Activity: Then and now	183
Activity: Into the future	183
Causes of change in demand	184
Activity: Costs and consumer demand	184
Activity: Advertising campaigns	185
Activity: Trends in your group	185
Planning, designing and producing promotional material	186
Types of promotion	186
Activity: Point-of-sale promotion	186
Activity: Spot the advertisement	188
Activity: Sponsorship	188
Constraints on promotional materials	189
Activity: What you see is what you get?	189
Planning, designing and producing materials	190
Activity: Target groups	191
Activity: Designing an advertisement	192
Activity: Costing advertisements	194
Activity: A competition leaflet	194
Evaluating the success of promotional materials	194
Case study: McDonald's – Comments	195
Activity: How is the new product going?	195
Providing customer service	195
Customer needs	195
Activity: Obtaining information	196
Activity: Exchange or refund?	197
Customer service	197

Case study: McDonald's customer service	197
Activity: Customer care	198
Activity: Customer charters	198
Business communications	198
Activity: Looking for communications	199
Case study: McDonald's communication	199
Activity: Business communications	199
Dealing with customer complaints	199
Case study: McDonald's – Complaints procedure	200
Activity: Dealing with complaints	200
Legislation to protect customers	200
Improving customer service	200
Case study: McDonald's – Customer satisfaction	201
Activity: Customer satisfaction	201
Activity: Suggesting improvements	202
Summary questions	203
Assignment: What do you know about consumers and customers?	204
Assignment: New promotions	205
Assignment: Setting up a travel agency	206
Assignment: What improvements can be made?	207
Assignment: Improving a reception area	208
Self-check questions	212

Unit 4 Financial and administrative support   **214**

The Elements	215
Identify and explain financial transactions and documents	215
Complete financial documents and explain financial recording	215
Produce, evaluate and store business documents	215
Financial transactions and documents	216
Activity: Financial transactions	216
Activity: What do businesses spend their money on?	217
Purchase documents	217
Activity: Purchasing goods	217
Activity: Completing a purchase order	219
Activity: Completing a goods received note	220
Sales documents	221
Activity: Completing sales documents	224
Payment methods and documents	224
Activity: Completing a petty cash voucher	225
Activity: Completing a cheque	226
Activity: Calculating interest	228
Receipt documents	229
Activity: Completing a receipt	230
Activity: Totalling takings	230
Activity: Checking a paying-in slip	231
Security and financial transactions	232
Recording financial transactions	232
Activity: The purchases day book	233
Activity: Producing a budget	235
Activity: Finding out about software	236
Producing, evaluating and storing business documents	236
Business documents	236
Activity: Company logos	236
Activity: Writing a memo	237
Activity: Writing a letter	238
Activity: Producing an invitation	239
Activity: Leaving a message	240
Ways of processing business documents	240
Activity: Which processing method?	241
Sending business documents	242
Activity: Ways of sending documents	242
Storing business documents	243
Activity: Filing alphabetically	243
Activity: Paper versus computer	244
Assignment: Exploring financial documents	245
Assignment: Completing documents	246
Assignment: Organising a sales conference	249
Core skills coverage grid	**252**
Useful addresses	**254**
Answers to self-check questions	**255**
Appendix: Key legislation	**256**
Index	**260**
Acknowledgements	**264**

The Intermediate GNVQ Business Team

The authors
Linda Daniel is an assessor with a specialist background in Business. She has been teaching Business and Business Studies for several years and is currently working at Castle Community School, Deal. She has been involved since the outset in the delivery and development of GNVQ Business at Key Stage 4.

Karen McCafferty is the GNVQ Intermediate Business Co-ordinator at Canterbury College, where she has taught Business and Finance for over ten years. She has taught Intermediate and Advanced GNVQs and their equivalents and has developed and run both GNVQ and NVQ courses.

Julia Joslin is a GNVQ Course Tutor at Canterbury College and teaches on both Advanced and Intermediate Business courses. Prior to teaching she worked for 15 years as a statistician and a manager within the Health Service.

Linda Porter is currently a freelance educational consultant and author of educational materials. She has previously worked with NCVQ in the development of GNVQ Business and has worked as a Business Advisory/support teacher for TVEI with responsibility for co-ordinating GNVQ. She has also been a GNVQ advisor and external verifier for RSA.

Amanda Thomas is in charge of Business Studies at Castle Community School, Deal. She is a specialist in the delivery and assessment of vocational qualifications at all levels and was involved in the original GNVQ pilot scheme. She has recently been actively involved in the training of new assessors to TDLB standards. Currently she is involved with the piloting of GNVQ Business at Key Stage 4.

The main contributors
Alec Main is Co-ordinator of the Curriculum Materials Unit at Thomas Danby College in Leeds.
Christine Woodrow has been a maths and numeracy teacher for 20 years. During this time she has supported students of various ages and levels. She is currently a GNVQ and Core Skills Co-ordinator in a growing Sixth Form College.

The advisers
Alison Atkinson is a senior lecturer in Business Education at the University of Brighton. She is an internal verifier for NVQs and has been a chief examiner for Business GNVQ.
David Holloway is a qualified barrister working in legal publishing where he is a commissioning editor in the areas of finance and trade. He has also lectured and written on commercial law and EU law.
Gary Holt has taught all levels of GNVQ from Foundation through to Management. He is currently Head of School – Business Studies at Wirral Metropolitan College and is an Executive Committee Member of the National Association of Business Studies Education.
Liz Norris is currently Head of Quality Enhancement Project at Mid-Kent College. She was Head of Business and Information Systems and GNVQ Co-ordinator at the College. Amongst other GNVQ projects she has worked with NCVQ on the Quality Framework and Assessing GNVQs in Business.

Thanks also to the staff from the many organisations who provided time and resources for our case studies and who validated our manuscript.

About this book

Intermediate GNVQ Business is a valuable qualification which will help you to:
- move on to further full-time education
- show prospective employers your potential
- prove your understanding of the business world
- show your ability to communicate well, and use numbers and information technology
- demonstrate that you are able to work on your own without constant supervision, knowing when to ask for help.

This book will help you achieve these things. It provides information and guidance on every aspect of Intermediate GNVQ Business, taking a lively approach to what is happening in the business world.

Using this book will help you to:
- understand the GNVQ Business units in the context of real businesses
- develop your own research and independent study skills
- prepare and present your portfolio of evidence for assessment
- prepare for end of unit tests.

The structure of the book
You will see that the book is divided into six sections:
- the Toolkit, which contains general information to help you with your GNVQ, in particular the core skills units in Communication, Application of Number and Information Technology
- Unit 1: Business organisations and employment
- Unit 2: People in business organisations
- Unit 3: Consumers and customers
- Unit 4: Financial and administrative support.
- The Appendices, which contain key legislation, useful addresses, a core skills coverage grid and answers to the self-check questions.

Each of the four units covers the elements, performance criteria and range for the mandatory Business units, and is made up of activities, assignments and case studies.

Activities give you a chance to practise your business skills and core skills, and you may be able to include some of them in your portfolio of evidence. Activities look like this:

A	**Seeing is believing**
Activity	Title of activity

At the end of each unit there are **assignments**, which enable to you collect evidence for the Business and core skills units. You should include your work towards these in your portfolio of evidence.

There are also **case studies** in each unit, which are examples based on real businesses. They give you insight into how businesses work.

Throughout the text you will see **cross-referencing buttons**, which show you where to find more information on a subject. Cross-referencing buttons look like this:

▶ Core skills coverage grid, page 252

Heading to look for in the text   Page to turn to for further information

At the end of the units there are two sets of questions:
- **summary questions**, which help you build up your own summary of the main points covered by the unit
- **self-check questions**, which are multiple choice questions (the answers are at the back of the book).

Both of these will help you prepare for your end of unit tests. As there is no test for Unit 4 at present, this does not include any questions.

Toolkit

Introduction

This Toolkit contains information to help you work towards your Intermediate GNVQ Business . As you read this book, you will probably find it useful to look back to this section for ideas, advice and information.

The Toolkit includes:
- general information on how to approach GNVQ assignments and activities
- advice and information to help you achieve the core skills units in Communication, Application of Number and Information Technology
- photocopiable resources you can use to practise different skills as you work through the book.

General skills for Business GNVQ

For your Intermediate GNVQ Business , you will need to collect and present evidence in your portfolio which shows that you:
- have covered all the Business units
- have covered all the core skills units
- can work independently, in order to get a merit or distinction grade.

You will also need to pass end of unit tests for three of the four mandatory Business units, to show that you have the knowledge, skills and understanding underpinning each unit.

This section of the Toolkit suggests some approaches and skills you can use in order to achieve these things and gain your GNVQ.

Carrying out research

During your GNVQ, you will need to find out information about subjects ranging from business organisations and legislation to personnel and employment. Finding out this information is called 'researching'. Good research involves looking for the right information in the right place.

You may find it helpful to carry out research with other students in your group. As well as saving time, this means that organisations aren't inundated with calls for the same information. Each of you should agree to carry out a particular piece of research and then share the findings with the rest of the group. For example, one person may agree to contact a local business, another the planning department, another the Economic Development Unit, and so on.

Collaborating in this way will also help you develop – and then claim – core skills in (for instance) Communication.

Toolkit

Where to find information
The following list suggests some starting points.

- Your **tutor** will be able to point you in the direction of good sources of information. You could also ask other subject tutors for help (for example, a geography tutor may have maps of the local area).
- **Librarians** can help you find information on particular topics, or show you how to use the IT system so you can find information yourself. Try the business sections in your school or college library and your town library.
- **Newspapers and magazines** can provide helpful, up-to-date information. Your local paper will tell you about businesses opening and closing in your area, activities and locations. Specialist magazines such as *The Economist* can also be helpful.
- **CD-ROMs** are a good source of information. Ask your IT department or library for titles which give you social trends, European statistics, or back copies of newspapers. You can print out information from CD-ROMs.
- **Radio and television** programmes often focus on business information and current affairs. Look at listings for the week ahead, and plan to listen to or watch programmes that might be useful.
- Get information from **people** by designing questionnaires and carrying out interviews. If you are interviewing someone from an outside organisation, you need to know in advance who you will see, when and where. Write down the questions you want to ask, and take them with you on the day.
- **Local business organisations** may also be able to provide useful information. Phone the organisation, and explain that you are researching business information for your GNVQ. Ask who is the best person in the company to give this information, and make a note of the person's name. Either ask for information to be posted (in which case send an SAE), or make an appointment for an interview. If you're finding it hard to get information from local organisations, try mentioning the promotional benefits they might gain from helping you.
- Your local **Job Centre** will be able to give you information about the employment situation in your area.
- Staff at your local **Economic Development Unit** may be able to provide you with information and statistics about the population and businesses in your area from local censuses. Ask your local Training and Enterprise Council (TEC) for their number.
- Various departments at your local **Civic Centre** will have information on plans to develop the area, the environment, trading standards, and so on.

▶ Questionnaires, page 20

A | Let's get started

Before you start working towards the units, it is helpful to find out who and what will be able to help you with your work. You will find some useful national addresses at the back of this book.

You will also need to find out what is available in your local area. Make a copy of the following table, complete it, and keep it in your portfolio so you can refer to it as you work.

Who can help me?

Suggestions	Contact name and hours of opening	Address	Phone number	Information/ resources they can provide
Job Centre				
Economic Development Unit				
Training and Enterprise Council				
Local government department				
Careers centre				
Local organisations (e.g. Citizens Advice Bureau)				
Local businesses				
Local library				
College/school library				
Other resources				
Other ideas				

Collecting information

During your research, you will probably collect a large amount of information. It is important to organise this information well so that you can use it to its best advantage.

- Prepare a **scrapbook** containing newspaper and magazine cuttings on business information and current affairs. You could include reviews of business-related radio and television programmes, commenting on the subject and your views.
- Keep a **resource folder** containing copies of leaflets, flyers, advertisements, financial documents, invoices, receipts, company reports and marketing communications from local businesses. These can provide useful examples for activities and assignments.
- Keep a **diary** of your independent GNVQ research (for example, keep records when you contact a local business organisation). This will provide evidence towards Communication core skills and show how well you plan your work and time.

© L. Daniel, J. Joslin, K. McCafferty, L. Porter, A. Thomas 1996. *Intermediate GNVQ Business.*

Toolkit

- Reports, page 19
- Drawing graphs, page 44
- Using images, page 24
- Making presentations, page 11

TO DO LIST

1	Go to the library
2	Type report
3	Phone local businesses
4	Hand in assignment 2
5	
6	
7	
8	
9	
10	

- Put together a **glossary** of business terms. This shows that you understand the words and phrases you come across in your studies, and will help you use them correctly in activities and assignments.
- Make a **list of useful business contacts**. You can build this up from local business surveys, contacts among your family and friends, and your own contacts from sports and leisure facilities, voluntary organisations, part-time jobs, and so on.

Presenting information

The following list suggests different ways you can present your research findings.

- Write reports – present your information in a set format and give it a clear structure and meaning.
- Produce graphs and tables – present statistical information pictorially to make a simple, effective visual impression.
- Draw diagrams and illustrations, and take photographs – to break up large amounts of writing and make your work more interesting.
- Use a computer to present your work – ask your IT tutor for help, and book computer time in advance.
- Make presentations and give talks – to show that you can communicate your work orally. It is always helpful to have written and visual materials, such as handouts and overhead transparencies, to back up your presentation.
- Make audio and video tape recordings – as an alternative to written work. Recordings can be a good way to provide evidence of Communication core skills (it can be particularly helpful to record presentations).

Managing your work

Sometimes, especially at the beginning of your GNVQ course, you may find that work appears bitty and unrelated. You may have different tutors, or go to different places for different parts of your course. As you progress through your studies, you should start making connections between different aspects of the work.

When this happens, you may find that you have lots of things to do at once, and need to decide the order in which to do them. The following guidelines should help you manage your work:

- Find out your deadlines – what needs to be done by when.
- Always approach your work by breaking it down into small, manageable chunks.
- Write a list of action points to be achieved each day or session, and tick them off as you achieve them.
- Always write down in advance what you want to find out or achieve from a phone call or visit, so that you won't forget anything at the time.
- Keep your diary and folder up to date. Catching up can be difficult.
- If you have a problem with meeting a deadline, discuss it with your tutor in plenty of time. It is easier to negotiate an extension to deadlines in advance.
- If in doubt about anything, ask! The chances are that other people are also unsure, but don't have the courage to ask themselves.

- If you're worried about anything, talk it over with a tutor as soon as possible.
- Enjoy your course – it should be fun as well as challenging!

Carrying out assignments

All businesses have to plan, monitor and evaluate their activities – and you need to do the same when you carry out assignments. The criteria to use can be grouped under two broad headings:

Processes	Outcomes
• Drawing up plans of action • Monitoring courses of action • Identifying information needs • Identifying and using sources to obtain information • Evaluating outcomes and justifying approaches	• Synthesis of knowledge and understanding • Command of language

Drawing up plans of action

Before carrying out an assignment, you need to work out a sequence of events and timings – an action plan. Get into the habit of spending time planning and prioritising your work. This means working out the most important things to do first, and breaking tasks down into small steps in a logical order. It is always helpful to get someone to check your action plan, to see if you have missed anything out.

Monitoring courses of action

Once your project is underway, you look back at your action plan regularly to see whether you need to make any adjustments. For example, if information is delayed or not available, you may need to change the timing or order of tasks.

▶ Managing your work, page 4

Identifying information needs

When you plan a research project, you need to work out what information will help you with your work. Your tutor will be able to help you identify what you need to find out, but it will help if you are able to identify your own information needs.

▶ Carrying out research, page 1

Identifying and using sources to obtain information

Once you know what sort of information will help with your project, you need to know where to get it and how to use it. Knowing the right people to ask and how to contact them will help.

Evaluating outcomes and justifying approaches

Evaluating your work is about reviewing what you have achieved – looking back at what you have done and seeing whether you have achieved your goals. As part of your evaluation, you need to show that you recognise what worked well, what didn't, and what you would do differently in the future.

▶ Where to find information, page 2

Not everything can always go according to plan. When it doesn't, you should be able to suggest alternative approaches for the future. For example, if you wasted an afternoon in the library because you didn't know where to find information, plan to talk to the librarian next time.

Synthesis of knowledge and understanding
Synthesis of knowledge and understanding means bringing together all the knowledge, skills and understanding you study throughout your GNVQ in producing your work. You can also show where you have linked any supplementary evidence and resources to your assignments and activities.

Command of language related to business
In all written work and presentations, you need to show a good understanding of the words, terms, concepts, ideas and phrases used by businesses. This will mean remembering and understanding words used by your tutors, employers and textbooks, and using them correctly in your own work. Compiling a glossary of business terms will help you with this aspect of your work.

If you meet the GNVQ grading criteria you may be awarded merit or distinction. Merit and distinction grades are particularly valued by employers because they show that you are able to work on your own without constant supervision, and that you are responsible enough to ask for help when necessary.

Preparing for assessment
Your collection of evidence for your GNVQ is referred to as your 'portfolio'. You will probably have a large folder containing all your written work, but your overall portfolio will also include other evidence such as videos, presentation materials, audio tapes and photographs.

Your tutors and assessors need to be able to find their way around your portfolio quickly and easily.

You should make sure that:
- you follow your tutor's guidance on preparing your portfolio
- your folder and other pieces of evidence are clearly labelled
- pieces of evidence are cross-referenced to the elements for both Business and core skills units
- you have a clearly defined section for all your action plans, review and evaluation sheets
- you have included all your feedback sheets
- you keep your records neat, tidy and legible
- you keep an up-to-date checklist of what you have achieved and what you still have to do.

Outcome flow chart
Once you think a piece of work is complete, you need to check that you have got everything together before presenting it to your tutor for final assessment. You will probably find it helpful to discuss the work with your tutor at this stage, and include any feedback in your portfolio.

Work through the following flow chart to see whether you are ready for assessment.

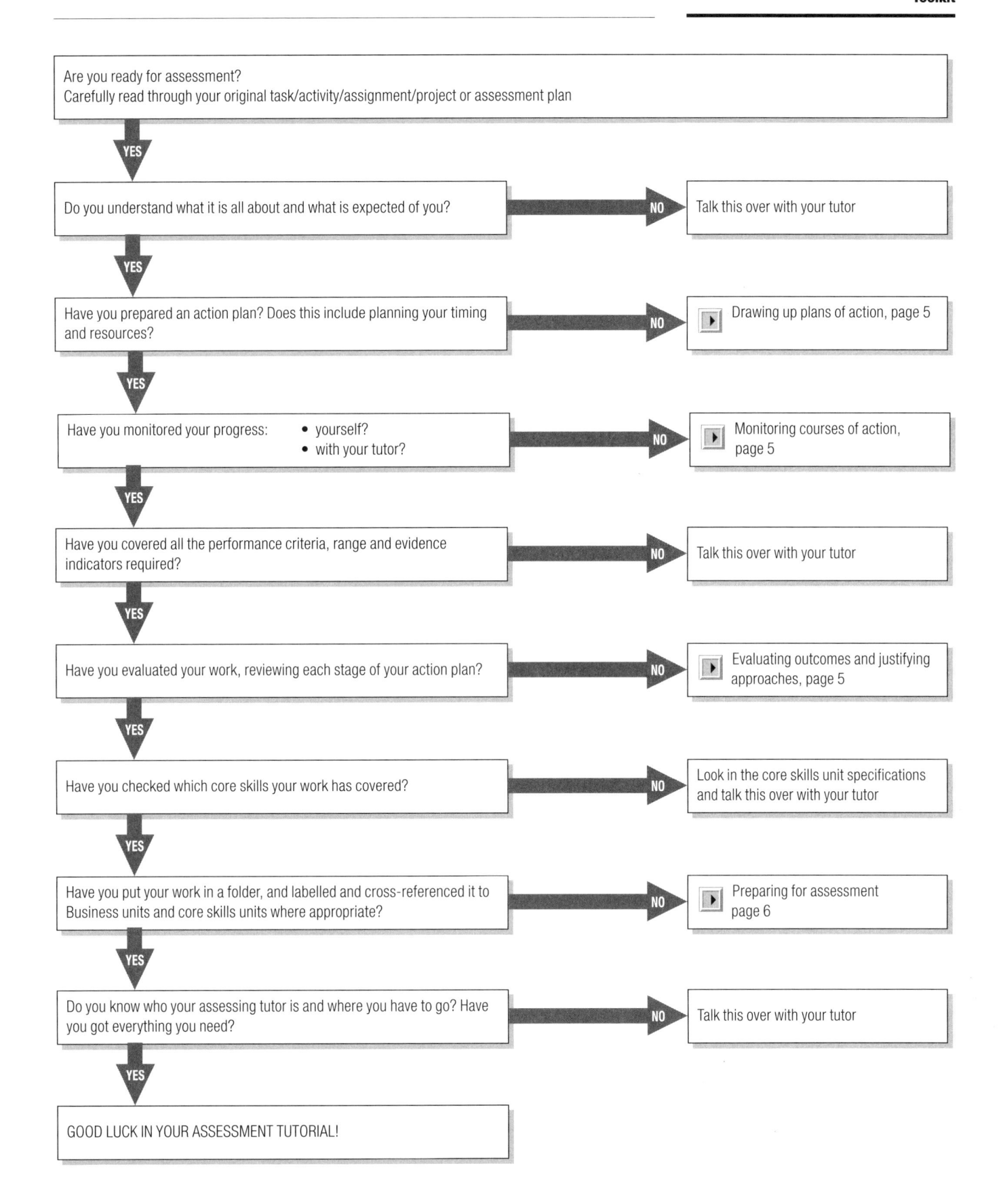

Are you ready for assessment?
Carefully read through your original task/activity/assignment/project or assessment plan

↓ YES

Do you understand what it is all about and what is expected of you? → **NO** → Talk this over with your tutor

↓ YES

Have you prepared an action plan? Does this include planning your timing and resources? → **NO** → Drawing up plans of action, page 5

↓ YES

Have you monitored your progress:
- yourself?
- with your tutor?

→ **NO** → Monitoring courses of action, page 5

↓ YES

Have you covered all the performance criteria, range and evidence indicators required? → **NO** → Talk this over with your tutor

↓ YES

Have you evaluated your work, reviewing each stage of your action plan? → **NO** → Evaluating outcomes and justifying approaches, page 5

↓ YES

Have you checked which core skills your work has covered? → **NO** → Look in the core skills unit specifications and talk this over with your tutor

↓ YES

Have you put your work in a folder, and labelled and cross-referenced it to Business units and core skills units where appropriate? → **NO** → Preparing for assessment page 6

↓ YES

Do you know who your assessing tutor is and where you have to go? Have you got everything you need? → **NO** → Talk this over with your tutor

↓ YES

GOOD LUCK IN YOUR ASSESSMENT TUTORIAL!

Unit tests

When it comes to working towards your end of unit tests, you may find the following approaches helpful.

- Remember you are being tested on the knowledge and understanding underpinning each unit.
- Do the multiple choice self-check questions at the end of each unit in this book to check your understanding. Mark them using the answer section.
- Try to answer the summary questions at the end of each unit in this book. These will help you summarise the information in the units.
- Having produced a summary, read it through and make an even shorter summary by putting the ideas into short sentences, or drawing a diagram which breaks down main headings into smaller headings and illustrates them with examples. You could do this on small cards to make a card index of information.
- A useful tip to help you remember important information is to turn it into a mnemonic. This involves making up a sentence or a word using the starting letters of points you are trying to remember. For example, the following sentence will help you remember the colours of the rainbow **R**ichard **O**f **Y**ork **G**ave **B**attle **I**n **V**ain.
- Try not to cram your work into the last minute. You are better off preparing in advance then relaxing the night before your end of unit tests.
- Tests are not threats which set out to fail you. They are opportunities for you to show everyone how much you know!

Communication

Good communication skills are very important in business. To work in business, you will need to be able to:
- take part in discussions with a range of people face to face, over the telephone and in presentations
- produce clear written material, including letters, memos, reports, minutes and questionnaires
- use images to help make communication clearer.

Taking part in discussions

People who work in business need to take part in discussions with a wide range of people on different subjects.

Preparing for a discussion

Prepare for all discussions, whatever their purpose, and whatever role you expect to play.

- Research the topic to be discussed, using:
  - books
  - periodicals
  - CD-ROMs
  - video and audio tapes
  - notes taken from texts and lectures
  - handouts.
- Brainstorm the topic, to bring to mind as many ideas as possible.
- Think positively about the other people in the discussion. Remind yourself what you know about their:
  - relevant experience
  - knowledge
  - attitudes
  - ways of presenting their views
  - ways of responding to others.
- Select half a dozen aspects of the topic you see as crucial. For each, jot down something you could:
  - ask
  - tell
  - suggest.

Listening to others

- **Listen** to what others say and how they say it. You can tell a lot about (for instance) how genuinely knowledgeable, sincere, committed or open-minded people are by the tone, pace and volume of their speech. These features are sometimes referred to as 'paralanguage'.
- Notice and interpret people's **body language**, which may:
  - add to, or change, the meaning of what they are saying
  - show how they are responding to other contributions to the discussion, including your own.
- **Don't interrupt:** let others finish making their point. It is courteous, it promotes good relations in the group, and you tend to learn more about the speaker *and* the topic.
- **Use the information you already have** to help you interpret and evaluate what others contribute:
  - 'I knew that, it was on Crimewatch UK!'

– 'Not true: I read the whole speech in my dad's paper.'
- **Concentrate on all contributions**, so you recognise (for example) where one builds on or challenges another.

Making your own contribution

If you have prepared well and listened well to others, you will be in a good position to:
- contribute facts, figures and views which are relevant
- link your contributions constructively to what others have said
- acknowledge what others have contributed, using language, paralanguage and body language.

Guidelines for contributing to discussions
- Sit up and lean forward slightly to show you are interested in the discussion.
- Avoid crossing your arms and making other barrier gestures which suggest you are not interested in other people's ideas and information.
- Smile at jokes, and nod when you agree with data and views offered.
- Frown or look puzzled by views or statistics you don't understand or accept.
- Voice your agreement, preferably with supporting data or a further reason.
- Repeat and endorse views expressed by someone else but overlooked by the rest of the group.
- Ask questions beginning 'what if...?' or 'why...?', to draw out further information, explanations or views.
- Invite others to repeat, develop or provide evidence for a point made.
- Congratulate others on valuable data or ideas they contribute – including challenges and queries.

If you follow these guidelines, your own contributions should:
- be relevant to the subject and purpose
- be suited to the audience and situation
- take the discussion forward
- confirm you have understood the contributions of others.

Talking on the telephone

Remember: no one can see you smile or frown over the telephone, so make sure your voice and the words you use send clear messages.

Preparing to make a call

1. Get a pen and paper so you can make notes.
2. Check that you have the phone number and extension.
3. Check the name and job title of the person you're calling.
4. Decide what information you want.
5. Prepare a list of questions to ask.
6. Make sure you know your number in case they need to return your call.
7. Check that you know your address – including the postcode – for any written reply.

The call itself

1. Give your name, and explain briefly why you are calling.
2. Give the name and job title of the person to whom you wish to speak.
3. Repeat (1) if necessary. When you ring a business, the call will often need to be transferred – make sure you don't off-load all your questions or information on the wrong person.
4. Ask your questions and/or give your information.
5. Speak clearly and avoid using slang.
6. Give the other person time to think, reply and/or take notes.
7. Where appropriate, show you're listening by saying 'uh-huh', 'yes, I see', and so on.
8. Make a note of important details (for example, quantities, dates, prices and reference numbers) and run through them at the end of the conversation to make sure you wrote them down correctly.
9. Give your details so you can be contacted by telephone or post.
10. Finish the call appropriately (for example, say 'thanks' or 'look forward to seeing you on Friday'), using the other person's name if possible.

Receiving calls

Most organisations have their own procedures for handling in-coming calls, but these will probably include the following steps.

1. Have pen and paper ready to make notes.
2. Announce the name of the organisation, followed by 'Can I help you?'. Many firms will expect you to give your own name, to personalise the relationship with the caller.
3. Speak clearly and avoid using slang.
4. If you are referring the call to someone else, tell the caller what you are doing.
5. If you are dealing with the call yourself, points 6, 7, 8 and 10 from 'The call itself' (see middle column) will apply.

Making presentations

Much of the work you carry out for your GNVQ, and many of the activities in this book, ask you to make oral presentations. You need certain skills to give a good business presentation, and this section will help you.

Preparing your presentation

- Make sure your presentation has a clear structure.
- Always start by telling people who you are and why you are there.
- Do you want people to ask questions as you go along? or at the end?
- Think about how you can use visual material. Overhead transparencies are a good idea, as you can prepare them in advance. If there isn't an overhead projector, see if you can borrow a flip chart with large sheets of paper. Practise in advance to make sure you write large enough for people to see and spell all the words correctly.
- Produce a timetable to remind yourself of your plan, like the one on the right.

PLAN FOR TALK

2 minutes	INTRODUCTION "Good morning my name is... I'm here to tell you about the new... drink"
5 minutes	WHY A NEW DRINK? "This drink is special because..."
1 minute	WHAT DOES IT LOOK LIKE? Show the drink with its packaging
5 minutes	WHY SHOULD YOU BUY THIS DRINK? An OHT showing: • price • flavour • availability • who will like it
2 minutes	CONCLUSION "Thank you for coming here today. This is to remind you that we have been talking about..."
5 minutes	QUESTIONS "Has anyone any questions they would like to ask?"

- Practise your presentation before you actually give it. If you practise in front of a mirror, you will get an idea of what the audience will see.
- Time your talk when you practise it – sometimes it's surprising how long or short it is.

Preparing yourself and the room
- Dress suitably – make sure that your clothes are neat and tidy. In a business presentation, customers will look at you as the representative of your company.
- Get to the room early (before your audience), so you can check everything is ready.
- Is the room set out the way you want?
- Are there enough chairs? Too many chairs?
- Can everyone see the overhead projector (OHP)?
- Is the OHP working?
- Is there a table for you?
- Do you need marker pens and a board cleaner? If so, have you got them?

Getting your message across

- Speak very clearly, and loud enough for the people at the back of the room to hear you.
- Stand up straight and look at your audience.
- Make sure you know what you are going to say in advance. Reading from notes muffles your voice and limits eye contact.
- If you want a reminder of your talk, write key words or sentences on small cards and keep them next to you.
- Don't fidget, use mannerisms or do anything that will stop your audience concentrating on what you are saying.
- Use visual materials to help explain your message.

Producing written material
As an Intermediate GNVQ student, you will use written material to:
- record information
- give and seek information
- offer your opinions and find out other people's opinions
- exchange ideas or put forward an argument

- communicate with people you know and people you don't know, although all will be familiar with the subject you are writing about.

Often, a single activity offers opportunities for you to work towards several aspects of core skills at once, as the following case study shows.

Case study: Sunday Opening

A group of Intermediate GNVQ Business students looked at the Sunday opening of local supermarkets. They:

- produced written material for people they knew (their tutor and colleagues)
- produced written material for people they didn't know (supermarket managers, customers, representatives of the Sunday Observance Society, trade union officials)
- used outline formats when taking minutes of group meetings, writing letters to supermarket managers, and writing reports on their findings and conclusions
- used pre-set formats when recording details, such as the name, address and manager of supermarkets.

They also produced evidence for:

- Communication core skills by taking part in discussions and using images in their reports
- Application of Number core skills by calculating Sunday rates of pay and displaying their findings in tables, bar charts and pie charts
- Information Technology core skills by using a computer to produce their reports.

Making notes

During your GNVQ you will often have to make notes as a record of something you hear or read. Notes may be made up of words, abbreviations, numbers, symbols, sketches or diagrams.

Linear (or 'sequential') notes record the points of something heard or read in the order in which they are made. You make your first note at the top of the page, the next a line or two below, the next a line or two below that, and so on.

To save time, you may use a range of shortening techniques when making linear notes:
- leave out details, illustrations and examples
- leave out all words except key words and essential link words
- use symbols to replace words and phrases (∴ for 'therefore', = for 'as a consequence)
- use sketches and diagrams if they are clearer than words.

Patterned notes – also known as 'spidergrams', 'scattergrams' or 'spraycharts' – give a visual picture of information.

```
        Public limited              Voluntary
        company
                                              Sole trader
                        ┌──────────────┐
                        │  BUSINESS    │──── Co-operative
                        │ ORGANISATIONS│
        Private ────────└──────────────┘
        limited
        company      Partnership        Franchise
```

A 'mind-map' can also be a useful way to make notes when brainstorming:

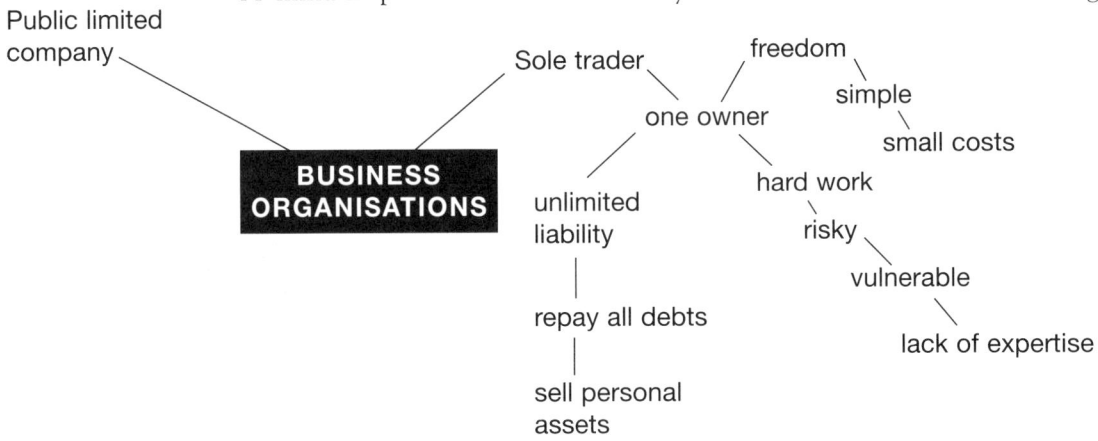

```
Public limited                              freedom
company                    Sole trader     /
                          \               simple
                           one owner     /
  ┌──────────────┐        /             small costs
  │  BUSINESS    │       /   hard work
  │ ORGANISATIONS│    unlimited
  └──────────────┘    liability      risky
                          │              vulnerable
                      repay all debts        \
                          │              lack of expertise
                      sell personal
                      assets
```

It is easy to add information to patterned notes. For example:
- a fresh spider leg
- a further toe on an existing leg
- a cluster of points (several legs close together) to record related points at once
- circles and arrows to link related points afterwards.

If your notes are recording information you are going to refer back to, you may need to rewrite them or elaborate on them to make sure they are easy to understand and read later. Just as important, you need to turn them from marks on a page to information or ideas in your mind. To do this, you might:
- rewrite the notes more fully
- underline or highlight key words and phrases

- convert them from linear to patterned, or vice versa
- add questions or comments, perhaps in a different colour
- sum up parts in sketches or diagrams
- try to apply the ideas to information to situations within your own experience.

Finally, file the notes (first and later versions) in a system that makes it easy to find them again whenever you want them.

Formal letters

All letters apart from those we send to family and friends are **formal letters**. When writing a formal letter on blank paper, you should always follow a traditional layout. This helps the person receiving the letter to see at a glance where it comes from, when it was written and by whom, and how to reply by post, telephone or fax.

Reference number – if there is one, quote the reference number from their letter to you and give them yours. This can help with filing and finding letters.

Recipient's name and address – to make it clear to whom you're sending the letter.

Greeting – use the person's name if possible.

Introductory sentence or paragraph – should expand on the title and prepare the reader for the rest of the letter.

Complimentry close – a polite, formal phrase before the signature. If the letter is written to a named person, use 'Yours sincerely'. Otherwise, write 'Yours faithfully'.

Your ref: 289/FO1

20 June 1996

24 Headley Road
Rainford
Surrey GU14 6QT

Mr J Timms
Personnel Manager
Atherton Systems Ltd
Bridge Street
Rainford
Surrey GU13 2JL

Dear Mr Timms

Application for the post of Junior Finance Officer

I would like to apply for the post of Junior Finance Officer at Atherton Systems advertised in the Evening Echo on 16 June 1996.

I am currently a student at Grays College in Rainford, studying for Intermediate GNVQ in Business and GCSEs in Computer Studies and Technology. I already have five GCSEs, as you can see from the enclosed CV.

I am leaving college in September and hope to work in an office as I enjoy working with people and would like to make the most of my business skills. I have already spent time on work experience in local offices, as well as having a part-time job in a local supermarket.

I am available for interview at any time and hope to hear from you in the near future.

Yours sincerely

Rachel Vaughan

Rachel Vaughan

Your address – should be clear and written in full (include your postcode, and write 'Road', not 'Rd').

Date of writing in full, including the word for the month, in the order day-month-year.

Title – a short heading that explains what the letter is about; for example, a job application or a letter of complaint.

The body of the letter – the main points, with detail.

Concluding paragraph – may be a single sentence that sums up what you will do, or would like the other person to do.

The signature – even if this is legible, you should print your name underneath.

Toolkit

- Always write as accurately and clearly as possible.
- Check your spelling using a dictionary, or a spell checker if you are working on a computer.
- Adapt your vocabulary, style and tone to suit your audience. Comparing a range of letters from different people will show the importance of tone. How is a letter from a friend different to a letter from a bank manager?

Letters sent by businesses are usually printed on special headed paper and laid out in the organisation's house style. Headed paper has the business's name, address and telephone and fax numbers, usually printed in a band across the top or bottom of the page.

▶ Formal letters, page 15

Memoranda (memos)

People within organisations use memoranda (usually shortened to 'memos') to communicate quickly and easily.

MEMO

atherton**SYSTEMS** *ltd.*
internal memorandum

From: John Timms Date: 12 June 1996
To: Freda Smith
Subject: Finance Officer vacancy

I confirm that an advertisement for the vacant post of Junior Finance Officer in your office will appear in the Evening Echo for 16 June.

I have the job description and person specification agreed with you and will prepare a short-list of candidates for your comments on 28th June.

Interview date: 5 July, 2.00 – 5.00, Room 7

J.T.

The headed memo form shows that this is an Atherton Systems internal memo.

The form prompts Mr Timms to supply the basic information: from whom, to whom, when, about what. This provides a record for filing.

The blank memo has enough space for a short message. It encourages people to be brief, and give the facts in plain language and simple style.

Initialling the memo gives a personal touch, and also confirms it is genuine.

Minutes of meetings

Records need to be kept of what is said at meetings so that information, ideas and decisions are not forgotten. When a group of people meet regularly, like a GNVQ team planning an event, they keep records of meetings called 'minutes'. Minutes should be written up and distributed as soon as possible after the meeting. They usually follow the same structure as the meeting's agenda (programme).

The amount of detail in minutes varies according to the group's purpose and its house style. Some simply record decisions and action points: others include details of the discussion leading to decisions and action points. There is generally more detail included if minutes are to be distributed to people who weren't at the meeting.

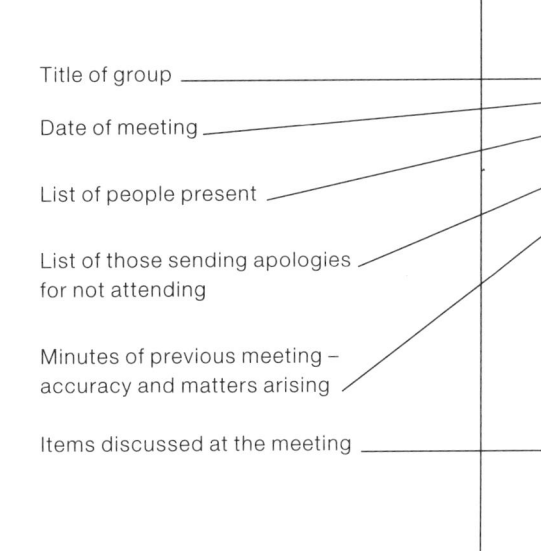

Title of group
Date of meeting
List of people present
List of those sending apologies for not attending
Minutes of previous meeting – accuracy and matters arising
Items discussed at the meeting

TADPOLE PROPAGATION GROUP
Minutes of meeting held on 25th January 1996.
Present: Jasbir Singh, Marcus Boyle, Linda Box (Chair), Toni Huxbury.

Apologies: Max Walker, Velda Blair.

Minutes of meeting held 11th January 1996.

Accuracy: Item 2 should read:
'MB was totally in favour' (the Minutes for 11 Jan read 'not really').
With this amendment, Minutes were accepted as accurate.

Matters arising: LB had put the group's request for a small budget for photocopying, postage and telephone calls to the Manager. This was agreed in principle; the figure is to be agreed within the next week.

Agenda
1. Group's name.
It was agreed that the present title is ungainly. JS proposed 'Save the Frog Group'; rejected as not precise. After considering suggestions, the group deferred a decision until the next meeting. Members to consult colleagues and bring ideas.

2. Marketing
TH believed few people understood the gravity of the plight of the frog. Until this was widely understood, there would be little demand for frog spawn among the general public. Wildlife groups were likely to be interested, but their membership was small. They would not generate enough demand to make start-up costs a reasonable risk. MB felt LB should approach the Manager for a significant marketing budget. This was agreed.

3. The legal position
MW had been given the job of establishing the legal position of 'farming' frog spawn for sale, and had not submitted a written report. It was felt the group had to have this matter resolved urgently. LB to ask MW to prepare a report as soon as possible, to be circulated with the minutes.

4. Pricing policy
It was felt that no progress could be made on this matter until (a) the legal position and (b) likely demand had been established.

5. Any other business
There was no other business.

Date of the next meeting

6. Date of next meeting
1st February 1996, 5.00 p.m., Committee Room B.

Notes of meetings

When meetings are 'one-offs', records are usually taken in the form of notes. These are less formal than minutes.

Possible Staff Association — Heading

5th March 1996 — Date of meeting
Present: J Armitage, S Bland, A Spray, C Cowper, L Williams, T Rooge, T Ahmad, V Proud, J Singh, P Richards, M Bigley. — List of people present
Apologies: W Willows, V Patel, B Murphy — List of people sending apologies for not attending

The meeting was called by T Rooge, arising from various conversations with people throughout the company. The purpose was to provide an opportunity for all those attending to share their ideas about forming a staff association. — The purpose of the meeting

After an hour's discussion, with T Rooge in the chair, it was generally agreed that there should be a full survey of staff interested in an association which would:
- be open to all employees of the company
- be non-political
- have no trade union role
- organise social activities
- have no membership fee
- charge for activities 'at cost'.

T Rooge, T Ahmad and A Spray agreed to carry out the survey as soon as possible. If enough interest was expressed, they would call a meeting to elect people to begin organising the association. — The outcomes

P Richards
6th March 1996

Reports

Reports are used to communicate research findings, information, ideas and opinions on a particular topic. Your reports shouldn't be mystery tours with surprising endings – they should follow a clear path, pointing to the end from the start.

Always prepare carefully before writing a report. Carry out research by reading class notes, handouts, books, periodicals, CD-ROM print-outs, and notes you have already made. Discuss with your tutor and other students what you need to do.

If you are asked to use a particular structure for your report, do so, carefully. If you are not given a particular structure for your report, use the one below.

- Title page – including the report title, your name and the date.
- Terms of reference – what you were asked to do. This may identify distinct tasks, or indicate the scope of your research (for example, the number of businesses to be studied, or the number of employees to be interviewed).
- Methods used – reading, observing, interviewing and so on.
- Findings – the facts, figures and views. You might present these in a variety of ways, including graphs and pictograms.

- Conclusions – what do your findings tell you?
- Sources – include a list of the books and periodicals you referred to, and the people and organisations you talked to. Books should be listed alphabetically according to author or editor, as appropriate. Periodicals should be listed alphabetically by title. In both cases, give the date of publication.

Produce a draft of your report, and run through the following checklist:
- Refer back to its purpose – does it do the job?
- Does it include all relevant details?
- Have you used appropriate vocabulary and tone?
- Is it accurate in terms of facts, layout, spelling and punctuation?
- Is the information easy to follow? Have you used clear headings, sub-headings and numbering?

Once you are happy with the draft, go on to produce a final version:
- Make sure you write as neatly as possible, or use a word processing package.
- If you word process your report, choose a clear font in a suitable size. Use bullets, indents and font characteristics to help make it clear how the information is organised and which items are most important.
- Make a final check on the accuracy of data, vocabulary, spelling and punctuation.
- Check that all items are addressed, dated and signed as appropriate.

Your report is then ready to go!

Statistical reports

When you use a questionnaire to carry out a survey, you need to write a special type of report – a statistical report – to communicate your findings.

▶ Questionnaires, below

A statistical report should include the following information:
- an introduction which explains:
  - what you were trying to find out
  - who you asked, where and when
  - why you asked certain important questions
  - a copy of your questionnaire
- an analysis of each question, including:
  - an explanation of how you are going to analyse the question
  - percentages
  - graphs (bar charts, pie charts, pictograms)
  - mean, mode and range
  - an explanation of what your analysis shows
- a conclusion based on your analysis, linking with the introduction (what you were trying to find out, and what you did find out)
- an evaluation of your survey, stating how it could be improved in the future.

▶ Percentages, page 32

▶ Graphs, page 44

▶ Mean, mode and range, page 56

Questionnaires

Carrying out surveys and designing questionnaires can be a good way to collect information directly, by:
- observing and recording behaviour or data
- asking people questions and using their answers to provide statistical information.

Follow these simple rules when using a questionnaire to carry out a survey.
- Keep your questionnaire short – aim at no more than a dozen questions. People you interview won't want to give up a lot of time, and analysis becomes complicated if you ask lots of questions.
- Make sure that you ask for all the information you need. Compare your questionnaire with an outline of what you want to find out.
- Choose topics carefully and suggest a range of possible answers to help you find out what people are, do, think and feel.
- Lay out your questionnaire so it is easy to read.
- Decide whether you're going to put your questions face to face, or give people a questionnaire form to fill in. This will affect the layout of your questionnaire and the sheet you design to collect responses ready for analysis.
- If you are going to hand out your questionnaire, make sure it is easy to read and encourages people to respond. It should be accessible, not 'impressive'.
- Test your questionnaire on a small group of people before you use it.
- Rewrite any questions that people don't understand.
- Think carefully about where to carry out your survey. The answers you get will be affected by where you ask the questions (you need to take this into account when analysing the results).

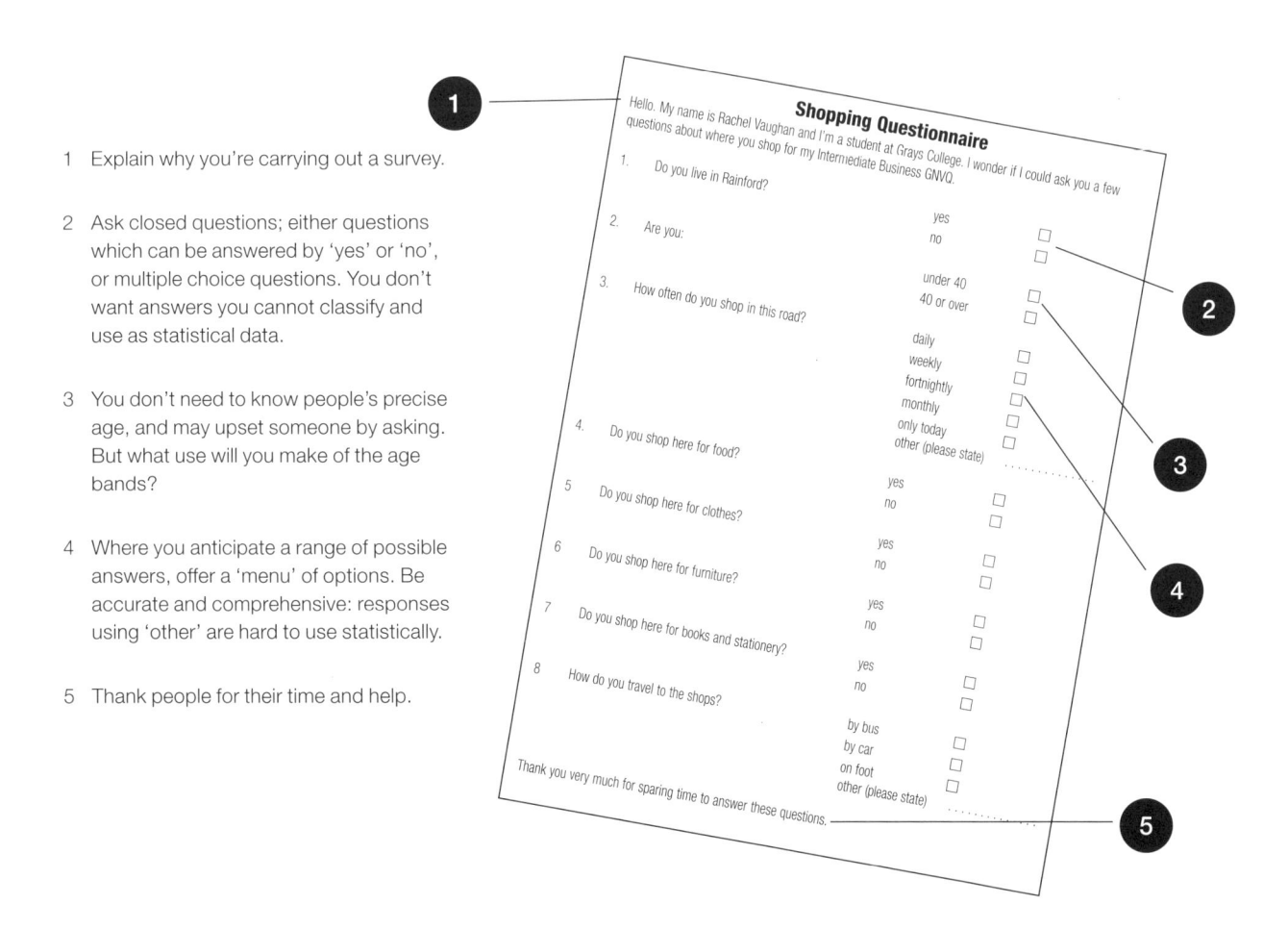

1 Explain why you're carrying out a survey.

2 Ask closed questions; either questions which can be answered by 'yes' or 'no', or multiple choice questions. You don't want answers you cannot classify and use as statistical data.

3 You don't need to know people's precise age, and may upset someone by asking. But what use will you make of the age bands?

4 Where you anticipate a range of possible answers, offer a 'menu' of options. Be accurate and comprehensive: responses using 'other' are hard to use statistically.

5 Thank people for their time and help.

Shopping Questionnaire

Hello. My name is Rachel Vaughan and I'm a student at Grays College. I wonder if I could ask you a few questions about where you shop for my Intermediate Business GNVQ.

1. Do you live in Rainford?
   - yes ☐
   - no ☐

2. Are you:
   - under 40 ☐
   - 40 or over ☐

3. How often do you shop in this road?
   - daily ☐
   - weekly ☐
   - fortnightly ☐
   - monthly ☐
   - only today ☐
   - other (please state) ☐ ....

4. Do you shop here for food?
   - yes ☐
   - no ☐

5. Do you shop here for clothes?
   - yes ☐
   - no ☐

6. Do you shop here for furniture?
   - yes ☐
   - no ☐

7. Do you shop here for books and stationery?
   - yes ☐
   - no ☐

8. How do you travel to the shops?
   - by bus ☐
   - by car ☐
   - on foot ☐
   - other (please state) ☐ ....

Thank you very much for sparing time to answer these questions.

Punctuation and grammar

Punctuation and grammar are closely linked, and both are covered in detail in English language textbooks. Ask tutors, friends and librarians to help you identify a user-friendly textbook to refer to as you work. If you have specific questions and problems, ask a friendly adviser for help.

It is easy to remember that:
- the beginnings of sentences and the names of countries, towns, people, newspapers, cinemas and brands of toilet paper all have capital letters
- all sentences end with a full stop.

It is harder to understand:
- what makes a sentence
- what a phrase is, and how it differs from a clause
- what a semi-colon is, and how it differs from a colon.

This is where your reference book, and friendly adviser, come in useful. In their absence, try these tests.

Is it a sentence?

Can you tick these statements about what you learn from the words between the capital letter at the start and the full stop at what you think is the end?

- I know the action.
- I know the tense – for example, whether the action 'was', 'might have been', 'is being', 'could be' or 'will be' done.
- I know whether the action is singular or plural.
- I know who or what did, might have done, is doing, might or will do the action.
- I know whether the doer of the action is singular or plural.

Four ticks? It is probably a sentence.
Three ticks or fewer? It probably is not a sentence – but consult that friendly adviser.

Phrase or clause?

If it is a **clause**, the test for a sentence will apply – except that the clause will be linked to one or more other clauses by a joining word or by being part of a list.

For example, each of the following sentences contains two clauses:

He wrote to the Personnel Officer and accepted the work-experience placement.

(clause 1)   (clause 2)

She shook the customer's hand and wished her good luck in the future.

(clause 1)   (clause 2)

> They decided that the profit margin was too low.
>
> (clause 1)   (clause 2)

This last sentence contains three clauses: can you identify them:

> They liked the product, could see a big market and negotiated for sole franchising rights.

If it is a **phrase**, there will be no tense, and possibly no doer or action. For example, 'the cost of living', 'the fight against inflation', 'the minister with responsibility for privatisation'.

Colon or semi-colon?

The most useful roles of the colon are:
- to introduce a list
- to announce evidence to support the statement made before the colon.

For example:

The government has to take into account a number of indicators: the number of people unemployed, the vacancies advertised, the nature of employment offered and the geographical distribution of the new jobs.

Here the **colon** says, in effect: 'Pay attention, because what follows will justify/explain/elaborate on what has just been said.' Often, as here, the justification takes the form of a list.

However, this is not always the case, as the following example shows:

She had no confidence in the minister's pledge: he had departed from declared policy on a number of occasions.

The **semi-colon** is often used to separate (or join!) two clauses which might have been separate sentences, but which are so closely related in subject matter that the writer wants to make their closeness clear to the reader:

The minister declared he was resigning to spend more time with his family; a month later he took up a post as Managing Director of Prosper UK.

Colons and semi-colons can also be used as a partnership, to build a long, complex sentence:

The company's position was deteriorating: there were, every month, fewer items on the order book; delivery dates were being missed frequently; production costs were, despite everything management tried, rising; and now competitors were appearing in the market-place.

Here the colon after 'deteriorating' announces evidence is coming to support the gloomy declaration about the company's position. The evidence takes the form of a list of statements, each providing some evidence of deterioration and closely linked to the others. They could have been presented as separate sentences; the semi-colons enable them to be kept as clauses within the single sentence, so emphasising the link.

You can also see that, with a sentence as complex as this, it would probably have been confusing if a comma had been used to separate the clauses.

Using images

Images – including maps, charts, tables, diagrams, sketches and photographs – can help make written communication clearer. Often, images are easier to understand than words:

- a map showing a route
- a plan showing the layout of a building
- pie charts, bar charts and pictograms showing proportions, ratios and trends.

Whether you create images yourself or take them from another source, it is important to use them appropriately. For example:

- a street map of a town centre is useful only if you explain whether the image is communicating the proposed site for a new supermarket, or the distribution of car parks
- a pie chart showing a company's markets is useful only if you point out the significance of the size of the segments
- a photograph showing different products produced by a company is useful only if you explain the link between the products.

Where should you place images?

If you need an image in order to understand the text (to follow the argument, or to interpret what the text is saying, for instance), the image goes where it is needed – in the text.

If the text is easy to understand without the image, and would be interrupted by the image, the image should go in an appendix. The reader can then turn to this when ready to examine more detailed evidence.

Application of Number and Information Technology

As well as being able to communicate well with people, you need to be able to use numbers and computers when working in business. This is why Intermediate GNVQ Business includes core skills units in Application of Number (maths) and Information Technology (using computers).

This section includes some information, advice and activities which might help you on your way.

Rounding

You don't always need exact answers to questions involving numbers. Instead, you can **round** numbers, making sure to keep them about the same size. For example, when we talk about the population of the world we usually talk about how many millions of people there are, rather than an exact figure.

Note!
When you round numbers, be careful not to change the overall size of the number.

Example

If we want to write 47 to the nearest 10, we're not interested in the number of units.

> 47 is between 40 and 50. 47 is nearer 50 than 40

47 is **more than half-way** between 40 and 50. So we need to **round up**:

> 47 = 50 to the nearest 10

Example

If we want to write 52,698 to the nearest thousand, we're not interested in the hundreds, tens and units columns – these should all be '0s'.

> Thousands above and below 52,698 are 53,000 and 52,000

52,698 is **more than half-way** between 52,000 and 53,000, so we need to **round up**:

> 52,698 = 53,000 to the nearest thousand

Toolkit

Short cuts for rounding

There are some short cuts you can use to speed up the process. Look at the number in the highest column you are not interested in.

- If this number is **less than 5** you need to **round down** as it is **less than half-way**.
- If this number is **more than 5** you need to **round up** as it is **more than half-way**.
- If this number **equals 5** it is **exactly half-way**. In this case, you also **round up**.

Example

Natalie's art teacher asked her to count how many art books there were in the college library, to the nearest ten. Natalie counted 342 books. She looked at the units column of this number (the next column down from tens), and saw that it was 2.

Therefore she **rounded down** the answer, and told her teacher:

> There are 340 books in the library (to the nearest 10)

Example

Natalie's teacher then asked her to find out how many students were registered at the college library, to the nearest hundred. Natalie found out from the librarian that there were 1250 students registered. She looked at the tens column of this number (the next column down from hundreds), and saw that it was 5.

Therefore she **rounded up** the answer, and told her teacher:

> There are 1300 students registered (to the nearest hundred)

Answers, page 64

A Rounding up and down

A leisure centre recorded the following attendance figures in one week.

Monday	274	Friday	345
Tuesday	136	Saturday	421
Wednesday	196	Sunday	169
Thursday	214		

1. What was the total number of people who attended during the week? Round this to the nearest ten.
2. Round each day's attendance to the nearest ten. Now find the total attending using these rounded figures.
3. Comment on your answer.

Rounding money

Sometimes you need to round amounts of money.

Example

Natalie's art teacher asked her to find out how much was paid in library fines the day before, to the nearest pound. Natalie found out that £6.86 was paid in fines. In the same way as before, she looked at the next column down from the pounds column, the 10p column, and found that it had 8 in it.

As this is more than 5, she **rounded up** the answer to the next pound, and told her teacher:

> The library took £7 in fines yesterday (to the nearest pound)

A — Rounding money

Answers, page 64

Moira had a limited amount of money, so when she went to the supermarket she needed to be careful how much she spent. As she shopped, she rounded each item to the nearest 10p and added the total up. The items she bought had the following prices:

52p, 34p, £1.35, 68p, 46p, 53p, 27p, £1.67, £2.35, 24p, 42p, 42p, 42p, 37p

1. Round each amount to the nearest 10p, and find out Moira's estimated total.
2. What would the actual total be?
3. Does using rounding give a reasonable estimate of the total?

Rounding decimal places

Decimal places are numbers after the decimal point – the decimal fractions.

Example

Round 3.64 to 1 decimal place.

This means round 3.64 so there is only **one number after the decimal place** (tenths only). If you look at the number in the next column down – the hundredths column – you see that it is 4.

4 is **less than half-way**, so you need to **round down**:

> 3.64 = 3.60 = 3.6 to one decimal place

You can lose the 4 without altering anything else.

> **Example**

Round 4.28 to 1 decimal place.

If you look at the number in the next column down – the hundredths column – you see that it is 8.

4.28 — this needs to 'go'

8 is **more than 5**, so you need to **round up**. To do this, you need to increase the first decimal place by 1.

4.28 = 4.3 to one decimal place
round up

> **Example**

Sometimes you get longer answers from a calculator, and need to round these.

Round 4.76324 to 2 decimal places. This means there needs to be 2 places after the decimal point.

4.76324
keep these – look at the next column

3 is **less than 5**, so you need to **round down**.

4.76324 = 4.76 to 2 d.p. (d.p. is short for 'decimal places')
don't change

> **Example**

Round 4.636363 to 2 decimal places.

4.636363
first number we don't need

6 is **more than 5**, so you need to **round up**.

4.636363 = 4.64 to 2 d.p.
   ↑
   round up

Example

Round 32.89583726 to 2 decimal places.

32.89583726
    ↑
    first number we don't need

This means that you need to **round up** 9 to 10. To do this, you **carry 1 to the next column**, just like you do when adding up numbers.

32.89583726 = 32.90 to 2 d.p.

A Rounding decimals

Mr Singh calculates how much he will have to pay on a bill which states:

Total   £123.97
Less 10% discount
Subtotal
Plus VAT at 17.5%
Total to pay

1 Calculate the discount, rounding your answer to 2 decimal places.
2 Calculate the subtotal.
3 Calculate the VAT, rounding your answer to 2 decimal places.
4 Calculate the total to pay.

Note: This activity uses percentages. You may need to work through the next section on percentages and then follow with the 'Rounding decimals' activity.

Percentages

It is very important to remember that a **percentage** is just a particular type of **fraction**.

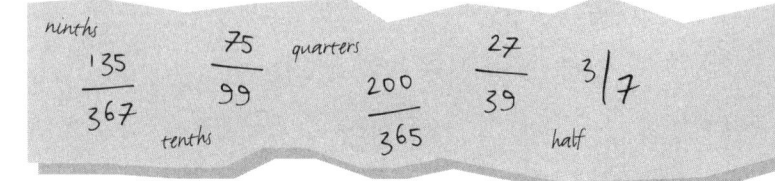

ninths: $\frac{135}{367}$ $\frac{75}{99}$ tenths   quarters $\frac{200}{365}$ $\frac{27}{39}$ $\frac{3}{7}$ half

Answers, page 64

- Percentages are fractions out of 100.
- Per cent means 'for each hundred' or 'out of a hundred'.

- **Fractions** can have **any** whole number as a **denominator** (bottom number). This means there are many different types of fraction.

$3.04 = 3\frac{4}{100}$ $0.78 = \frac{78}{100}$

Toolkit

- **Decimal fractions** can only have powers of **10** as denominators (tenths, hundredths, thousandths and so on), so we can put them in columns to match whole numbers. We use the decimal point to show where the whole numbers stop and the fractions start.

We use a special sign as a quick way of writing per cent – %. This means the same as $\frac{}{100}$.

So...

$$7\% = \frac{7}{100} \qquad 26\% = \frac{26}{100} \qquad 100\% = \frac{100}{100} = 1$$

- Watch out! 100% does not mean 100.

To **use** a percentage you need to write it as a fraction.

Example

To find 6% of £40, change 6% to its fraction form and multiply by £40.

$$6\% \text{ of } £40 = \frac{6}{100} \times 40 = £2.40$$

Using a calculator:

`6 ÷ 1 0 0 × 4 0 = 2.4`

We write **money** with **two** numbers after the decimal point to represent the pence, so 2.4 becomes £2.40.

VAT and discounts

People in business most often use percentages to work out:
- VAT (Value Added Tax), which is stated as a percentage (currently 17.5%)
- discounts (an amount taken off the price of something).

Example

If you need to add VAT to £65 and the rate of VAT is 17.5%, change 17.5% to its fraction form then multiply by £65.

$$17.5\% \text{ of } £65 = \frac{17.5}{100} \times 65 = £11.375 = £11.38$$

Using a calculator:

`1 7 . 5 ÷ 1 0 0 × 6 5 = 1 1 . 3 7 5`

This gives you too many decimal places, so you need to **round** the answer to the nearest penny, giving you £11.38.

This is the amount of VAT. Add this to the original price to get the total:

$$£65 + VAT = £65 + £11.38 = £76.38$$

Example

A tennis racket originally cost £35, but now has a discount of 20% in the sale. To find out the discount and the new sale price of the tennis racket, you need to find 20% of £35:

$$20\% \text{ of } £35 = \frac{20}{100} \times 35 = £7$$

Using a calculator:

`2 0 ÷ 1 0 0 × 3 5 = 7`

So to find the racket's new selling price, take £7 from the original price of £35:

$$£35 - £7 = £28$$

Using percentages to describe situations

We use percentages to describe situations when one quantity is 'part of' or is a 'change in' another, or to compare two or more similar situations. All percentages are linked to the same number – **100**. Percentages show information as a **proportion** of 100.

Example

In a letter to the Brinton Observer, Mr Jackson, an irate parent complaining that his daughter Sally had not been included in the Brinton West football team, included the information shown here.

168 girls go to Brinton East Primary School whilst only 70 go to Brinton West. This shows girls prefer Brinton East – and I can see why!

Toolkit

Two days later the Observer printed the response on the right from Mrs Ahmed, a teacher at Brinton West.

Mr Jackson had tried to compare two schools which were not the same size. By using percentages to show what the situation would have been if each school had exactly 100 pupils, Mrs Ahmed was able to compare like with like.

> Mr Jackson needs to get his facts right! Brinton East has 350 pupils while Brinton West is a smaller school and has only 125 pupils. Surely Mr Jackson can see that, using his figures, 48% of Brinton East pupils are girls, and 56% of Brinton West pupils are girls. These figures *could* be used to show that girls prefer Brinton West! The truth is, of course, that both schools provide quality education for both boys and girls.

Working out percentages

The first step in working out percentages is to find the right fraction.

Example

Mrs Ahmed found out that there were 168 girls at Brinton East Primary School, out of a total of 350 pupils. She then wrote 168 out of 350 as a fraction:

$$\frac{168}{350}$$

The second step is to change this fraction to a percentage. This means finding an equivalent fraction with 100 at the bottom.

Sometimes this is easy:

$$\frac{25}{50} \text{ is the same as } \frac{50}{100} = 50\%$$

But often it is more complicated than this, so we need to find a way that works for all fractions. Mrs Ahmed knew that:

- she needed to get '%' in the answer
- $100\% = \frac{100}{100} = 1$
- if she multiplied a number by 1, the answer would be the same size as the question.

So she realised that she could also multiply by 100% without changing the size of the fraction:

$$\frac{168}{350} \times 100\% = 48\%$$

% means '$\frac{}{100}$', or 'out of 100'. We don't actually do this at this stage, so % is in the answer.

Hints for fractions

- When trying to decide what should go at the bottom of your fraction and what at the top, try to write (or think of) a sentence in words which includes the phrase '...out of a total of...' or '...out of the original amount...'
- Remember that sometimes you may not be given the total or the original amount – you may have to work this out from other information.

Using a calculator:

`1 6 8 × 1 0 0 ÷ 3 5 0 = 4 8` or

`1 6 8 ÷ 3 5 0 × 1 0 0 = 4 8`

From this, Mrs Ahmed knew that 48% of pupils at Brinton East were girls.

Similarly, at Brinton West 70 out of 125 pupils were girls.

$$\frac{70}{125} \times 100 (\%) = 56\%$$

Using a calculator:

`7 0 × 1 0 0 ÷ 1 2 5 = 5 6` or

`7 0 ÷ 1 2 5 × 1 0 0 = 5 6`

From this, Mrs Ahmed knew that 56% of pupils at Brinton West were girls. This meant that the proportion (share) of girls at Brinton West was higher than at Brinton East.

What is 100%?
In this case, the whole school represented 100%. So if 48% of the pupils at Brinton East are girls, the other 52% must be boys (100 – 48%).
In the same way, 56% of the pupils at Brinton West are girls, so 44% must be boys.

A Using percentages

Swish Leather Shop offers credit to its customers at a rate of 9% per year. The customer repays money in 12 monthly repayments. If the amount to be repaid does not divide exactly by 12, the 'extra' is paid in the first instalment, which acts as a deposit. The shop also has a sale, in which everything is reduced by 10%.

1. Find the credit cost of a jacket bought in the sale which originally cost £225.
2. How much would the customer have to pay:
   a. in the first month as a deposit?
   b. in each following month?

SwishLeather

OUR CREDIT OFFER

REPAY IN 12 MONTHLY INSTALMENTS

ADD ONLY 9% TO THE COST OF YOUR SWISH LEATHER GOODS

Answers, page 64

Ratios
When we describe situations using fractions (or percentages), we write the appropriate amount 'out of' the **total**.

Example
A group of 30 students were offered a cup of tea or coffee. Three of the students chose tea, while 27 chose coffee.

Using fractions, you would write the fraction preferring tea as:

$$3 \text{ 'out of' } 30, \text{ or } \frac{3}{30} \left(= \frac{1}{10} = 10\%\right)$$

But when we write information as a **ratio**, we show how the total is shared out. So in the example above, where we know that the 30 students are 'shared out' 3 teas to 27 coffees, we can write it as:

$$3 \text{ to } 27, \text{ or } 3:27$$

We can cancel ratios in the same way that we cancel fractions, by dividing both 'sides' of the ratio by the same number. So in this case:

$$3:27 \text{ is the same as } 1:9$$

Ratios can also be used to compare more than two different shares.

Example

Another group of 20 students were asked what drink they liked best – 4 said tea, 6 said coffee, and 10 said cola. As a ratio, you can write this as:

$$4:6:10 \text{ (tea : coffee : cola)}$$

which simplifies to:

$$2:3:5$$

A Writing ratios

Amwar's Bakery employs the following staff:

Senior management
1 managing director
2 assistant directors
2 senior supervisors

Middle management
5 supervisors
5 junior supervisors

Shopfloor staff
60 bakers

One of the directors is looking at the number of staff employed at different levels in the organisation. She sees that there are 5 senior managers, 10 middle managers, and 60 shopfloor workers. She compares these figures in different ways:
- The ratio of senior to middle managers = 5 : 10 = 1 : 2
- The ratio of middle managers to shopfloor workers = 10 : 60 = 1 : 6
- The ratio of all managers to shopfloor workers = 15 : 60 = 1 : 4
- The ratio of senior to middle to shopfloor workers = 5 : 10 : 60 = 1 : 2 : 12

Crossman's Toolworks employs the following staff:

Senior management
1 managing director
6 assistant directors

Middle management
12 section managers
12 assistant managers

Shopfloor staff
40 turners
60 machinists
20 packers

1. Write the following information as ratios in their simplest form.
   a. The number of senior managers to middle managers at Crossman's Toolworks.
   b. The number of middle managers to shopfloor staff at Crossman's Toolworks.
   c. The number of managers to shopfloor staff at Crossman's Toolworks.
   d. The number of senior managers to middle managers to shopfloor staff at Crossman's Toolworks.
2. Compare the proportion of managers and shopfloor workers employed by Amwar's Bakery and Crossman's Tools.
3. Investigate the staff employed by your school or college. How many are senior and middle managers? How many are teachers and tutors? Compare your own organisation with Crossman's Tools. Is it top-heavy with management? Is it balanced? Does it have more teachers and tutors than managers?

▶ Answers, page 64

Using ratios

Example

Sally worked out that the ratio of the amount she takes home each month to the amount deducted from her salary is approximately 2 : 1. If she earns £18,000 per year she can work out how much she expects to take home.

Toolkit

Sally will take home 2 shares, and 1 share will be deducted (a total of 3 shares).

```
Each share = £1500 ÷ 3 = £500
2 shares = £500 × 2 = £1000
1 share = £500
```

So Sally expects to take home £1000 and have £500 deducted.

Example

In the same way, if you know that Jazwinder takes home £630 per month and that her take home to deductions ratio is 7 : 1, you can work out her annual salary.

Jazwinder takes home £630, which is 7 shares.
1 share = £630 ÷ 7 = £90
Her total pay is 7 + 1 = 8 shares
8 shares = £90 × 8 = £720 per month

So Jazwinder's annual salary is £720 × 12 = £8,640 per year.

A Using ratios

1. If Ben earns £22,500 per year and his take home to deductions ratio is 7 : 3, how much does he expect to take home each month?
2. Manraj has a take home to deductions ratio of 7 : 3. He takes home £1225 per month. How much does he earn each year? (Note: he takes home 7 shares)

▶ Answers, page 64

Measure

In Britain, we currently use two systems of measurement – the Imperial System and the Metric System.

Systems of measurement

The **Imperial System** has been used in Britain for many years. It includes different systems for **weight**, **length** and **capacity** (measuring liquids and volumes) developed a long time ago. For example, the measurement of one foot was about the length of a man's foot, and a yard about one stride! We still use some of these measures, even though we have 'gone metric'.

The **Metric System** was introduced in Britain fairly recently. It is widely used in the rest of Europe. Each metric measure uses a number system based on **thousands**. There is a base unit for each type of measurement (the metre for length, the gram for weight, and the litre for capacity). Each of these can be broken down into 1000 small pieces (millimetres, milligrams and millilitres), or 1000 can be joined together to make a larger measurement (kilometre, kilogram and kilolitre). Because the millimetre (mm) and millilitre (ml) are very small, we also use the centimetre (10 mm) and the centilitre (10 ml).

*Beer is measured in **pints***

*Wine is measured in **centilitres***

36

The Metric System was designed to link different units:

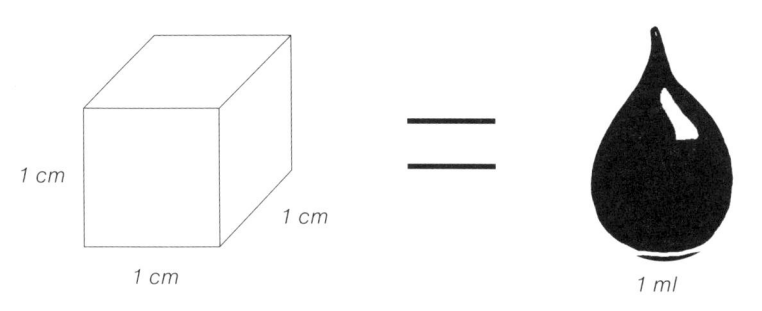

1 cubic centimetre of water has a volume of 1 millilitre and weighs 1 gram

You should try to use metric measurements as much as possible.
Look out for imperial and metric measures in shops:
- What is the normal weight of a bag of sugar or a bag of flour?
- How do you buy your milk?
- Would you ask your grocer for a pound of apples or a kilo of apples?
- Do we buy petrol by the litre or by the gallon?

Systems of measurement

The Imperial System
Length
12 inches = 1 foot (12" = 1')
3 feet = 1 yard (3' = 1 yd)
1760 yards = 1 mile
Weight
16 ounces = 1 pound (16 oz = 1 lb)
14 pounds = 1 stone (14 lb = 1 st)
112 pounds = 1 hundredweight (112 lb = 1 cwt)
20 hundredweight = 1 ton (20 cwt = 1 t)
Capacity
20 fluid ounces = 1 pint (20 fl oz = 1 pt)
2 pints = 1 quart (2 pt = 1 qt)
8 pints = 1 gallon (8 pt = 1 gal)
Temperature
Measured in degrees Fahrenheit (°F)
Water freezes at 32°F
Water boils at 212°F
Body temperature should be 98.6°F
The legal minimum working temperature in offices is 60.8°F

The Metric System
Length
1000 millimetres = 1 metre (1000 mm = 1 m)
1000 metres = 1 kilometre (1000 m = 1 km)
10 millimetres = 1 centimetre (10 mm = 1 cm)
100 centimetres = 1 metre (100 cm = 1 m)
Weight
1000 milligrams = 1 gram (1000 mg = 1 g)
1000 grams = 1 kilogram (1000g = 1 kg)
1000 kilograms = 1 tonne (1000 kg = 1 t)
Capacity
1000 millilitres = 1 litre (1000 ml = 1 l)
(the kilolitre is not often used)
10 millilitres = 1 centilitre (10 ml = 1 cl)
100 centilitres = 1 litre (100 cl = 1 l)
Temperature
Measured in degrees Celsius or Centigrade (°C)
Water freezes at 0°C
Water boils at 100°C
Body temperature should be 37°C
The legal minimum working temperature in offices is 16°C

Changing between metric and imperial

Approximately:
2.5 cm = 1 inch
30 cm = 1 foot
1 metre = 39 inches =
1 yard 3 inches

8 kilometres = 5 miles
1 kilogram = 2.2 pounds (lb)
1 litre = 1.75 pints

To change:
°F to °C, subtract 32, multiply by 5 and divide by 9
°C to °F, multiply by 9, divide by 5, and add 32.

Toolkit

Estimating measurements

To estimate measurements (lengths, weights and so on), keep a measurement that you know in your mind and compare this with the one you are estimating. For example:

- if you know that a door is approximately 2 metres tall, you can use this to estimate the height of a room or a person
- if you know that your hand span (from the tip of your thumb to the tip of your little finger when your hand is spread out) is approximately 20 cm, you can use this to estimate the length of a table – measure yours for use in the future
- if you know that the top joint of your thumb is 2 to 3 cm, you can use this to estimate smaller lengths – measure yours for use in the future.

Paper

Businesses use a great deal of paper. Most will be of standard 'International Paper Size' – the most common is called the 'A' Series. This includes:

- A0 paper, which has an area of 1 square metre. It measures 841 mm x 1189 mm (to the nearest millimetre).
- A1 paper, which is half the size of A0
- A2 paper, which is half the size of A1; and so on.

The diagram below shows the relative sizes of paper from A0 down to A6 size, although there are also smaller sizes. The most common size for letters is A4, which measures 210 mm x 297 mm.

Paper is usually bought in reams (500 sheets) or quires (25 sheets).

	Size in mm
A0	841 x 1189
A1	594 x 841
A2	420 x 594
A3	297 x 420
A4	210 x 297
A5	148 x 210
A6	105 x 148
A7	74 x 105
A8	52 x 74
A9	37 x 52

A0

[Diagram showing the relative sizes of A1, A2, A3, A4, A5, A6 paper within an A0 sheet]

Shape

People working in business often need to use different shapes in their work. The most important points for you to remember are:
- perimeter
- area
- volume.

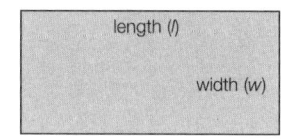

Perimeter is the distance round the edge.
The perimeter of a rectangle
= length + width + length + width
= $2l + 2w$

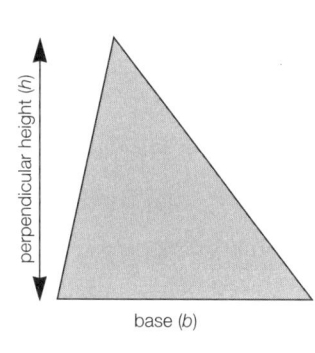

Area measures the surface of a shape in squares; for example, square centimetres, square metres, square feet, square inches.

To find the area of a triangle, multiply half the base by perpendicular height:
area of a triangle = $\frac{1}{2} \times b \times h$

To find the area of a rectangle, multiply length by width:
area of a rectangle = $l \times w$

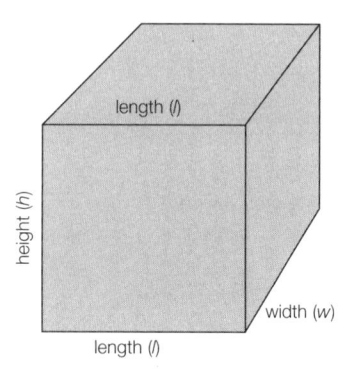

Volume measures the amount of space in a shape. Volume is measured two ways:
- in cubic units (for example, cubic centimetres, cubic metres, cubic inches, cubic feet)
- in liquid measure (for example, litres, millilitres, pints, gallons).

The volume of a cube or cuboid is found by multiplying length by width by height:
volume of a cube or cuboid = $l \times w \times h$

Using π

π (pronounced 'pie') is a Greek letter which we use to represent a very special number. Scientific calculators have a button labelled π which, when pressed, shows the number:

3.1415927

This is a small part of a number which has been calculated to millions of decimal places! One of the good things about using the letter π instead of the actual number is that you can round it to whatever is best for the circumstances. So:
- when estimating, you can round to a whole number – π = 3
- when calculating to one or two decimal places – π = 3.14 or 3.142.
  So why is this number special?

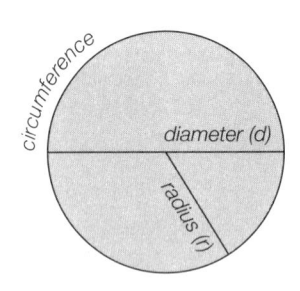

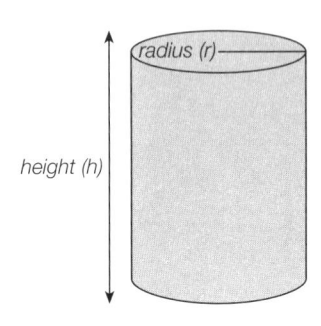

Toolkit

Measure the distance round the outside of any circle (the circumference), and the distance across the circle, through the centre (the diameter). Divide the circumference by the diameter, and the answer is always π (how accurately depends on how accurately you measure).

You can use π whenever you want to find the circumference, area or volume of any shapes or solids which involve circles.

- The circumference of a circle = $\pi \times d$ (d = diameter) or $2\pi r$ ($d = 2 \times$ radius)
- The area of a circle = πr^2 ($\pi \times r \times r$)
- The volume of a cylinder = $\pi r^2 h$ (h = height or length)

A Using shape

1 You have been asked to work out the cost of redecorating your office. The office is the size of your classroom.
   a Measure the length, width and height of the room. What will you use to take these measurements? Explain why.
   b Draw a plan of the room using an appropriate scale (for example, 1 cm represents 1 metre). Your plan should show the position of doors and windows.
   c Find the area of the walls. To do this, you need to multiply the length of each wall by its height, then find the area of any doors and windows and take this away from the total wall area to find the area for painting. Include the ceiling in your calculations.
   d Visit a local DIY store to find out the area covered by 1 litre of paint. From this, work out how many litres of paint you will need to buy. Assume you need to apply 2 coats of paint.
   e Find out the cost of a tin of emulsion paint. Are there different sized tins? What would be the best way to buy the paint?
   f Around the walls of the office there is a picture rail. What is the length of this picture rail? If it is going to be varnished at a cost of 30p per metre, what will be the total cost of revarnishing the rail?

2 As part of your responsibilities, you organise the tea and coffee for your office. There is a kettle which holds a maximum of 1.7 litres. You need to decide whether this is going to be big enough, or whether the office should buy a small boiler.
   a Each person in the office has a mug of about the same size. Each mug is 6 cm tall and has a diameter of 7.4 cm. Assuming each mug is a cylinder, work out the volume of a mug. Change your answer to millilitres.
   b Each time a mug is used, it is filled to four-fifths of its volume (capacity). How many mugs can be filled from a full kettle?
   c If there are six people in the office, will the kettle be big enough?

▶ The Metric System, page 36

▶ Answers, page 64

40

Conversion

If you need to change from one unit of measurement to another (for example, from litres to gallons), you can use:
- a conversion factor
- a conversion table
- a conversion chart or graph.

Conversion factors

A **conversion factor** is useful if you only have one or two calculations to do and you're not going to need to do them very often. If you use a conversion factor you can be as accurate as you want to be.

If you convert measurements only occasionally, you will probably use a conversion factor

> Example
>
> - the conversion factor to change litres to gallons is 0.22
> - the conversion factor to change gallons to litres is 4.546

This means that **1 litre is 0.22 gallons**, and there are **4.546 litres in 1 gallon**.
- to change litres to gallons you need to multiply by 0.22
- to change gallons to litres you multiply by 4.546

So if you buy 30 litres of petrol you are buying:
30 × 0.22 gallons of petrol = 6.6 gallons

This information is useful if someone wants to check how many miles they can travel using 1 gallon of petrol (car economy is often given in 'miles per gallon').

Conversion tables

Conversion tables and graphs are useful if you have to change measurements from one unit to another regularly.

With a **conversion table**, numbers are worked out once, using the conversion factor, and the answers are put in a table. This means that you can read the table instead of working out the answers each time. You can read a conversion table in two ways:
- read the middle column as gallons and the right-hand column as litres; or
- read the middle column as litres and the left-hand column as gallons.

You can design a conversion table to go as high as you think you might need – you could make this table go up to 100 litres if you thought it would be useful.

A conversion table for gallons and litres might look like this:

Gallons		Litres
0.220	1	4.546
0.440	2	9.092
0.660	3	13.638
0.880	4	18.184
1.101	5	22.730

If you convert measurements regularly, you will probably use a conversion table or graph

Toolkit

Each of the numbers in the table can be rounded to the degree of accuracy you need; for example:

$$1 \text{ gallon} = 4.546 \text{ litres} = 4.5 \text{ litres}$$

However, a conversion table does not answer all problems – could you use this table to change 3.5 gallons to litres?

Conversion graphs

To do this, it might be useful to draw a conversion graph or chart. Using the answers already worked out for the conversion table, you can plot three useful points on a graph:
- 0 litres = 0.0 gallons
- 10 litres = 2.2 gallons
- 20 litres = 4.4 gallons.

By joining these points together to give a straight line, you can read all other conversions from this graph, as shown below.

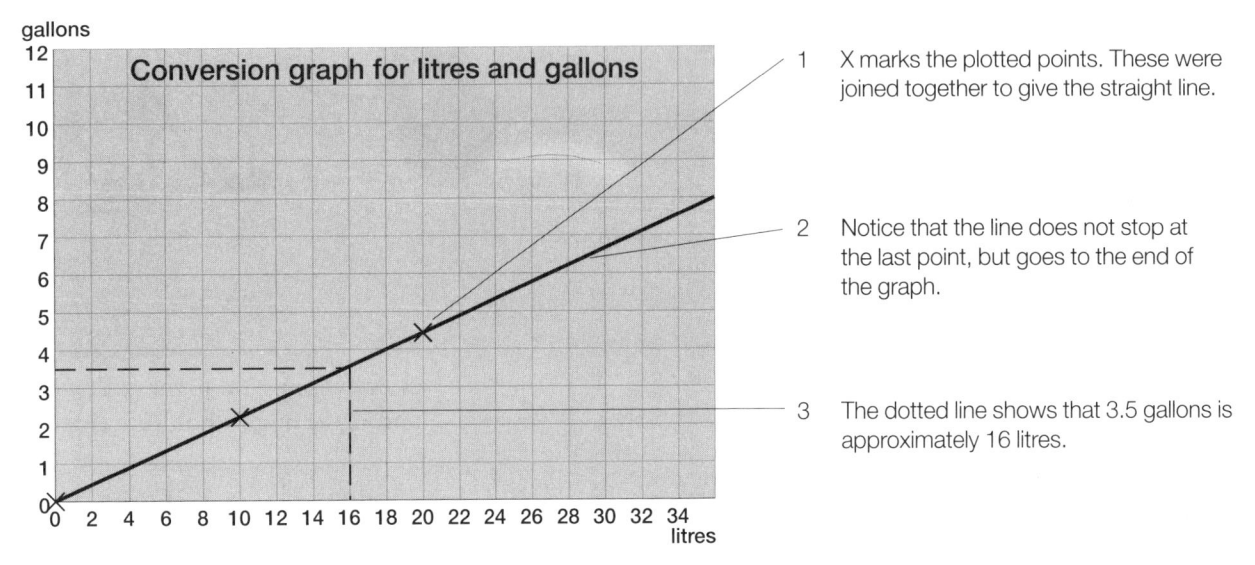

Conversion graph for litres and gallons

1. X marks the plotted points. These were joined together to give the straight line.
2. Notice that the line does not stop at the last point, but goes to the end of the graph.
3. The dotted line shows that 3.5 gallons is approximately 16 litres.

A conversion graph is often not as accurate as using a conversion factor or conversion table (using the conversion factor 3.5 gallons = 15.911 litres) but it is a quick and often easy way to change between units.

A Converting measurements

During 1995 the Government of the day decided that industry needed to be encouraged to use more metric measures by stating that goods sold 'loose' could continue to be sold by the pound, but goods sold in packs or bags must all be sold by the the kilogram. This particularly affected the way fruit and vegetables were sold. Trident Supermarket bought and sold all their apples by the kilo, Granny's Grocers had to buy their apples from the wholesaler by the kilogram but sold them in pounds.

1. Use the fact that 1 kilogram = 2.2 pounds to draw a conversion graph in 5 kg intervals, up to 30 kg.
2. Granny's Grocers can buy boxes with the following sizes: 20 kg, 24 kg and 30 kg. How many pounds of apples are there in each of these boxes?

Answers, page 64

Negative numbers

The numbers we use are usually **positive numbers** – they are **more than 0** (zero). But sometimes we need to describe numbers which are **less than 0**. We call these **negative numbers**.

Temperature can be measured in °C (degrees Celsius or Centigrade). Water freezes at 0°C. When the temperature falls below this freezing point, we use negative numbers. We usually call them **minus numbers**. If the temperature falls 1 degree below freezing, this is written as −1°C (minus 1 degree Centigrade). If the temperature falls to 5 degrees below freezing, this is written −5°C.

When a bank or building society account is overdrawn, the amount which is overdrawn can be written as a negative number, or as an amount followed by O/D (overdrawn). If an account is £30 overdrawn, this can be written as −£30 or £30 O/D.

1995	STATEMENT DATE	5 JAN 1996		ACCOUNT NO. 12345678
DATE	DETAILS	WITHDRAWALS	DEPOSITS	BALANCE (£)
6 DEC	BALANCE FROM SHEET NO. 317			88.32
11 DEC	0230034	62.42		25.90
16 DEC	0230035	30.00		4.10 O/D
17 DEC	LEEDS CENTRAL		20.00	15.90

A Using negative numbers

1. During a very cold winter, a gardener recorded the temperature outside his greenhouse. At lunchtime on Tuesday the temperature was 3°C. By midnight the temperature had dropped by 10 degrees. By the following lunchtime, the temperature had risen by only 5 degrees.
   a What was the temperature at midnight?
   b What was the temperature on Wednesday lunchtime?

2. Bashir had £32.45 in his bank account. If he wrote a cheque for £46.50, what would be the new balance of his account? If he put £20 into his account, how much would he now have in his account?

Answers, page 64

Drawing graphs and charts

We often draw graphs and charts as part of a presentation. They give a good picture of data, and make it easier to see the general result. Remember, because they are pictures they often do not provide detailed information. For detail, you should look at the original information.

The different graphs and charts we can use include:

Bar charts
- all bars are the same width
- each bar should be labelled
- the height of the bar shows 'how many' (the frequency)
- only one axis has a scale, the other has labels
- bar charts can be horizontal or vertical

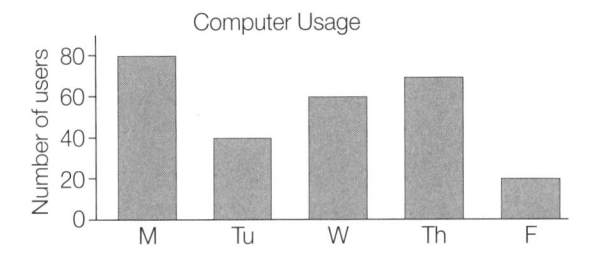

Pictograms
- also known as pictographs
- use symbols (pictures) rather than bars
- all pictures should be the same size
- pictures are chosen to emphasise the topic

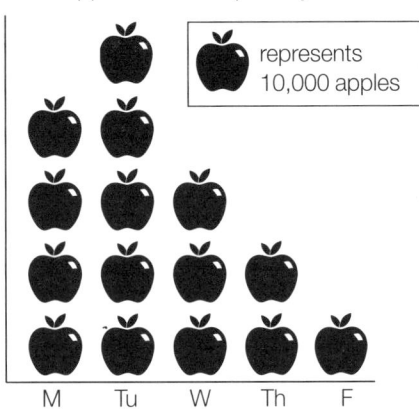

Pie charts
- show proportion (the way things are shared out)
- show the fraction of the whole for each area
- don't usually show detail
- two pie charts are often used to compare different-sized samples

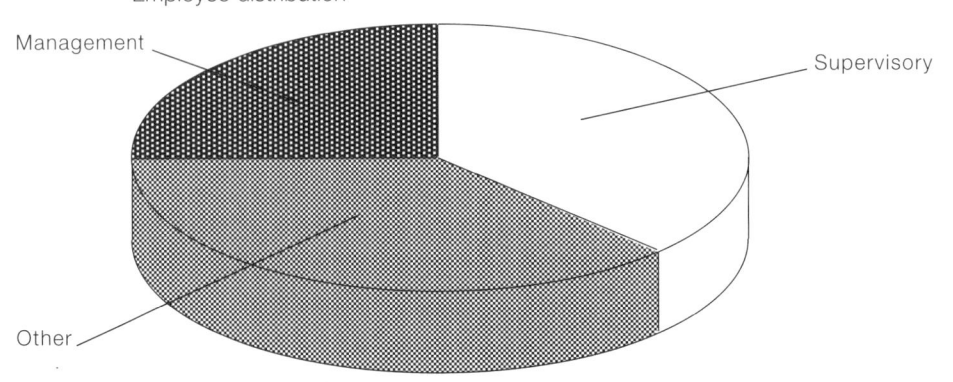

Bar charts

- Bar charts, or graphs, can be drawn with the bars horizontal or with the bars vertical. Vertical bar charts are the most common.

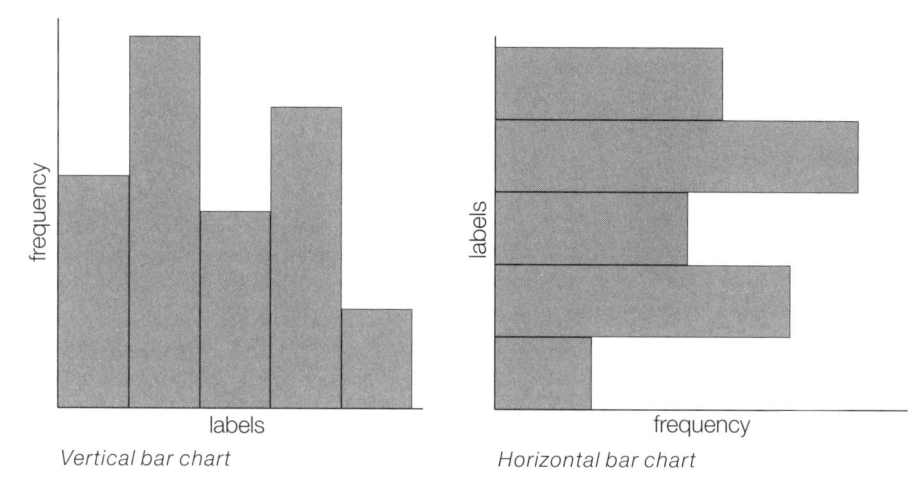

Vertical bar chart

Horizontal bar chart

Choosing a scale

The axis for frequency must be to **scale** – evenly spaced. Working on graph paper, each square must be worth **the same amount**.

CORRECT — one square = 5

CORRECT — one square = 2

WRONG — one square = 5, one square = 2

The main decision you have to make is **what scale to use**. Look at the frequency information and, if you are drawing your chart by hand, the number of squares on your graph paper. Choose a scale which will fit the paper well. Be careful not to choose a difficult scale – keep to 2's, 5's, 10's, 20's, 25's, 50's, 100's. Avoid 3's and other awkward numbers.

Make sure you understand the meaning of your scale and the smaller parts of it; for example, what does 0.5 cm show on your graph?

A Choosing a scale

Get a piece of graph paper 30 cm long.

1. How would you fit a frequency of up to 50?
2. How would you fit a frequency of up to 100?
3. How would you fit a frequency of up to 550?

Answers, page 64

Toolkit

Drawing a bar chart

Having decided on the scale for your frequency, you need to draw bars to the correct height. Each bar must be the **same width**. You can leave gaps between the bars if you wish, or you can keep them next to each other. Make the graph fit neatly on the page.

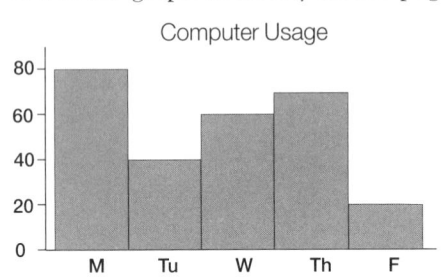

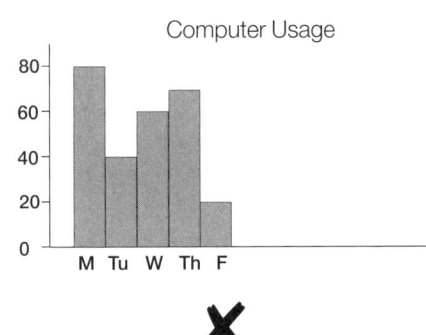

The height of each bar should match its 'frequency' (how many times it occurs). There is no need to put the bars in order of size.

Give the graph a title, and label the axes and bars to make sure it is clear what the graph shows.

Reading a bar chart

Having drawn the graph, you can use it to find information.

Example

The following table shows the daily takings of a sweet shop over one week:

Day	Mon	Tue	Wed	Thurs	Fri	Sat
Takings (£)	40	30	45	10	30	50

The sweet shop manager drew the following bar chart to show this information. She joined each bar together to make a **line graph** as this gave her a clearer picture of the shape of the graph. You can draw a line graph without drawing thr bar chart first, but you must remember to use the mid-point of any grouped data.

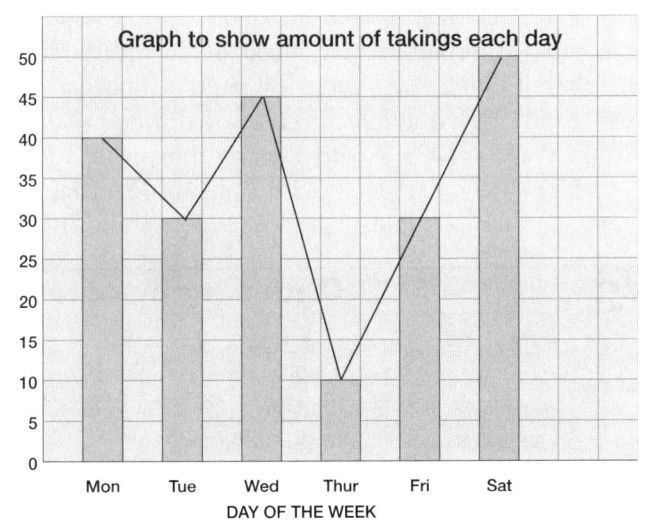

46

By looking at this, she could see that Saturday is the most popular day (the highest point) and Thursday is the least popular day (the lowest point).

Composite bar charts
Composite bar charts are used to:
- compare two or more sets of similar data
- display more than one set of data on a graph.

Sets of data side by side
To compare two or more sets of data, bars for each set of data are drawn side by side.

Example

The following table shows the Randall family's monthly expenses for 1970, 1980 and 1990.

	Housing	Food	Clothing	Fuel	Savings
1970	£44	£52	£24	£38	£30
1980	£135	£170	£80	£75	£60
1990	£290	£280	£110	£100	£40

Drawing a composite bar chart can make it easier to compare these sets of data.

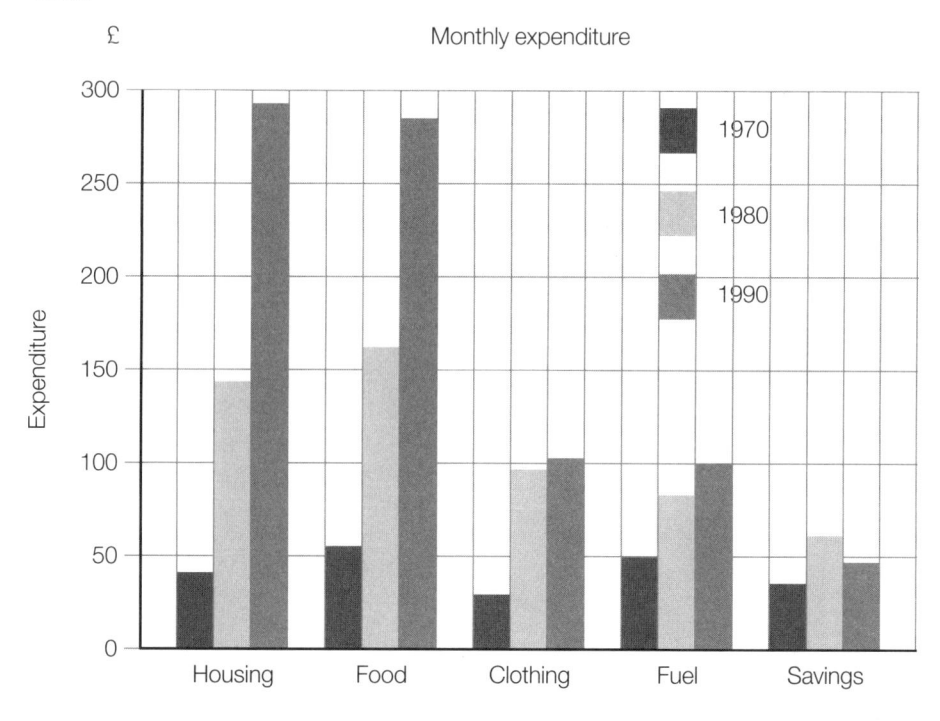

By looking at the chart, you can see that:
- most expenditure is on housing and food
- savings is the only category to decrease
- the greatest actual increase was in housing from 1980 to 1990
- expenditure on clothing more than doubled in the first ten years, then changed little in the next ten years.

Totals subdivided into different sections

This type of composite bar chart emphasises totals, but divides them into sections to show how they were made up.

The Randall family's monthly expenses can be totalled as follows:

	Housing	**Food**	**Clothing**	**Fuel**	**Savings**	**Total**
1970	£44	£52	£24	£38	£30	**£188**
1980	£135	£170	£80	£75	£60	**£520**
1990	£290	£280	£110	£100	£40	**£820**
Totals	**£469**	**£502**	**£214**	**£213**	**£130**	

You could draw a composite bar chart showing this in two ways:
- by year – with three bars (one for each year) split into five sections (one for each type of expense). This would show how the Randall family's total monthly expenditure changed over each ten-year period. What they spent money on would be of secondary importance
- by type of expenditure – with five bars (one for each expense) split into three sections (one for each year). This would show what the Randalls spent their money on. The change in expenditure over each ten-year period would be of secondary importance.

Monthly expenditure (by year)

Monthly expenditure (by type)

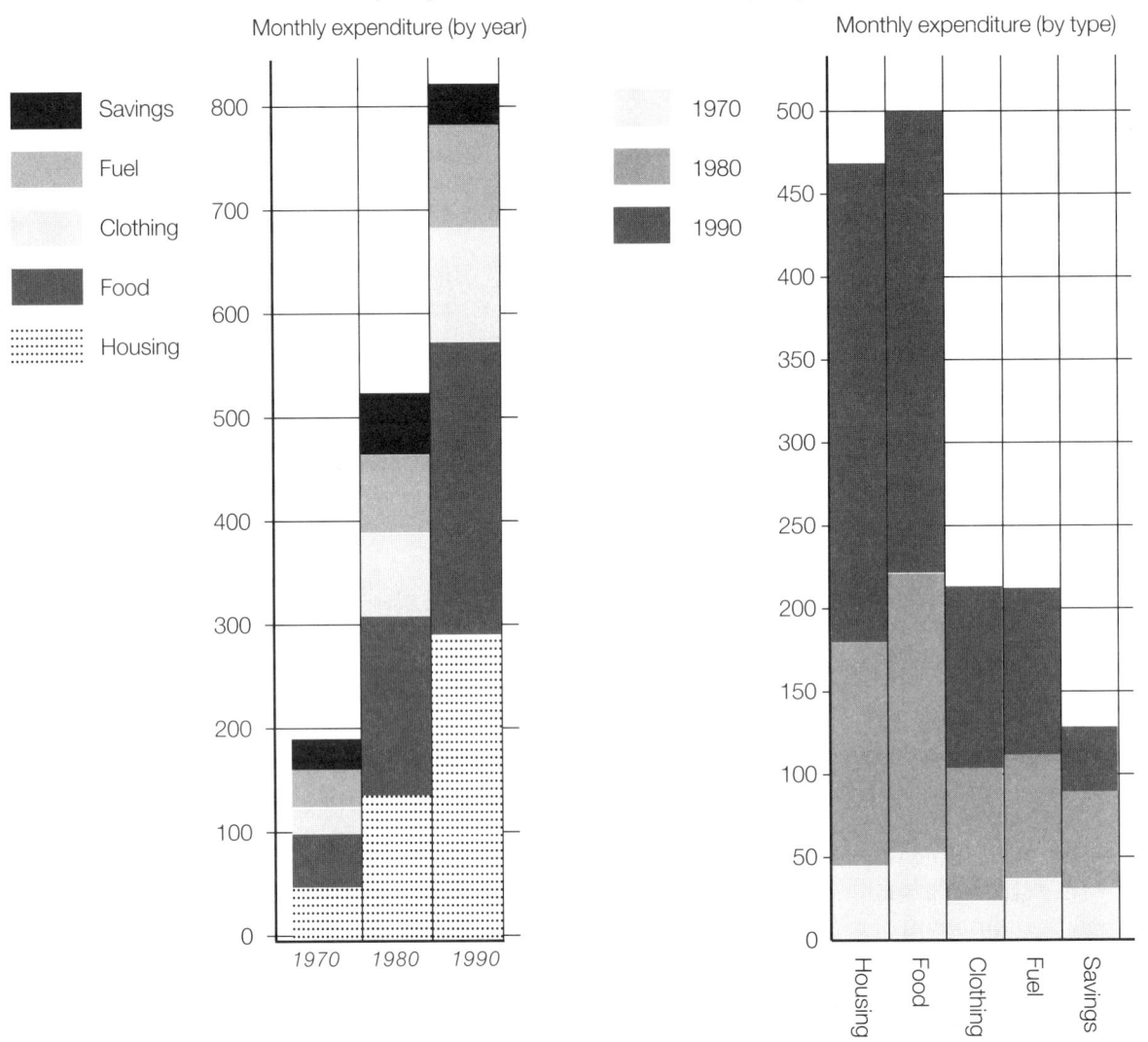

A Reading and drawing composite bar charts

1 The composite bar chart below shows what percentage of British Rail trains were cancelled in 1990-1. Make three comments about the graph.

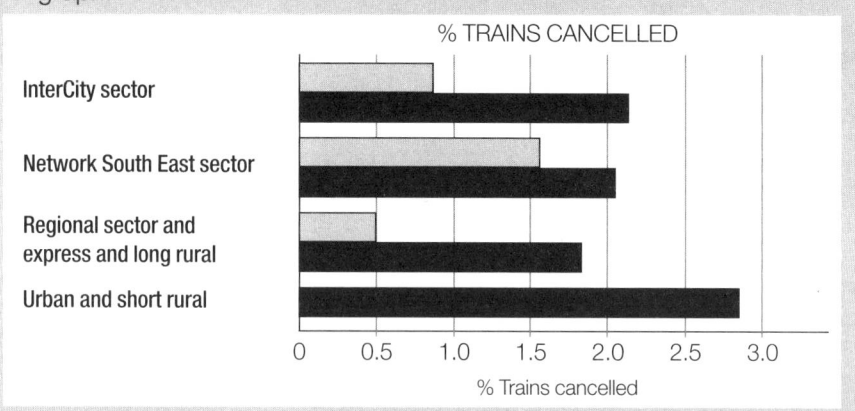

% TRAINS CANCELLED

- InterCity sector
- Network South East sector
- Regional sector and express and long rural
- Urban and short rural

% Trains cancelled

Legend:
- 1986–1987
- 1990–1991

Source: *Social Trends*

2 The following table shows the different vehicles which travelled down a road between midday and 7 p.m.

	12–1	1–2	2–3	3–4	4–5	5–6	6–7
cars	8	8	6	9	15	20	13
vans/lorries	4	3	1	3	5	4	2
buses	3	4	4	5	6	7	4
other	2	1	1	0	3	2	1

Draw a composite bar chart to show the total traffic distribution from 12 p.m. to 7 p.m. and the different traffic types.

▶ Answers, page 64

Pictograms

Pictograms are graphs which use pictures to emphasise the topic. For example:
- if your topic is cigarette smoking, you might use pictures of cigarettes
- if your topic is the number killed in a war, you might use pictures of crosses or coffins
- if your topic is traffic, you might use pictures of cars, lorries or buses.

Note! Each picture in a pictogram must be the same size, even if you use different pictures in the same graph.

To save time and effort, we usually let one picture represent more than 1. For example:

might represent 200 buses

might represent less than 200 buses

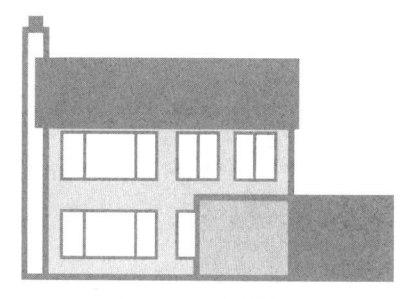

might represent 1000 houses

Toolkit

One of the problems with pictograms is that it is difficult to show the difference between similar numbers, for example 691 buses and 695 buses. You could show part of a bus to represent less than 200 buses, but you couldn't make detailed differences.

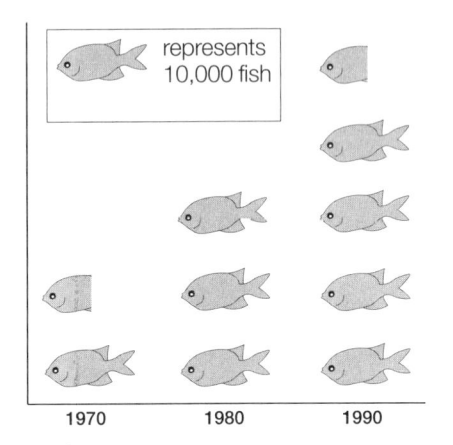

Example

This pictogram shows the increase in number of fish caught by Tubbs & Co. over a 20-year period.

This doesn't show exactly how many fish Tubbs & Co. caught each year – you can't tell how many the 'part fish' represents. The important thing is that it shows that the number of fish being caught is increasing quickly.

Number of fish caught by Tubbs & Co.

A Using pictograms

1 The women's support group at Johnson's biscuit factory asked Margaret to research the number of women in middle and senior management posts at Johnson's during the last ten years. Margaret realised that the total number of people working at Johnson's had changed over the years and that this might affect the figures, so she also worked out the percentage of managers who were women. Her findings were as follows:

Year	Numbers	Percentage
1985	45	7%
1990	62	12%
1995	73	9%

a Use a computer to draw a pictogram showing the changing number of women in management at Johnson's. Use a draw package to draw the axes for your graph, and add labels and titles. Find an appropriate piece of clip art and use it to produce the chart. Make sure all the pictures are the same size.

b Draw a bar chart to show how the percentage of women in management jobs has changed, and comment on the results.

2 Queenstown Plant Nursery plants tomatoes each year. Mr Davies, the nurseryman, measures the height of each plant at the beginning of each month to check they are growing well. He records the results on a pictogram.

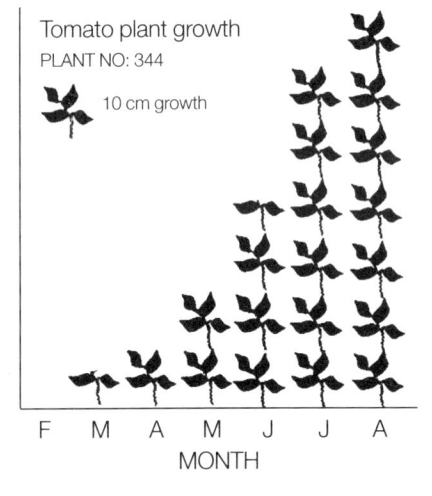

Use the pictogram to answer the following questions:
a In which month did Mr Davies measure the plant for the first time?
b Approximately how much did the plant grown in April?
c In which month did the plant grow by the largest amount?
d What was the approximate height of the plant at the beginning of August?

Tomato plant growth
PLANT NO: 344
10 cm growth

Answers, page 64

Pie charts

Pie charts are so called because they are like sharing out a pie!

Pie charts show the proportion of the results in different sections. The pie is always the same basic size, even though the size of the circle may change. It is the angle at the centre of the circle which is shared, and this is always 360 degrees (360°).

Reading pie charts

Example

This pie chart shows how 180 people like to spend their spare time.

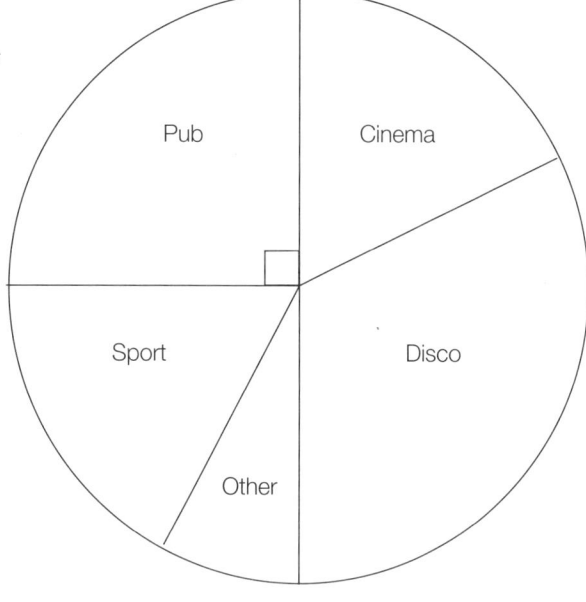

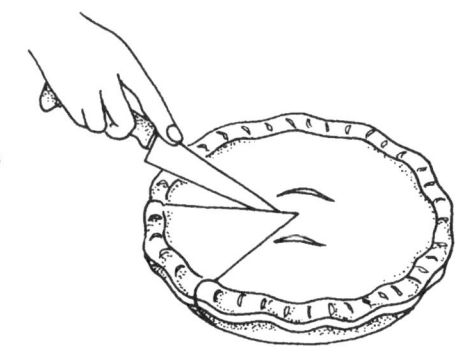

It shows that the biggest group are people who like going to discos, then people who like going to the pub, and so on.

Drawing pie charts

The first step in drawing a pie chart is working out the angles. There are several ways to do this.

Note! The total angle of a pie chart is always 360°.

Example

Swan Village Sports Centre carried out a survey into people's favourite sports. These were the results (the 'Frequency' column shows the number of people who chose each sport as their favourite).

Favourite sport	Frequency
Football	80
Squash	30
Swimming	40
Other	30

Kim Harding, the manager of the sports centre, wanted to present this information in a pie chart. To do this, she needed to work out the angles for the chart. She could do this in two ways.

Toolkit

Method 1
Find the total number of responses.

80 + 30 + 40 + 30 = 180

Write the number in each section as a fraction of the total (180).

Football = $\frac{80}{180}$ Squash = $\frac{30}{180}$ Swimming = $\frac{40}{180}$

Other = $\frac{30}{180}$

Find these fractions of 360° (the total angle in the pie).

Football = $\frac{80}{180} \times 360 = 160°$ Other = $\frac{30}{180} \times 360 = 60°$

Squash = $\frac{30}{180} \times 360 = 60°$

Swimming = $\frac{40}{180} \times 360 = 80°$

Method 2
Find the total number of responses.

80 + 30 + 40 + 30 = 180

Find the angle for each group by 'sharing' the 360 between the total.

360 ÷ 180 = 2 (angle per response)

Multiply this angle by the frequency of each group.

Football = 80 × 2 = 160°

Squash = 30 × 2 = 60°

Swimming = 40 × 2 = 80°

Other = 30 × 2 = 60°

Once she had worked out the angles, Kim was ready to draw the pie chart. To do this, she needed a protractor.

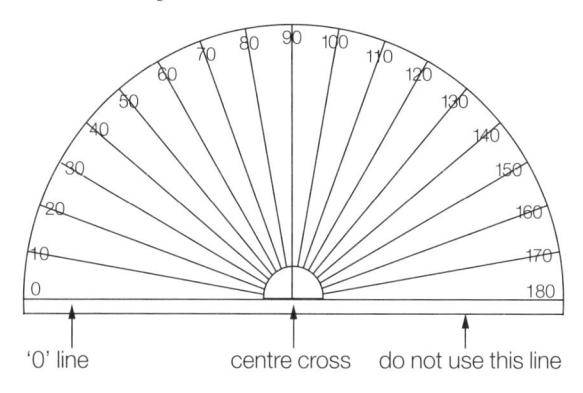

'0' line | centre cross | do not use this line

Using protractors
A protractor has an extra strip on the bottom for protection. When measuring, you should ignore this.

There are two scales on most protractors, so you can measure in either direction. Make sure you always start at '0' and measure towards '180'. Make sure the 'centre cross' is positioned at the 'point' of the angle, and the '0' line rests exactly on your first line.

To draw her pie chart, Kim worked through the following steps.

Step 1:
Using a compass, she drew a circle and drew in a radius (a line from the centre to the edge of the circle).

Step 2:
She set the '0' line of the protractor on the radius, and the centre cross on the centre of the circle. She decided to begin by drawing the angle for football, which she knew was 160°. She measured the angle round from '0', and made a mark at 160°. She then drew a line from the centre of the circle to the edge, passing through this mark.

Step 3:
She then moved the protractor round so that the '0' line was on the new line (the centre cross was still on the centre of the circle). From here, she measured the next angle and carried on drawing lines and measuring angles until the pie chart was complete. She found that the last angle fitted in the space available – if it hadn't she would have had to measure again more accurately!

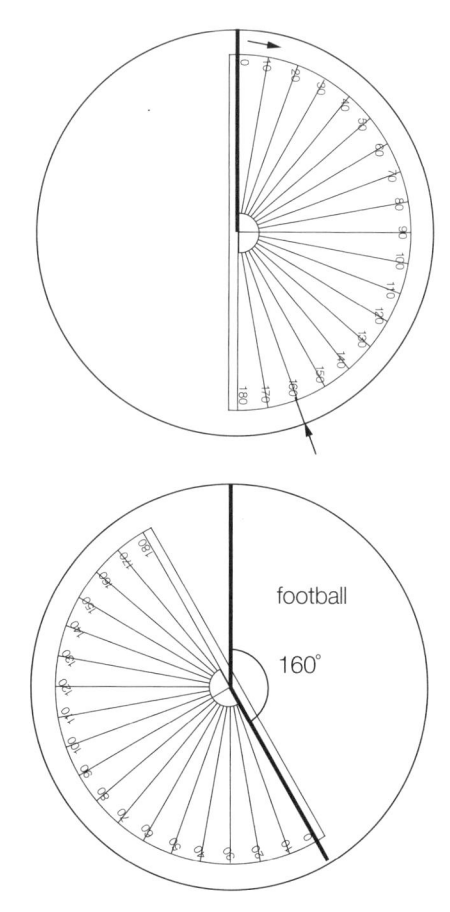

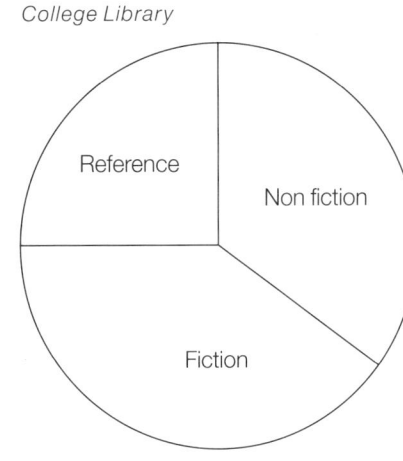

Toolkit

Her final pie chart looked like the one on the right.

Using pie charts

Pie charts are often used for comparison; for example, to compare figures for 1980 with figures for 1990. They are particularly useful for comparing different size samples, such as the results of a small, local survey and a large, national survey.

College Library (pie chart: Reference, Non fiction, Fiction)

Central Library (pie chart: Reference, Non fiction, Fiction)

(Pie chart: Other, Football, Squash, Swimming)

Example

These pie charts compare books in a busy library in the city centre with books at a small college library.

The pie charts show that there is a higher proportion of reference and non-fiction books at the college library than at the central library, where fiction books are most popular. Because the central library is bigger, it may in fact have a larger number of reference and non-fiction books than the college library.

When samples (in this case, the total number of books at each library) are different sizes, pie charts help you compare proportions, not actual numbers. Whether the sample size is 100, 1000 or 10,000, all pie charts have a central angle of 360°. Therefore you can say that each pie shows how the sample would be divided if it was scaled down or up to 360 (you can think of it as 'out of 360').

To get the same sort of results with bar charts, you need to change all frequencies to percentages of the total. This would have the effect of scaling up or down to 100 (think of it as 'out of 100').

A Using pie charts

The Co-op in Swan Village and the Co-op in Queenstown sent the following sales figures to head office. They show the amount of sales (in £s) in the different sections of the stores in one week.

	Swan Village	Queenstown
Tins and packets	200	5600
Fresh fruit & veg	148	2100
Meat/fish counter	120	2340
Dairy	84	960
Other	24	520

Draw two pie charts – one for each shop – and comment on the results.

▶ Answers, page 64

Probability

Probability is a measure of how likely it is that something will happen. The higher the probability, the more likely it is that it will happen.

Example

Multilux produces light bulbs. The company expects one bulb in every 100 to be faulty in some way.

This means that the **probability** of a light bulb being faulty is $\frac{1}{100}$.

The managing director of Multilux wanted to know how many bulbs were likely to be faulty for every 2000 produced. He knew that the probability of a bulb being faulty was $\frac{1}{100}$, and realised that he needed to find this fraction of 2000 bulbs:

$$\frac{1}{100} \text{ of } 2000 = 20 \text{ bulbs}$$

From this, he knew that he could **expect** 20 bulbs in every 2000 to be faulty – in reality, there might be more or less.

To get the original figure of 1 in 100 bulbs likely to be faulty, Multilux carried out research by checking batches of 100 bulbs. Probability is often based on the findings of research like this.

Multilux sign

Example

In a group of GNVQ Business students, 6 out of 30 had blue eyes. They worked out that the probability of a student having blue eyes was:

$$\frac{6}{30} = \frac{1}{5}$$

This would mean that in a group of 100 students you would expect:

$$\frac{1}{5} \times 100 = 20 \text{ students to have blue eyes}$$

A Working out probability

1. At Amwar's Bakery, the probability of a biscuit breaking before it is packed is $\frac{1}{500}$. If the Bakery bakes 5000 biscuits, how many can it expect to break?
2. Find out how many students in your group are left-handed. Use your results to write down the probability that a member of your group is left-handed. If this probability was true for your whole school or college, how many students would you expect to be left-handed? How could this information be used by a firm producing left-handed scissors?

Answers, page 64

Toolkit

The mean, the mode and the range

The mean

This is the best known average, also known as the **arithmetic mean**.

Example

To help you understand, imagine six people have money as follows:

At the moment, the money isn't shared out equally – some people have more than others! Calculating the mean is like finding out how much each would have if the money was shared out equally. The total amount of money must stay the same.

To work this out they could put all their money on the table and then share it out. In our example, the total amount of money would be:
£6 + £5 + £3 + £2 + £1 + £1 = **£18**

Sharing this out equally between the six of them would give each one:
£18 ÷ 6 = **£3 each**

£3 is the mean.

> To find the mean, find the total, then divide it by the number of pieces of data. When you find the mean, always use every piece of data.

Example

To find the mean of £34, £56, £65, £72, £84:
find the total: £34 + £56 + £65 + £72 + £84 = £311
divide it by the number of pieces of data: £311 ÷ 5 = £62.2 = £62.20

The mode

This is the simplest average to 'work out'.

The mode is the most popular or most frequent figure – the value that crops up most often.

Example

The following figures are the amount of time, in minutes, that 15 patients spent with their doctor in one day:

6, 4, 4, 7, 4, 4, 6, 5, 4, 4, 6, 4, 5, 8, 4

From these figures you can draw a frequency table – a table showing how many people had to wait for each length of time.

A quick way to do this is to tally the data – for each number put a mark. To help keep track (especially for large numbers) we group marks into fives as shown on the right. This is called a '5-barred gate' – the fifth mark is put across the other 4 to 'tie' them together.

From our numbers, we can compile the tally chart on the right. As you can see, 8 patients spent 4 minutes with the doctor. Therefore 4 minutes was the modal time spent with the doctor.

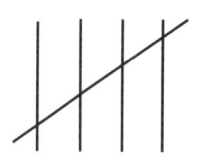

Data	Tally	Frequency
4	⦀⦀⦀ ⦀⦀⦀	8
5	⦀⦀	2
6	⦀⦀⦀	3
7	⦀	1
8	⦀	1

Note: You can also use a tally chart to help you find the **mean**:
4 minutes occurred 8 times. This adds up to 32 minutes
5 minutes occurred twice = 10 minutes
6 minutes × 3 = 18 minutes
7 minutes × 1 = 7 minutes
8 minutes × 1 = 8 minutes

From this, you can work out that the total number of minutes spent with the doctor was
32 + 10 + 18 + 7 + 8
= 75 minutes, and that there were
8 + 2 + 3 + 1 + 1 = 15 patients.

Therefore the mean
= 75 ÷ 15 = 5

Answers, page 64

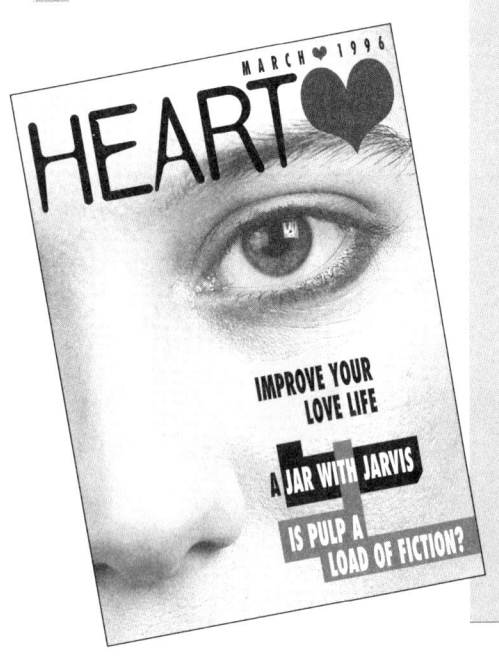

The range

Dispersion measures the degree of **spread**. The simplest measure of spread – dispersion – is the **range.**

The range of a set of numbers is the difference between the largest and the smallest.

Example

Work out the range of 3, 8, 6, 9, 2, 7
The largest number is 9, and the smallest number is 2.
Therefore the range is 9 – 2 = 7

So to find the range of a set of numbers, simply look for the largest value and the smallest value, and calculate the difference.

Example

Look again at the amount of time 15 patients spent with their doctor.
The range is 8 – 3 = 5 (this means that there was 5 minutes difference between the shortest and longest times).

A   Mean, mode and range

A publishing company was planning to introduce a new magazine for young people, and produced a questionnaire to find out how much they were prepared to pay for a good new magazine. This was the frequency table the company produced from the results of the survey (prices were rounded to the nearest 50p):

Amount (in £s)	Frequency
0.50	1
1.00	21
1.50	35
2.00	25
2.50	58
3.00	39
3.50	15
4.00	3
4.50	2
5.00	1

1. Add a column to this table to multiply frequency by amount. Use these amounts to find the total and mean amount young people would be prepared to pay. Round your answer to the nearest penny.
2. What is the modal amount young people were prepared to pay?
3. What was the range in the amounts they were prepared to pay?
4. If you were publishing the new magazine, what price would you give it? Explain your decision.

Using information technology

Computers are very good at dealing with numbers and producing graphs. Although it is important that we know how to produce graphs by hand, a large business would always use IT. Computer packages not only save time and effort, but also produce well-finished graphs and charts.

To produce a graph or chart on the computer, you have to begin with a spreadsheet or database.

Using a spreadsheet

The following information is generally true, but you must learn how to use the spreadsheet package you have at school or college as they are all slightly different.

When you use a spreadsheet or database, you put all the information into a table like the one below. These are the sales figures sent to head office by a grocery shop with branches in Swan Village and in Queenstown. The table shows the amount (in £) taken by different sections of the stores in one week.

	A	B	C	D
1	Item	Swan Village	Queenstown	
2	Tins & packets	200	5600	
3	Fresh fruit/veg	148	2100	
4	Meat/fish	120	2340	
5	Dairy	84	960	
6	Other	24	520	
7				
8				
9				
10				

Each piece of information is placed in a **cell**, described using the letter at the top of the column and the number at the beginning of the row. In the example here, the word 'Item' is in cell A1. The number 5600 is in cell C2.

Managers need to compare figures like this several times a year. Therefore it is important that they show the date they produced each set of data. One way to do this is to type the date into cell C9. A better way is to use the computer to 'insert the current date' in this cell.

	A	B	C	D
1	Item	Swan Village	Queenstown	
2	Tins & packets	200	5600	
3	Fresh fruit/veg	148	2100	
4	Meat/fish	120	2340	
5	Dairy	84	960	
6	Other	24	520	
7				
8				
9	22nd April 1996			

Producing graphs

By using the graph option in the spreadsheet or database package, you can produce graphs and charts like these:

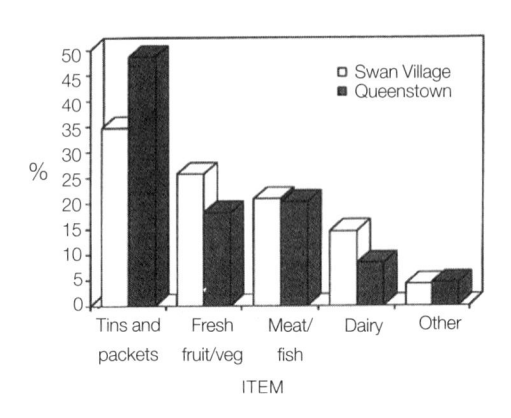

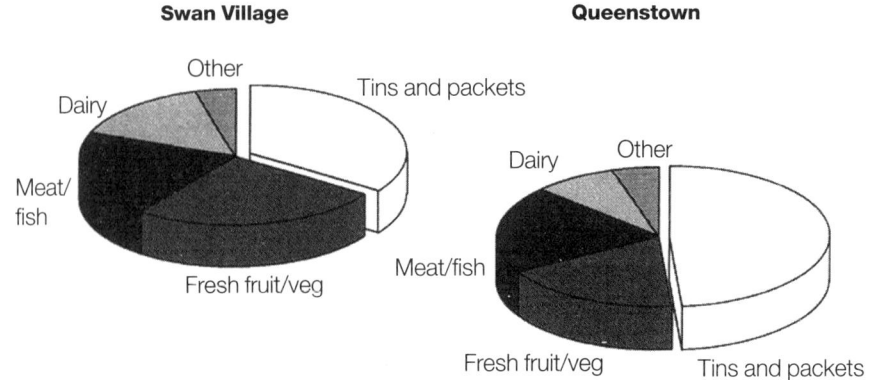

For the bar chart, the information has been changed to percentages. You can do this by using a calculator and typing in the answers, but it is better to use the power of the spreadsheet by putting in a formula.

Use a spreadsheet package to work through the following steps. Find out how your package inserts the current date, and insert it into cell A9.

Step 1: working out totals

The total number of sales for Swan Village should go in cell B7. To do this, you need to select B7, then enter a formula.

	A	B	C	D
1	Item	Swan Village	Queenstown	
2	Tins & packets	200	5600	
3	Fresh fruit/veg	148	2100	
4	Meat/fish	120	2340	
5	Dairy	84	960	
6	Other	24	520	
7				
8				
9	22nd April 1996			
10				
11				

The formula might look like this:
=B2+B3+B4+B5+B6
or like this:
=SUM(B2:B6)

This should give a total of 576.

Repeat this process for Queenstown. You should get a total of 11,520.

Step 2: working out percentages

The percentage of Swan Village's total sales that came from tins and packets should go in cell D2. This will be:

$\frac{200}{576} \times 100$ (200 as a percentage of the total number of sales – 576)

The formula might look like this:
=B2/B7*100

Notice that / is used to divide and * is used to multiply, and that we use B2 and B7 instead of the numbers 200 and 576.

The answer is 34.722222. If you don't need this number of decimal places, you can **format** the cell to give whole numbers only. This will give you the answer 35%.

If you work out percentages for all the other amounts from Swan Village, and repeat the process for Queenstown, your spreadsheet should look something like this:

	A	B	C	D	E	F
1	Item	Swan Village	Queenstown	%1	%2	
2	Tins & packets	200	5600	35	49	
3	Fresh fruit/veg	148	2100	26	18	
4	Meat/fish	120	2340	21	20	
5	Dairy	84	960	15	8	
6	Other	24	520	4	5	
7	Total	576	11520			
8						
9	22nd April 1996					
10						
11						

The percent columns should always add up to approximately 100%. (You might get 99% or 101% if figures are rounded up or down.)

Once you have produced your graphs or charts, one of the best ways to use them is to include them in a written (word processed) report. By inserting graphs at appropriate points in the text you can make reports clearer and more attractive.

Toolkit

> **Example**
>
> The following extract is taken from the sales manager's report to the board of directors of the grocery shop with branches in Queenstown and Swan Village.

The following bar chart shows sales in five categories – tins and packages, fresh fruit and vegetables, meat and fish, dairy, and 'other'. It compares sales at one of our smaller branches (Swan Village) with one of our larger branches (Queenstown).

The graph shows the percentage of sales in each of the categories in each of the stores. It shows that:
- fresh fruit/veg and dairy are not as popular in the large store as in the small store
- meat and fish are roughly the same
- tins and packets and 'other' have a higher proportion of the sales in Queenstown than in Swan Village.

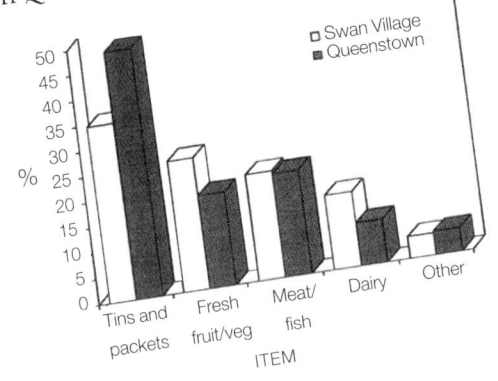

This may be due to:
- local competitors
- each store's marketing strategy
- a difference in lifestyle of the two sets of customers.

I suggest we investigate our local competitors in each area and discuss marketing strategies with managers (with particular reference to those sections of sales which do not compare favourably with other stores).

Safety first!

It is important to take safety into account when using IT equipment. How would you do things differently to the person below?

Store disks away from heat and electrical equipment

Keep drinks away from equipment

Position screen to avoid reflections

Keep cables tidy. Make sure cables are connected properly.

Note!
Make sure you take precautions to avoid losing or corrupting your work.
 Use security systems to prevent others accessing your work.

Dealing with errors and faults

When you use computers you may find that you make mistakes (errors) which affect your work. It is all too easy when you learn a new computer package to press the wrong key or click the mouse on the wrong icon, creating an effect you did not want.

When you make a mistake, you can deal with it in one of two ways:
- sort it out yourself
- ask someone for help.

Hopefully you won't have done anything which can't be undone.

Sometimes the actual hardware or software generates a fault – for example:
- the computer network breaks down
- the setup of the computer is wrong
- there is a bug in the software.

In these cases it is unlikely that you will be able to sort the problem out yourself, and you will need to ask for help.

Always record errors and faults you come across in a **log**. Make notes on how they were sorted out and which ones couldn't be put right. Record whether you solved the problem yourself, or whether you asked for help.

Answers

Activity: Rounding up and down (p. 26)
1. 1755 = 1760
2. 1760
3. You get the same answer both ways. This won't always be the case – it will depend how much is rounded up and how much is rounded down.

Activity: Rounding money (p. 27)
1. £10.10
2. £10.04
3. Yes

Activity: Rounding decimals (p. 29)
1. £12.40
2. £111.57
3. £19.52475 = £19.52
4. £131.09

Activity: Using percentages (p. 33)
1. Sale price = £225 − £22.50 = £202.50.
   Credit price = £202.50 + £18.23 = £220.73
2a. £18.39 + 5p = £18.44
 b. £18.39

Activity: Writing ratios (p. 34)
1a. 1 : 2   b 1 : 5   c 3 : 10   d 1 : 2 : 10
2. Middle to senior managers are in the same ratio at Amwar's Bakery and Crossman's Toolworks. Amwar's Bakery has a slightly higher ratio of middle managers to shopfloor workers. Ratios of 1 : 4 and 3 : 10 are slightly more difficult to compare (1 : 4 would be 2.5 : 10). Crossman's Toolworks has a higher ratio of managers (both senior and middle) to shopfloor workers.

Activity: Using ratios (p. 36)
1. £1312.50
2. £1750 per month = £21,000 per year

Activity: Using shape (p. 40)
2a. The radius of the mugs is 3.7 cm.
   The volume of each mug is $\pi \times 3.7 \times 3.7 \times 6 = 258$ cubic cm
   258 cubic cm = 258 ml
   $\frac{4}{5}$ of 258 = $\frac{258}{5} \times 4 = 206.4$ ml
2b. 1.7 litres = 1700 ml. 1700 ml ÷ 206.4 = 8.2. Just over 8 mugs can be filled from the kettle
2c. Yes, the kettle is big enough for the staff

Activity: Converting measurements (p. 42)
 a. 20 kg = 44 lb
 b. 24 kg = 52.8 lb
 c. 30 kg = 66 lb

Activity: Using negative numbers (p. 43)
1. a −7 °C   b −2 °C
2. −£14.05 (overdrawn), £5.95

Activity: Choosing a scale (p. 45)
1. 2 per cm, this gives a frequency of up to 60
2. 5 per cm, this gives a frequency of up to 150
3. 20 per cm, this gives a frequency of up to 600

Activity: Reading and drawing composite bar charts (p. 49)
1. Comments can include: there is a definite increase in all areas; the greatest increase is in 'urban and short rural'; Network SouthEast has a bad record for both years; the worst section changed from Network SouthEast to 'urban and short rural'; 'Regional sector express and long rural' has more than doubled.

2.

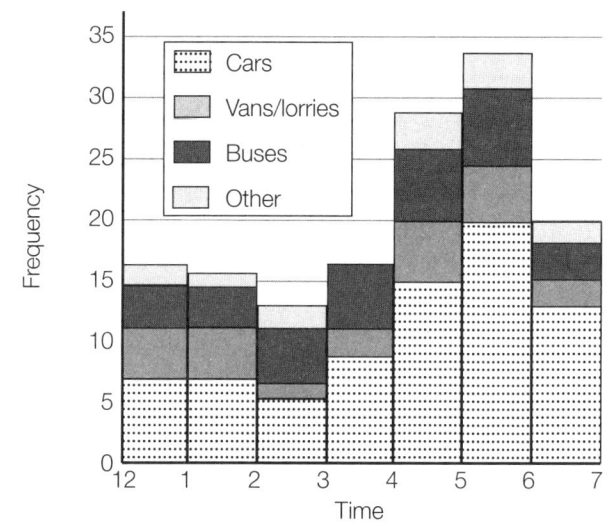

Activity: Using pictograms (p. 50)

1a.

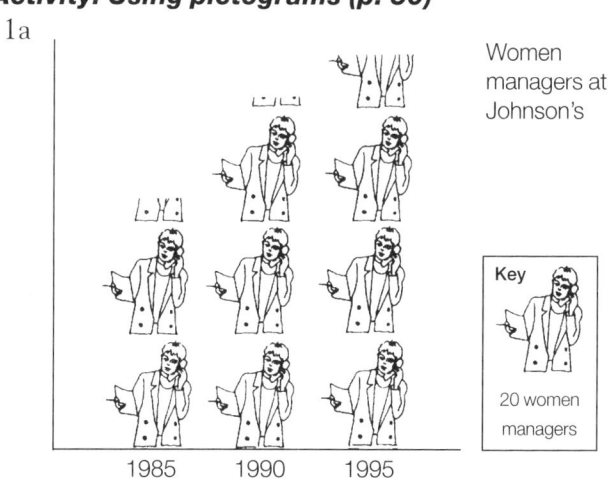

64

b

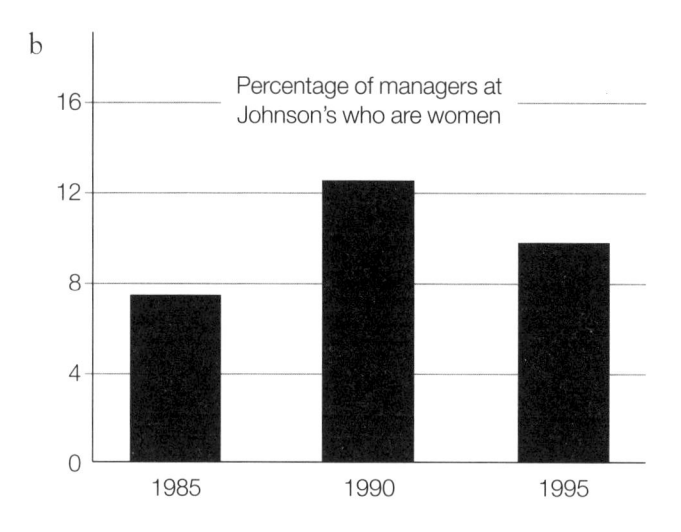

Percentage of managers at Johnson's who are women

[Bar chart showing: 1985 ≈ 7%, 1990 ≈ 12.5%, 1995 ≈ 9.5%]

c The graphs show that the number of women managers has increased. The percentage of women managers increased in the first five years, then dropped back down to 9% (still above the 1985 figure).

2 a March   b 5 cm   c June   d 70 cm

Activity: Using pie charts (p. 54)

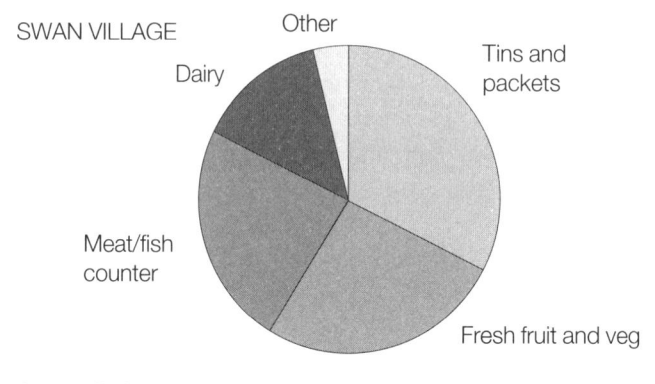

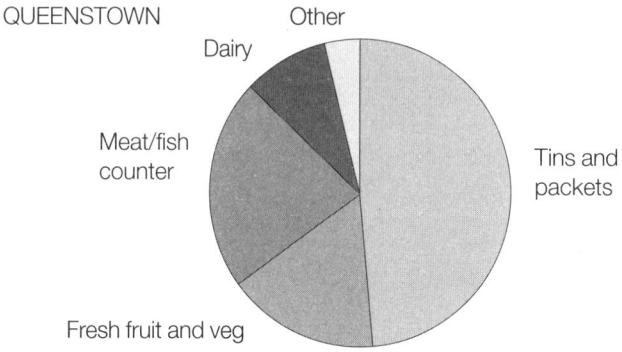

SWAN VILLAGE

[Pie chart with segments: Other, Dairy, Meat/fish counter, Fresh fruit and veg, Tins and packets]

QUEENSTOWN

[Pie chart with segments: Other, Dairy, Meat/fish counter, Fresh fruit and veg, Tins and packets]

The pie charts show that a higher proportion of income in Queenstown comes from tins and packets than in Swan Village. Fresh fruit and veg is the second largest source of income in Swan Village and the third largest in Queenstown. The meat and fish counter provides about the same proportion of income in both stores, but dairy sells better in Swan Village.

Activity: Working out probability (p. 55)

1   10

Activity: Mean, mode and range (p. 58)

1   £2.3225 = £2.32
2   £2.50
3   £5 − £0.50 = £4.50
4   Probably £2.50, as the mode is £2.50 and the mean is just below this amount. It would be sensible to start at a low price to get people to buy the magazine in the first place.

Toolkit

Documents for you to photocopy

In this section you will find a range of blank documents that you can photocopy and use to practise the skills you learn as you work through this book. The logos on the documents are for Rackets & Runners and Foster Stationery, the companies you will find out about in Unit 4. If you want to fill out documents for other companies, blank out the logo area when you photocopy the document, and then add the appropriate logo.

RACKETS & RUNNERS

81 HOPE STREET · GLASGOW · G2 6AJ · TEL: 0141 221 3424

PURCHASE ORDER

Date:

Order No:

Delivery address:

Ref No:	Quantity	Description	Unit Price

Signature . . . .   Date . . . .

© L. Daniel, J. Joslin, K. McCafferty, L. Porter, A. Thomas 1996.
Intermediate GNVQ Business.

foster**stationery**ltd

UNIT 55 · ALBION INDUSTRIAL ESTATE
EDINBURGH · EH20 1LF

advice note

customer:	deliver to:

YOUR ORDER NUMBER	GOODS SENT BY	DATE SENT	INVOICE DATE	INVOICE NUMBER

QUANTITY	DESCRIPTION	UNIT PRICE	AMOUNT

GOODS RECEIVED IN GOOD CONDITION BY:

Toolkit

RACKETS & RUNNERS

81 HOPE STREET · GLASGOW · G2 6AJ · TEL: 0141 221 3424

goods received note

Supplier: Date:

                                             Invoice No:

Order No:	Description	Quantity

Signature . . . .

© L. Daniel, J. Joslin, K. McCafferty, L. Porter, A. Thomas 1996.
Intermediate GNVQ Business.

foster**stationery**ltd

UNIT 55 · ALBION INDUSTRIAL ESTATE
EDINBURGH · EH20 1LF

invoice 39621

customer:

account no:

date:

tax point:

QUANTITY	DESCRIPTION	UNIT PRICE £	TOTAL EXCLUDING VAT	VAT RATE	VAT NET

VAT

TOTAL

TERMS

E & O E

© L. Daniel, J. Joslin, K. McCafferty, L. Porter, A. Thomas 1996.
Intermediate GNVQ Business.

foster**stationery**ltd

UNIT 55 · ALBION INDUSTRIAL ESTATE
EDINBURGH · EH20 1LF

credit note 4126

customer:

date:

account no:

our ref:

your ref:

REFERENCE	QUANTITY	DESCRIPTION	UNIT PRICE	TOTAL (INC VAT)

REASON FOR CREDIT:

foster**stationery**ltd

delivery note

UNIT 55 · ALBION INDUSTRIAL ESTATE
EDINBURGH · EH20 1LF

customer:

deliver to:

YOUR ORDER NUMBER	GOODS SENT BY	DATE SENT	INVOICE DATE	INVOICE NUMBER

QUANTITY	DESCRIPTION	UNIT PRICE	AMOUNT

GOODS RECEIVED IN GOOD CONDITION BY:

© L. Daniel, J. Joslin, K. McCafferty, L. Porter, A. Thomas 1996.
Intermediate GNVQ Business.

RACKETS & RUNNERS

81 HOPE STREET · GLASGOW · G2 6AJ · TEL: 0141 221 3424

STATEMENT OF ACCOUNT

customer:

account no:
date:
credit limit:
terms:

DATE	REFERENCE	DESCRIPTION	DEBIT	CREDIT	BALANCE

AMOUNT NOW DUE

REMITTANCE ADVICE

account no:
cheque no:

DATE	DESCRIPTION	AMOUNT DUE

TOTAL CHEQUE ENCLOSED £

© L. Daniel, J. Joslin, K. McCafferty, L. Porter, A. Thomas 1996.
Intermediate GNVQ Business.

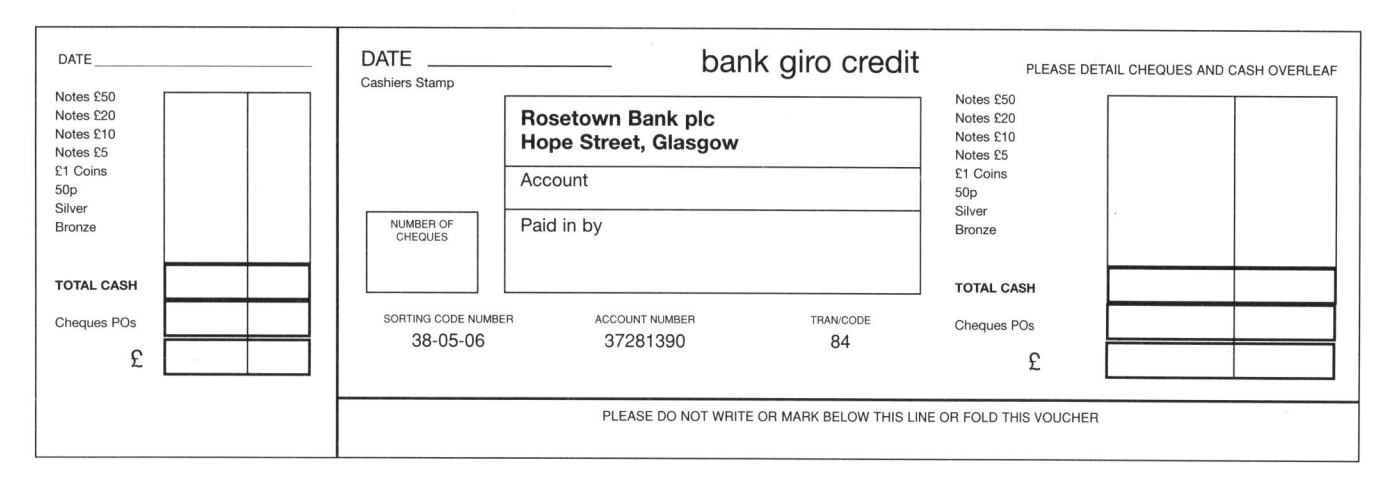

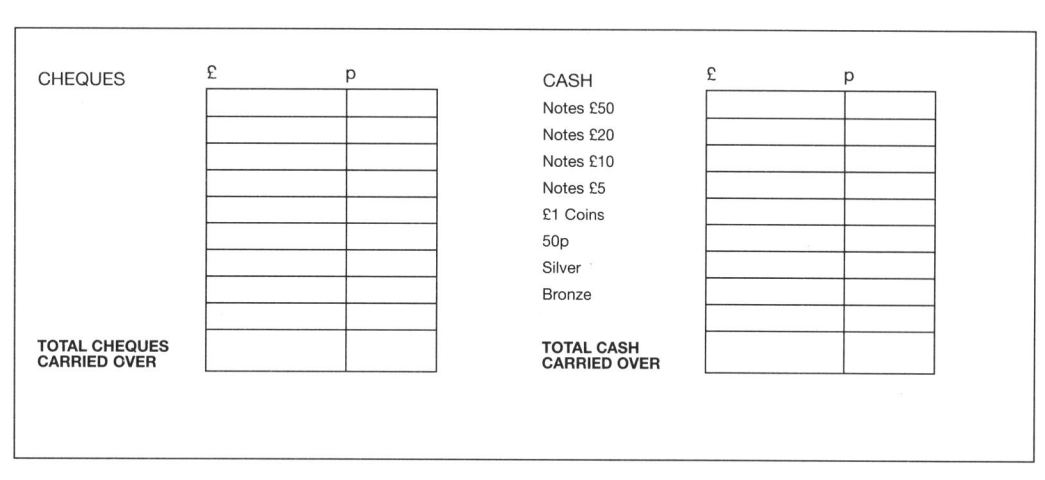

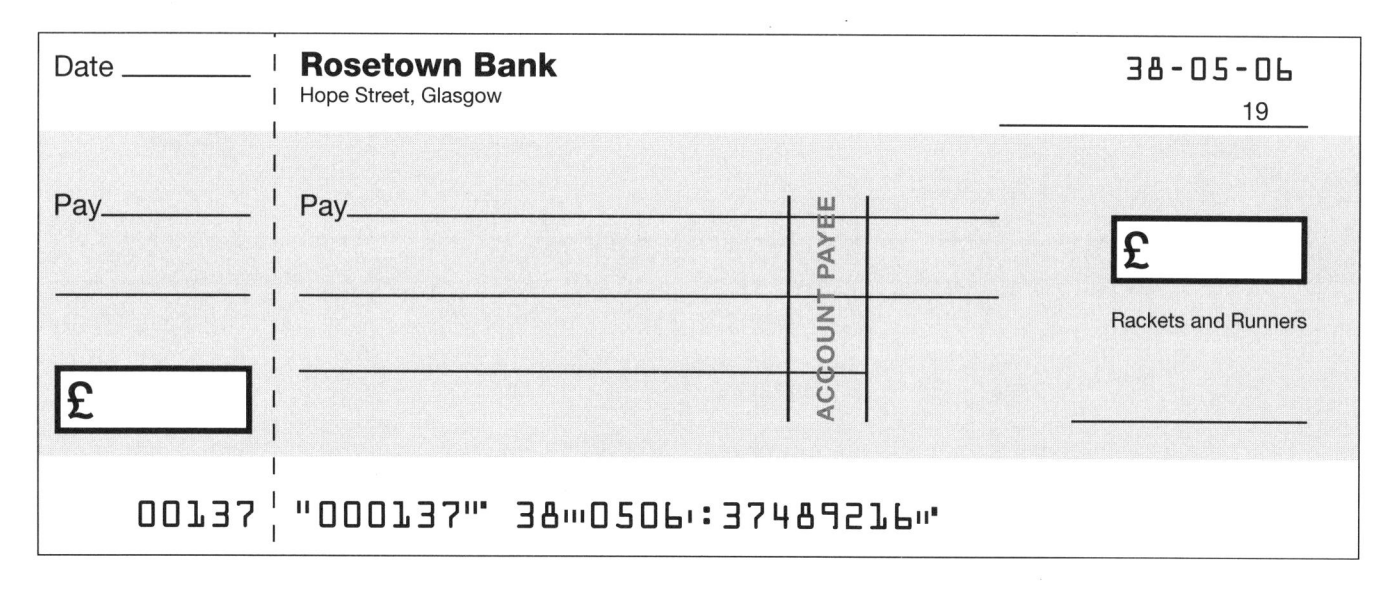

Toolkit

DATE _____	DATE _____	**bank giro credit**	PLEASE DETAIL CHEQUES AND CASH OVERLEAF
Notes £50	Cashiers Stamp		Notes £50
Notes £20		**Rosetown Bank plc**	Notes £20
Notes £10		**Hope Street, Glasgow**	Notes £10
Notes £5			Notes £5
£1 Coins		Account	£1 Coins
50p	NUMBER OF		50p
Silver	CHEQUES	Paid in by	Silver
Bronze			Bronze
TOTAL CASH			**TOTAL CASH**
Cheques POs	SORTING CODE NUMBER	ACCOUNT NUMBER TRAN/CODE	Cheques POs
£	38-05-06	37281390 84	£

PLEASE DO NOT WRITE OR MARK BELOW THIS LINE OR FOLD THIS VOUCHER

CHEQUES	£	p	CASH	£	p
			Notes £50		
			Notes £20		
			Notes £10		
			Notes £5		
			£1 Coins		
			50p		
			Silver		
			Bronze		
TOTAL CHEQUES CARRIED OVER			**TOTAL CASH CARRIED OVER**		

Date _____   **Rosetown Bank**   38-05-06
                  Hope Street, Glasgow   _____ 19

Pay _____   Pay _____

                                                                        £ _____
   £ _____   Rackets and Runners

00137   "000137" 38⑯0506⦂ 37489216⦀

Toolkit

PETTY CASH VOUCHER

Folio _____

Date _____

Date	Purpose	£	p
	Total spent		

Received by	Approved by

8234

81 HOPE STREET · GLASGOW · G2 6AJ · TEL: 0141 221 3424

receipt

customer ....

date ....

Received with thanks ....

© L. Daniel, J. Joslin, K. McCafferty, L. Porter, A. Thomas 1996.
Intermediate GNVQ Business.

RACKETS & RUNNERS

To ....

From ....

Message

Taken by ....

Date .... Time ....

---

foster stationery ltd
statement of account

UNIT 55 · ALBION INDUSTRIAL ESTATE
EDINBURGH · EH20 1LF

customer:

account no:
date:
credit limit:
terms:

DATE	REFERENCE	DESCRIPTION	DEBIT	CREDIT	BALANCE

AMOUNT NOW DUE

---

remittance advice

account no:
cheque no:

DATE	DESCRIPTION	AMOUNT DUE

TOTAL CHEQUE ENCLOSED £

© L. Daniel, J. Joslin, K. McCafferty, L. Porter, A. Thomas 1996.
Intermediate GNVQ Business.

1 | Business organisations and employment

We all rely on business organisations every day of our lives – whether we're travelling, shopping, eating, studying or simply sitting at home watching television. But what are these businesses? Why, where and how do they exist?

This unit looks at the purposes, ownership, location, products and customers of different types of business organisations. By looking at organisations in your area and across the UK, it will help you to gain an understanding of the aims and activities of businesses.

All business organisations rely on the skills and knowledge of the people they employ. As part of this unit, you will carry out a detailed investigation of employment in different areas, giving you insight into the types of jobs available in businesses.

The Elements

Explain the purposes and types of business organisations
- describe developments in industrial sectors
- explain the purposes of business organisations
- explain the differences between types of business ownership
- explain the operation of one business organisation

This element explains how business organisations are grouped depending on what they do and who owns them. It also looks at the purposes of different businesses, and gives you an opportunity to look in detail at how one business organisation operates.

▶ Purposes and types of business organisations, page 78

Examine business location, environment, markets and products
- explain the reasons for location of businesses
- explain influences of the business environment on business organisations
- describe markets for businesses' products based on demand
- identify products provided by business organisations
- explain activities undertaken by businesses to improve their market position
- propose products which would meet market demand

In this element you will look at some of the reasons why businesses are located in particular areas. You will discover that their success depends on being able to provide what their customers need, when they need it, at the right price. You will then put your knowledge and understanding into practice by investigating a business organisation in your area.

▶ Business location, environment, markets and products, page 94

Present results of investigation into employment
- describe and give examples of types of employment
- collect, analyse and explain information about employment in different regions
- compare working conditions for employees in different organisations
- present results of investigation into employment, or comparison of working conditions

The third element looks at the different types of jobs available and what affects employment opportunities. You will look at information about employment in different areas in order to draw your own conclusions about what is happening and why. You will then go on to research what is happening in two EU regions, and present the results of your investigation.

▶ Investigating employment, page 111

Business organisations and employment

Purposes and types of business organisations

Have you ever stopped to consider how different types of business organisations affect your daily life?

Let's think about your day yesterday, for example. Here's what Anna, a GNVQ Business student, did.

'Yesterday I had scrambled eggs on toast with a glass of milk for breakfast. Then I caught the bus to college and went to lectures. We watched a video on advertising and I made some notes. At lunchtime I went to the shops and bought a sandwich and a packet of crisps. Then in the afternoon I used a computer to work on my assignment. After catching the bus home, I went out to the local pizza restaurant for the evening and had my usual favourite – seafood topping!'

The fact that Anna was able to do all these things was the result of a chain of industries and business organisations exchanging skills, labour or services, money, and natural resources. How many different types of industries and business organisations can you think of which were involved in providing Anna's breakfast? Or in helping her travel to and from college?

Developments in industrial sectors

Business organisations can belong to one of three industrial sectors:
- primary sector
- secondary sector
- tertiary sector.

Primary sector

Business organisations in the primary sector extract raw materials or resources from the land (or sea). This is the first stage – called 'primary production' – in the chain of manufacturing and distributing goods.

Primary sector industries include:
- the farming sector, responsible for the eggs, milk and crops you eat
- the extraction industry, which provides coal, gas and oil to heat your home and workplace
- quarrying companies, which extract stone used to make the roads you travel along
- the forestry industry, which provides the raw materials for making your tables, chairs and paper
- the fishing industry, responsible for catching the fish you eat.

Employment in the primary sector has declined in the UK since the Industrial Revolution. This is mainly because machines have made the extraction of crops and raw materials less labour intensive. However, the primary sector is still a major employer in other, less industrialised parts of the world.

The primary sector involves extracting raw materials.

Many people still work in the primary sector in Sri Lanka, famous for growing and exporting tea

Secondary sector

Business organisations in the secondary sector use raw materials to produce and manufacture goods. This is the second stage – known as 'secondary production' – in the chain of producing goods for people to use.

78

Secondary sector industries include:
- the manufacturers which produce the furniture you use
- the construction industry that built your home
- the public utilities industry that brings you heat and water
- the public transport system that takes you where you need to go
- the telecommunications system that enables you to use the phone.

Secondary sector business organisations either:
- manufacture 'producer' goods, which are bought and used by other businesses
- manufacture 'consumer' goods, which are bought and used by the general public.

Employment in the secondary sector has declined in this country over the last 25 years. Manufacturing companies in the UK now face more competition from recently industrialised countries, which keep costs down by paying low wages. For example, it is cheaper to assemble electronic components in Taiwan than in the UK, as wages are lower. In turn, Taiwan is gradually being overtaken by countries which pay even lower wages, such as Thailand and the Philippines.

Businesses in the secondary sector often manufacture goods for other businesses, rather than for consumers

Tertiary sector

Business organisations in the tertiary sector provide services to make sure manufactured goods reach the people who need them. The tertiary sector also includes professional services, administration, financial services and public services. For example, tertiary sector services are provided by:
- the tutor in your tutorials
- transport and distribution companies, which take food to retail companies
- retail companies, which sell food to you
- advertising companies, which promote goods and services
- computer companies, which install and maintain the computers you use
- banking and financial service organisations, which support business organisations in every industrial sector.

In recent years, the number of people employed in the tertiary sector in this country has grown as a result of the decline of the primary and secondary sectors. The tertiary sector has also grown in other developed economies abroad, such as Japan.

There is a growing demand today for sevices that make life easier for us

Business organisations and employment

```
PRIMARY SECTOR                    Business Organisations            TERTIARY SECTOR
Extraction of raw materials and                                     Services, e.g. banking, distribution,
resources, e.g fishing, mining, farming.                            leisure, insurance.
                                  SECONDARY SECTOR
    [EXAMPLE 1]                   Manufactures, builds or provides, e.g. engi-    [EXAMPLE 1]
                                  neering, construction, public utilities.
    [EXAMPLE 2]                                                                    [EXAMPLE 2]
                                  CONSUMER           PRODUCER
                                  e.g. food, TVs     e.g. machinery
    [EXAMPLE JOB                                                                   [EXAMPLE JOB
    ADVERTISEMENT]                [EXAMPLE 1]        [EXAMPLE 1]                   ADVERTISEMENT]

                                  [EXAMPLE 2]        [EXAMPLE 2]

                                  [EXAMPLE JOB       [EXAMPLE JOB
                                   ADVERTISEMENT]    ADVERTISEMENT]
```

A Industrial sectors

Include your work for this activity in your portfolio of evidence.

1. Copy out the chart from the top of this page, making sure you leave enough space for information.
   a. Carry out research to find examples of business organisations in each industrial sector. Look in your local area, or research local directories. Ask your tutor for help if necessary.
   b. Go through the job advertisement pages of your local papers and find examples of advertisements for jobs in each sector.
   c. Complete the chart with details of two business organisations in each sector. Include: the name of the business – its address and telephone number – the nature of the business (its main business activities). Then either copy details of the job advertisements, or stick them straight onto your chart.

2. By examining different sources of information about industrial sectors – for example, employment figures over a number of years – you can identify patterns and trends.

▶ Carrying out research, page 1

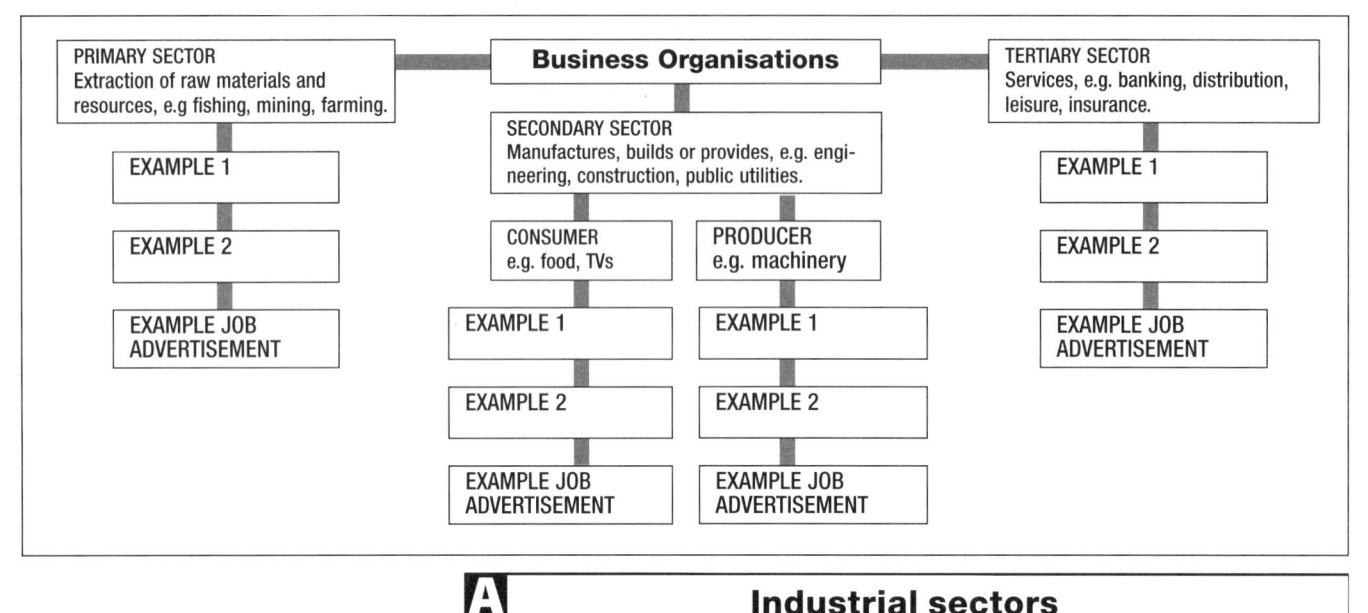

▶ Employment trends, page 112

Look at the information below from *The Monthly Digest*. This is a magazine produced for the government by the Central Statistical Office.

Table 1.1: Employees in employment by industrial sector

- All figures in the table are shown in thousands.

Industrial sector	1971	1979	1981	1986	1993	1994
Total manufacturing sector	8,065	7,253	6,222	5,236	4,615	4,534
Total services sector	11,627	13,580	13,468	14,486	15,349	15,363
Agriculture, forestry, fishing, energy and water supply industries	1,248	1,102	1,073	808	609	565

a Which sector has lost the most jobs? What occupational areas might be hit? What sort of business activities might be declining?
b Which sector has gained the most jobs? What occupational areas might be growing? What sort of business activities might be growing?
c Which sector is currently the largest employer? What occupational areas does this include?
d What do you think might happen in each sector over the next two or three years?
e Examine the patterns that seem to be occurring in the primary, secondary and tertiary sectors from 1971 to 1994, and comment as fully as possible on these trends. Include comments on which sectors you think seem to be growing, and which are decreasing.
f Draw bar charts to compare the number of people employed in each sector.
g Calculate the mean number of employees in each sector. What is the range for each year?

▶ Bar charts, page 44

▶ Mean and range, page 56

Types of business organisation

As well as being grouped by industrial sector, business organisations can be put into different groups depending on their:
- size
- ownership.

Small, medium and large business organisations

Businesses can be classified as small, medium or large. Which category they fall into depends on a number of factors:
- their **annual sales turnover**. This is the total amount of sales made in a year
- their **market share**. This is 'the sales turnover of the business expressed as a percentage of the total turnover of its competitors' sales in the same line of business.' To put it simply, market share tells you how much business a company has got compared to its competitors
- their **number of employees** (or money spent on technology, machinery and property). This is known as capital employed.

In line with this:
- Granada Group PLC is a large business organisation. Its annual turnover in 1995 was £2.4 billion. It owns Granada Television, which produces popular television programmes like Coronation Street. This is considered a market leader, with a market share of 40% of programmes sold to the ITV network. In its Rental and Computer Services Division alone, the Granada Group PLC increased the number of employees from 9,830 in 1994 to 10,106 in 1995
- Dodd Engineering – a company which paints industrial machinery, large equipment and street lamps – is classed as a medium-sized business organisation. It has an annual turnover of £5 million and employs 60 people
- Comp-U-Clic – a computer company – is classed as a small business organisation. It had an annual turnover of £750,000 in 1995, and increased its employees from two in 1994 to six in 1995.

▶ Market share, page 89

Granada has become a market leader in leisure and recreation

Business organisations and employment

In 1995, Companies House used the following criteria to define small, medium and large businesses:

SMALL	MEDIUM	LARGE
< £2,800,000 turnover	Between £2,800,000 and £11,200,000 turnover	> £11,200,000 turnover
Balance sheet total < £1,400,000	Balance sheet total between £1,400,000 and £5,600,000	Balance sheet total > £5,600,000
< 50 employees	Between 50 and 250 employees	> 250 employees

Companies House: an organisation established by the government to set up and register private companies.

A Small, medium and large businesses

Include your work for this activity in your portfolio of evidence.

1. Look at the number of people employed by Granada Group PLC and Comp-U-Clic in 1994 and 1995. What was the actual increase in staff in each case? What was this increase as a percentage of the numbers employed in 1994?

2. Look at the table showing the criteria for small, medium and large businesses. What does > indicate? What does < indicate?

3. As a group, either design a questionnaire to use with your local Training and Enterprise Council (TEC) or to send to chosen businesses, to find out whether businesses in your area would be classed as small, medium or large.

   Your questionnaire will be sent by post, so you need to consider this as you design it. Work out carefully what sort of information you need to ask for. You may want to include some questions which ask about the local businesses in general (background questions), and then questions on more detailed subjects such as turnover and number of employees. It might be helpful to give a choice of answers to a question, for example:

   Is your turnover: less than 2.8 million   ☐
                       2.8 to 11.2 million   ☐
                       greater than 11.2 million ☐

   Carry out the survey as a group, to make sure no business is asked the same questions twice! Include a short letter with your questionnaire, explaining what you are doing, why you have asked the business, and what you are going to do with the information. Don't forget to thank them for their help and include an SAE (stamped addressed envelope).

▶ Percentages, page 29

▶ Designing questionnaires, page 20

Training and Enterprise Council (TEC): *TECs encourage local economic growth through developing skills and knowledge needed for competitiveness. There are 81 TECs in England and Wales.*

From looking at Granada Group PLC, Dodd Engineering and Comp-U-Clic, you can see that the size of a business organisation is largely determined by the amount of finance available to fund its activities. This in turn may reflect the ownership of the business.

The ownership of business organisations

Business organisations can also be put into groups depending on who owns them. Ownership falls into two broad categories:
- private sector
- public sector.

The private sector is made up of business organisations which are owned or controlled by one or more individuals.

The public sector is made up of organisations owned by the government. They exist to meet the needs of the public as identified by the government, and this affects their main purposes, decisions and policies. Public sector organisations include:
- public services, such as London Transport
- public corporations, such as the Bank of England and the BBC
- nationalised (state-owned) industries, such as the Post Office.

In recent years many nationalised industries – such as British Airways, British Telecom and British Gas – have been privatised. This means that they have been sold off, and have become large business organisations in the private sector. When a nationalised industry is privatised, shares (of ownership) are bought by members of the public, who then have the right to elect directors to represent their interests in running and controlling the organisation.

Public sector, or private sector?

Business organisations in the public and private sectors are often divided into seven more specific categories, depending on their type of ownership.

Sole trader

A sole trader is someone who owns and controls his or her own business. A sole trader:
- makes day-to-day decisions about running the business
- keeps all the profits made by the business
- has unlimited liability. This means that legally the owner is the business, and is responsible for all the debts it runs up.

Sole traders have responsibility for keeping all aspects of their business together

Business organisations and employment

Unlimited liability: people have unlimited liability if they are liable to pay any debts or losses run up by the business.

Sole traders are often under a lot of pressure, as they are responsible for finding finance, time and resources to make the business work.

Case study: Linda Penn

Linda Penn
AROMATHERAPIST

12 THE LARCHES · MORESBY · DORSET · DK5 6TN
TEL & FAX: 01647375384

Linda Penn gave up a full-time job training people in NVQs and retrained as an aromatherapist. Once qualified, she set up a business using aromatherapy to treat people, and training others as aromatherapists. Her overheads were low as she worked from home, but because of limited space she could only train students on a one-to-one basis. Her only other expenses were buying materials to use in her practice.

- What are the advantages and disadvantages of Linda Penn's business?

Overheads: the costs of running a business. These can be direct, such as buying raw materials and paying wages; or indirect, such as heating and lighting.

Partnerships

Business organisations offering professional services – such as doctors, solicitors and estate agents – are often partnerships. There can be anything from two to twenty partners in a partnership, all of whom own the business. Partners who are not involved in the day-to-day running of the business are referred to as 'sleeping partners'. Taking on new partners is a good way for a business to raise extra finance and to introduce extra skills into the business.

Each partner shares the legal responsibilities of the business. They can have either unlimited liability or limited liability.

Limited liability: if a business fails, people with limited liability are only liable to pay out the amount of money they originally invested in the business.

Most partnerships draw up a legal agreement known as the 'Deed of Partnership', which sets out who is responsible for what and how the profits are divided.

Case study: Linda and Michelle

Linda Penn's aromatherapy business proved very successful, with many clients being helped by her treatments. Linda needed to take on some extra help, and thought of Michelle, with whom she had trained. Michelle was already working as a book keeper for a local company, but wanted to reduce her hours of book keeping and build up her own aromatherapy practice. She had some money and time to invest, so talked to Linda about the benefits of a partnership.

- What advice and actions would you recommend for Linda and Michelle next? Give your reasons for this advice.

Private limited companies

Often, a business may wish to raise finance by asking for investment from people who are not involved in the day-to-day running of the business. In order to do this, the business organisation must register as a limited company through Companies House.

Private limited companies:
- have the letters Ltd after their name
- can sell company shares privately (these shares are not available to the general public on the stock exchange)
- do not have to publish their company accounts in full.

The shareholders – owners – of private limited companies have limited liability. This means that they do not lose their personal assets (such as their home) if the business fails. This gives people the confidence to invest in private limited companies. In turn, they receive a share of the profits – a dividend – as a reward for risking their money by investing in the business.

Dividend: companies keep some of their profit to reinvest in the business, and pay the rest to shareholders as a dividend.

All limited companies have to file certain documents at Companies House, including:
- a memorandum of association, which provides details of the company, its address, its directors and secretary, the share capital, the number of shares, who holds shares, and how much capital needs to be raised
- articles of association, which give details of the day-to-day running and control of the company.

Case study: Linda and Michelle – private limited company?

If Linda and Michelle decide to register their business as a private limited company, they will have to contact Companies House and file a memorandum of association and the articles of association. These will have to be printed, with numbered paragraphs, and signed. Once the Registrar of Companies receives these documents, a Certificate of Incorporation will be issued if everything is in order. This is the company's 'birth certificate', and Linda and Michelle will then be able to trade as a private limited company.

Public limited companies (PLCs)

Public limited companies – such as Marks & Spencer and British Airways – are the largest business organisations in the private sector.

Public limited companies:
- have the letters PLC after their name
- sell shares to the general public through the stock exchange
- must produce a prospectus giving information about share investment
- must have a minimum share capital of £50,000. This means that a public limited company's shareholders have to invest a total of £50,000, which then stays in the business.

Shareholders in public limited companies share ownership of the business, and have a right to attend annual general meetings and elect directors of the company. Some companies offer shares in the company to employees, to increase their commitment to the success of the business.

Shares for public limited companies are bought and sold on the stock market

All shareholders receive copies of the annual report and accounts, which gives details of the company's financial position. Like shareholders in private limited companies, they are paid a share of the profit as a dividend in return for their investment. They also have limited liability – they do not lose their personal assets if the business fails.

A Share performance

Find out how Marks & Spencer's shares have performed on the stock market recently. Has the value of its shares gone up, or down?

Franchises

Today, more and more businesses in the UK are franchises. This means that the owner, who is self-employed, buys into a large company which provides training, advertising, equipment and products. The owner loses some control over the running of the business, but in return receives advice and support from the company.

The owner of a franchise (called the 'franchisee'), usually keeps the profits of the business, although sometimes the franchise agreement states that profits are shared between franchisee and franchisor (the parent company). Depending on the agreement, the franchisee may have limited or unlimited liability.

All franchises – an increasingly popular type of business ownership

Case study: Linda's franchise alternative

Many of Linda Penn's students achieved NVQs in aromatherapy, and she considered offering them support in setting up businesses in their own homes. In addition to training, she intended to provide them with high-quality aromatherapy oils and products, and a network of support and help in dealing with clients and their conditions.

- What might the advantages be to both Linda and her students of this franchised arrangement?
- Can you think of any disadvantages of this type of arrangement? Consider the quality of the products and services, ownership, who keeps the profit, and the control of the business.

Co-operatives

There are two major types of co-operative business organisations in this country.

The first are co-operative retail and wholesale societies. In this type of business organisation:
- each owner (or member) has one vote in controlling the business, no matter how many shares s/he owns
- shares are not available on the stock market, and can only be bought or sold through the company
- members share the profits in the form of dividends paid out on shares, and reduced prices which are offset by the profits
- the owners have limited liability – they don't lose their personal assets if the co-operative fails.

The second type of co-operative business organisation is the worker or 'producer' co-operative. In worker co-operatives, ownership of the business is shared equally among the workers themselves. Each worker has one vote, and helps to make decisions on how the business is run and controlled. If the co-operative needs extra finance, it can raise it by increasing the number of members. Like a limited company, co-operatives have to be registered.

The workers who own the business have limited liability, and agree between them how to share out the profits.

Case study: Linda's co-operative alternative

Linda Penn's reputation grew, and so did the size of her practice. One day she was contacted by a local doctor who wanted to establish a complementary health care practice at the back of his surgery. His aim was to set aside two consulting rooms for three three-hourly sessions, seven days a week, to a few qualified and experienced complementary therapists (including, he hoped, Linda). He would then be able to refer his patients to the different therapists.

He was seeking advice from the regional co-operative development agency and applying for a loan to support the project from the Co-operative Bank.

- What would be the advantages of Linda becoming involved in this co-operative arrangement?
- Can you think of any disadvantages?

State-owned business organisations

State-owned business organisations – including public corporations and nationalised industries – are in the public sector. They are owned by the government, not shareholders or private individuals. The interests of the general public are looked after by 'watchdogs' such as OFWAT and OFTEL.

As they are owned by the government, no individuals are liable if the business gets into difficulties. Any profits made by state-owned businesses are reused as government central funds.

Purposes of business organisations

Business organisations all share the objective of being successful. However, they may focus on any of the following purposes in order to achieve or maintain success:
- to make a profit
- to increase market share
- to provide customer service
- to provide public service
- to benefit the community (charitable organisations).

Profit

Generally, business organisations are run to create wealth by making a profit.

There are two ways of working out profit:
- gross profit – the amount of money made through sales, with just the cost of purchases deducted
- net profit – the money left for the owners of a business after all business costs have been deducted. In other words, it is what's left when business costs are taken away from income. Net profit is the best measure of how successful a business has been in its trading activities.

Making as much profit as possible is one of the main purposes for the owners and shareholders of a business. They then have to decide how much of the profit to pay out in dividends to make their investment worthwhile, and how much to plough back into the business, to enable it to grow and become competitive.

Putting profit back into the business is very important. Profit:
- provides money to support the business' activities; for example, to buy materials and services, to pay for labour, and to meet overheads such as rent, power and administration
- enables the business to expand and remain competitive by investing in new technology
- acts as a measure of success, which encourages future investment in the business and helps it raise capital from outside sources.

A Calculating Linda's profit

Linda Penn's aromatherapy business made a gross profit of £7,313 in 1995. Her expenses for that year were:

	£
use of her house for the business	405
telephone and postage	384
car expenses (petrol, services etc.)	520
legal fees	528
sundry expenses	186
depreciation (car, fixtures etc.)	558

Calculate her net profit for the year.

Market share

The success of a business organisation is often measured by its market share. Market share is a business' sales turnover expressed as a percentage of the total turnover in its line of business.

One of the major purposes of many businesses is to become a market leader – to sell more of a particular product or service than their competitors. To do this, they often invest a lot of time and money in research to find out why consumers choose to buy products and services from one business rather than another. They can then decide on policies to expand their market share e.g. BT has the largest share of the telephone market in the UK.

▶ Market share, page 81

C Case study: Linda's market share

In 1996 Linda Penn's total annual sales of pure aromatherapy oils to her clients and students was £500. The total annual sale of aromatherapy oils in the UK reached £50 million.

This means that Linda's market share was:
500/50,000,000 × 100% = 1/1000% = 0.001%.

- What could Linda do to increase her market share?

Customer service

In the retail industry there is a saying that success depends on:

'getting the right goods of the right quality to the right place at the right time in the right quantities at the right price.'

If a business achieves this aim, it can guarantee customer satisfaction.

Business organisations and employment

Many businesses have become experts in providing a fast and efficient service to other businesses

Every business organisation has its own customers who need to be satisfied. Satisfied customers come back, spend more money, and are likely to tell their family and friends about the good service they have received. All of these things help a business to make more profit and succeed.

Therefore, one of the main purposes of many business organisations is to provide good customer service. To do this, they carry out research into what customers want and need, and then decide how they can best meet customers' needs.

▶ Customer needs and wants, page 105

▶ Customer service, page 195

A Finding out more about customer service

1. Make a list of business activities which depend on providing good service to customers.
2. Make a list of businesses which depend on providing good customer service to other businesses.
3. Can you think of some of the ways local organisations provide customer service? Think about how they improve quality, provide after-sales service, offer support, deliver goods and services, and provide credit facilities.

Public service

Business organisations with the main purpose of providing public service are financed by the government. They include:

- the National Health Service, state education and social services on a national level
- ambulance, fire and library services on a local level.

These businesses receive their income through taxation or other public funding. Central or local government, acting in the best interests of the general public, decides how much income a business should receive and how this should be spent. Some public sector organisations, such as the National Health Service, which offer a free service receive all their income from the state. Other organisations, such as local business companies which charge for their services may receive a government subsidy to ensure they continue to provide this service,

▶ Public sector organisations, page 83

Subsidy: *a sum of money given by the government towards the cost of producing goods or providing a service. For example, a business organisation providing rail travel might be offered a subsidy so it could keep its prices low.*

C Case study: From public to private – a change of purpose

When nationalised industries are privatised and move from the public sector to the private sector, their main purpose changes. In the public sector, their main aim is public service – to provide the best possible service to the general public and to reduce costs for consumers. In the private sector, their main aim is to increase profits for shareholders.

However, this change of purpose does not always mean worse public service. Increased competition between private companies can force organisations to provide better customer service in order to remain competitive. Once a business is privatised, it still has to take account of the public, as they buy the products and services the business produces. To look after the public interest the government set up 'watchdogs' such as OFGAS and OFWAT.

Charitable

A charitable business organisation exists to benefit the community in some way. Charitable organisations have one of five main purposes:
- the relief of poverty – for example, Shelter
- educational provision – for example, RSA Examinations Board
- religious provision – for example, The Bible Shop
- research – for example, Cancer Research
- benefiting the general public – for example, Help the Aged, Scouts and Guides.

In order to gain the benefits of having charitable trust status, an organisation has to register. Once registered, a charitable organisation may not have to pay taxes, as the profits from the organisation are ploughed back into benefiting the community. Having a registered charity number can also help organisations raise funds.

Examples of different types of business	Public sector organisations	Small private sector organisations	Medium private sector organisations	Large private sector organisations
Sole trader				
Partnership				
Private limited company				
Public limited company				
Franchise				
Co-operative				
State-owned				

A Classifying business organisations

Include your work for this activity in your portfolio of evidence.

Make a copy of the chart above, filling a sheet of A4 paper so you have plenty of space to fill in information.

1. Find out the names of local businesses that fit into each category of business organisation. You will need to find an example of a sole trader, a partnership, a private limited company, a public limited company, a franchise, a co-operative, and a state-owned organisation.
2. Fill in details of the organisations on your chart, putting them in the correct column according to whether they are public sector, small private sector, medium-sized private sector, or large private sector organisations. You don't need to complete each space on the chart, but you should have at least one example of each type of business and each sector category. Your final chart should include seven examples in total.

© L. Daniel, J. Joslin, K. McCafferty, L. Porter, A. Thomas 1996. *Intermediate GNVQ Business.*

Business organisations and employment

Examples of different types of business	Public sector organisations	Small private sector organisations	Medium private sector organisations	Large private sector organisations
Sole trader		Apples & Pears 57 High Street Manton Greengrocer		

3 Provide a key for each example, and state:
 – the name of the business
 – its address and telephone number
 – its major purpose
 – the nature of the business activity
 – the type of liability
 – how profit is used.

The operation of a business organisation

Case study: Steve Parker and Comp-U-Clic

Steve Parker was made redundant by Granada Computer Services in 1991. He was employed as a trainer of computer field engineers who carried out maintenance and repairs on computers owned by different business organisations. When he was made redundant the whole training division was closed down, reflecting the drop in demand for maintaining and repairing specialist mainframe computer equipment, as more businesses were installing and using PCs.

With his redundancy payment and a business enterprise allowance from the local Training and Enterprise Council, Steve decided to start his own computer company – Comp-U-Clic. The business began in a computer 'studio' above a carpet shop. The studio was in a block of shops on one of the busiest commuter routes in and out of Wolverhampton in the West Midlands. There were good parking facilities outside the studio, whereas the main town was a pedestrianised zone.

Steve developed the business around his in-depth working knowledge of how computers are built and work. He:
- provided support and information to customers on how to get what they wanted out of their PC, using what he called 'Comp-U-Chat' to establish their particular needs
- built customised computer systems to customers' specifications
- repaired hardware
- provided software support.

Many of Comp-U-Clic's competitors in the town did not have such detailed knowledge and understanding, as they only sold computers which they had bought from other companies. Soon, Comp-U-Clic's reputation spread and the business grew.

Eighteen months after the business was set up, it moved to bigger premises with a shopfront, just 20 metres down the road. The business has since expanded, with one other full-time member of staff and four part-time members of staff.

Steve built Comp-U-Clic's business reputation on friendly personal service and technical support to customers

Business organisations and employment

Today the main feature of the business is building, supplying and installing PCs for home and business use, repairs, upgrades and installing networks.

The overheads (running costs) are now much higher, and there is increasing competition in the town centre.

Being located in the right position is vital for a business' success

A The operation of Comp-U-Clic

Include your work for this activity in your portfolio of evidence.

After reading through the background information, prepare a report for Steve Parker on the business operation of Comp-U-Clic. Divide your report into the following sections.

1. **Type of business.** Classify Comp-U-Clic as an organisation as fully as possible.
2. **Trends and location.** Comment briefly on recent past, present and future trends for the types of products and services offered by Comp-U-Clic. You will need to take into account the recent growth in the home and business use of computers and software, the business' expansion to larger premises with extra staff, and the possible competition.
3. **Products.** Having moved to larger premises, what products and services do you feel Comp-U-Clic should now offer? Consider the advantages and disadvantages of being a specialist supplier of a select line of computer products and services, rather than a general supplier of a wide range of products and services.
4. **Links with other businesses.** What links should Comp-U-Clic establish with other businesses and organisations? To help you with this, consider potential suppliers and customers, locally, regionally, nationally and internationally. How might Comp-U-Clic make these links? Who could help?
5. **Purposes.** What do you think should be the main purposes of the business for the present and near future?
6. **Recommendations.** Make recommendations for the future business expansion of Comp-U-Clic. Consider ownership, legal responsibility, and raising finance How do you think the business should use its profits to support the main purposes of the business? Allow the overall net profit to represent 25% of the annual sales turnover.

▶ Types of business, page 81

Business organisations and employment

Business location, environment, markets and products

The success of a business organisation depends on a number of factors, including:
- where it is located
- the business environment it is operating in
- the market for its goods and services
- the products and services it has to offer.

Business location

There is a saying in the business world that:

'the three most important considerations for a business are position, position and position!'

The location of a business needs to be convenient for customers and suppliers

So what factors does an organisation need to consider when deciding where to locate the business?

Labour supply

There must be a ready supply of labour – people with the right skills, qualifications and experience who are available for employment. Without the right workers, a business will fail.

Sometimes, colleges design courses especially to train people in the skills needed by businesses in their area. For example, a college of art and technology in the West Midlands runs link courses with local schools and training courses in leatherwork. This is because the area is renowned for its leathercraft, and the courses make sure that there is a supply of skilled people ready for employment in the industry.

Can you think of any local courses run in your school or college, or at schools or colleges near you, which train a regular supply of workers for industries in your area?

▶ Geographical factors, page 124

Some businesses choose their location because of the availability of natural resources

Natural resources

Many business organisations take into account the supply of natural resources or raw materials when choosing a location. For example, there are a lot of chemical manufacturers and oil refineries at Ellesmere Port on Merseyside. This is because the businesses have easy access to oil tankers coming into port carrying crude oil, saving on transport costs.

Business organisations and employment

C Case study: Aromatherapy resources

Linda Penn needed a range of herbs and oils for her aromatherapy business, which she made into remedies and blends. She did not grow these herself, as the process was time-consuming and costly. Instead, she bought them from a local shop in town that specialised in selling high-quality organically-grown herbs and oils.

- What are the advantages of Linda being close to a supplier of the resources she needs? What problems might she have encountered if she couldn't get hold of the raw materials easily?

Other businesses in the area

When choosing a location, business organisations need to look carefully at the other businesses in the area. If there are lots of similar businesses nearby, there might be too much competition – too many businesses trying to attract the same customers. In this case, organisations have to lower their prices and profit margins, which can put them out of business.

But sometimes competition is a good thing. Some areas are known for specialising in particular goods or services, and attract customers because of this. For example, Hatton Garden in London is the home of lots of shops selling jewellery. Customers wanting to buy jewellery go to the area because they know they will find something to meet their needs.

Businesses also need to consider how close they are to businesses which can supply them with products. For example, it was convenient for Linda Penn to have a shop selling natural herbs and oils close to her aromatherapy business.

Access to customers

All businesses need customers. When choosing a location, business organisations need to consider whether:
- there are plenty of customers nearby
- people living in the area have enough money to make regular purchases of the goods or services on offer
- customers can travel to the business easily (for more on transport services, see below).

Competition isn't always bad for business

▶ Incentives, page 96

A Where were the customers?

Find an example of a business which has closed down in your area. Work out some reasons why the business might have been in the wrong location. Who were its customers? Why were there not enough customers to keep the business going?

Business organisations and employment

Transport services

All businesses need to be close to good transport links so that:
- customers can reach them easily
- finished goods, partly-finished goods and raw materials can be moved easily and cheaply around the local area and region, and then on to the rest of the country and world.

When looking at transport services, businesses should consider roads, rail links, coastal ports and airports.

A Moving goods around

A food manufacturing company is looking for a new site for its factory and headquarters. It has a fleet of lorries which need to transport its products quickly and efficiently to retail companies throughout the UK.

Look at the map of the motorways and major roads in the UK. In what area of the country would you suggest the company starts looking for premises?

▶ Incentives, page 96

Incentives

In some parts of the UK, incentives are offered to new businesses locating in the area. These incentives may be offered:

- by local government. Funding is given to regional development agencies, who work closely with TECs to provide financial help for new businesses. This is most common in areas of high unemployment, where old industries have been lost and the local council is keen to attract new businesses
- by national government. Funding for businesses is channelled through particular government departments, such as the Department for Trade and Industry, and the Department for Education and Employment
- by the European Union. Funding is available to support business development in certain regions of the UK.

Incentives might be offered in the form of:
- grants
- loans with low interest rates
- matched funding (where money provided by the business is matched by funding)
- assistance towards rent or business rates.

Motorways and major trunk roads

Case study: Barnaby's new department store

In practice, very few businesses are free to decide their location. Most have to weigh up the advantages of a good position against the disadvantages of paying high overheads, and find a compromise.

Barnaby's is a small chain of department stores, started by James Barnaby in 1850. There are now four stores throughout the UK – in Liverpool, Oxford, Wales and Scotland. Barnaby's now wants to open another branch in the Midlands.

There are two possible locations:
- The Mander Centre in the middle of Wolverhampton
- Shrewsbury town centre.

The Wolverhampton option

The Wolverhampton option

The Mander Centre is a large, privately-owned shopping centre in the heart of Wolverhampton. Wolverhampton is near several major population centres, including Birmingham, Coventry, Walsall, Worcester and Stafford. Good motorway links bring in shoppers from across the Midlands, and there are 12 off-street car parks as well as a multi-storey car park attached to The Mander Centre. Bus and rail stations are only ten minutes walk away, and there is a taxi rank in front of the Centre.

The possible premises in the Mander Centre offers:
- a new shop on several floors
- 2000 square metres of sales area
- the facilities of a purpose-built shopping centre, including car parking
- an underground delivery and rubbish removal service
- a security service
- a wide range of shops in the same centre, including BHS, Boots the Chemist, WH Smith, Our Price, Mothercare and Superdrug.

Please note these figures for the overheads are to be used purely for educational purposes. They are not indicative of the actual figures for the Mander Centre.

Overheads would be:

Rent	£575,000
Rates	£85,000
Service charge	£17,000
Wages	£1,000,000
Heat, light etc.	£140,000
Start-up costs (including shop fittings, fixtures and decorating)	£600,000

- The total population in the area is 191,020.
- The working population is 112,002 (58.6%).
- 15,927 people are unemployed (14.2%).

The Shrewsbury option

The Shrewsbury option

Shrewsbury in Shropshire services the needs of a rural area, and attracts tourists from across the UK to its attractions and events. It is an hour's drive from Birmingham, and has nine off-street car parks. It also has good rail links with other parts of England and Wales, and regular buses serving the main Shropshire towns.

The possible premises in Shrewsbury town centre offers:
- a modernised Victorian building on two floors
- 2400 square metres of sales area
- a shopping centre nearby, with Sainsbury's, Next, Marks & Spencer, McDonald's, Ratners the jewellers, a restaurant, Littlewoods, Boots and Argos
- delivery facilities at the rear of the building.

Overheads would be:

Rent	£624,000
Rates	£75,000
Service charge	£0
Wages	£1,000,000
Heat, light etc.	£127,000
Start-up costs (including shop fittings, fixtures and decorating)	£650,000

- The total population in the area is 64,443.
- The working population is 28,572 (44.3%).
- 1,800 people are unemployed (6.3%).

Business organisations and employment

A Locating a business

1. Look at the information in the case study above. Where would you recommend Barnaby's opens its new store? Give your reasons why, bearing in mind labour supply, other businesses in the area, access to customers, and transport services.

2. Barnaby's decided to find out more about The Mander Centre, and got a plan of the shops already in the centre. Which shops do you think would be in competition with Barnaby's? What would be the advantages and disadvantages of having so many shops nearby?

3. Wolverhampton is in the West Midlands region. Barnaby's found out these facts about the West Midlands:
   - the southern part of the region is well known for fruit farming
   - the south western part of the region is a popular tourist centre, in particular Stratford-upon-Avon
   - the area to the north, around Stoke, is known as the Potteries.
   - there are still a number of pottery and china companies in the area
   - one of the largest out-of-town shopping centres in Europe, The Merry Hill Centre, is about ten miles away from The Mander Centre.

   How would each of these factors affect businesses in The Mander Centre? Are there any useful natural resources or suppliers in the area? Looking at the plan, which shops would they help?

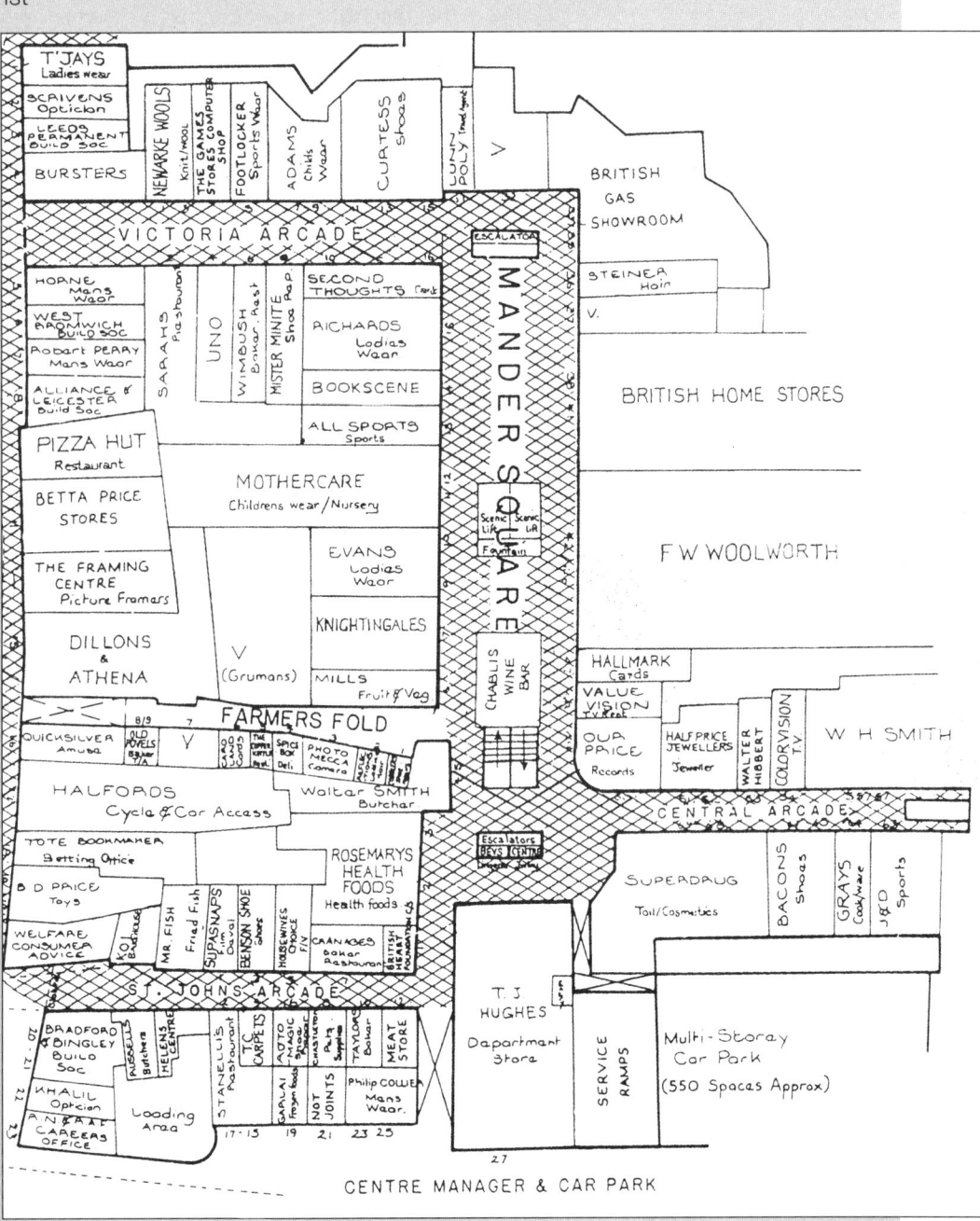

The Mander Centre

Business organisations and employment

Legislation, page 256

How does the business environment affect a business?

As we have just seen, a competitive business environment can have both positive and negative effects on a business. Within the business environment, business organisations can also be influenced by legal, environmental and public factors.

Legal influences

A range of legislation exists to make sure that businesses operate safely and honestly. For example, a business which manufactures goods has certain legal responsibilities:
- it has to follow the Health and Safety at Work Act 1974, which ensures the well-being of employees
- it is insured against claims in case products are faulty and a consumer is harmed (this is called 'product liability')
- it has to follow any legal specifications for the goods it is producing.

Consumer Protection and Safety Acts lay down safety standards on behalf of the consumer for many goods, in particular:
- electrical equipment
- toys
- children's clothes
- nightclothes
- heating appliances and oil heaters
- cooking utensils
- crash helmets
- baby goods, such as prams, pushchairs and mattresses.

The British Standards Institution (BSI) works closely with the European Union to draw up legislation on the safety of goods. All manufacturers are required to meet these standards, and inspectors from the BSI, Trading Standards Department and Consumer Protection Department make checks to ensure they are being met.

A   Meeting standards

Labels that reassure us about the quality and safety of goods are known as 'kitemarks'. Here are some examples of kitemarks which have been provided by the Trading Standards Department.

Visit your local shopping centre and find examples of kitemarks. What types of goods and services do they appear on? What do they mean? How do you think they influence the businesses which manufacture these goods and services?

Environmental influences

Businesses must also be aware of their impact on the environment. This can include:
- noise pollution – for example, night clubs have to monitor noise levels at night
- air, sea and land pollution – for example, manufacturing companies have to dispose carefully of the by-products of manufacturing goods.

The Department of the Environment is responsible for legislation on environmental issues such as air pollution, noise emission and waste disposal. It also sets up working parties and advisory committees which provide advice and encourage businesses to adopt 'environmentally-friendly' practices.

With the Department of Trade and Industry, the Department of the Environment has set up an environmental helpline (0800 505794) to advise businesses on best practice and to advise people with environmental concerns. If a member of the public has a complaint about the effect of a business' activities on the environment, it is usually dealt with by the local Environmental Health Department. There are also trading standards departments and consumer advice organisations in every area, which can help the general public.

Can you think of any businesses that affect the environment in your area? What do they do?

Public influences

Business organisations should never underestimate the influence which public feeling can have on business success.

People concerned about issues such as the environment and consumer safety often set up pressure groups. They may try to discourage people from buying certain goods, and aim to influence public opinion, legislation, and policies. For example, conservationists were up in arms at the acid rain caused by two power stations sited in the same area of the UK, and campaigned to close or move them. Often, members of the public concerned about issues like this join organised pressure groups like Greenpeace or Friends of the Earth.

Markets

The word 'market' literally means a place where people buy and sell their goods or services. When you think of a market you tend to think of it as a particular place where goods are bought and sold, e.g. Oldham market. Shoppers who want to buy vegetables meet stall-holders who are selling vegetables; purchases and sales are made.

Most markets, however, are not like this. The markets for airline tickets or coal are not located in one place. The market for airline tickets is an international market where buyers and sellers are linked by telephone and fax, and millions of pounds or dollars may change hands in a typical deal. Goods can now also be bought on the Internet. Markets, in fact, come in all shapes and sizes, from the local market for vegetables and clothing to the countrywide (or **domestic**) market for coal and the international market for gold and diamonds.

A business needs customers to buy its goods or services

Wherever a business is located, it has to be able to sell its goods or services at a profit. In other words, it needs customers.

Businesses need to find out who their customers are by asking questions such as:
- Who will buy and why?
- How much will they buy and how often?
- How much will they pay?
- Where else can they buy from?

In finding out the answers to these questions, a business is said to be defining its market.

Business organisations and employment

▶ Market share, page 89

All businesses aim to improve their market share – to get more customers to buy their products and services, rather than those of their competitors. If all the businesses selling any one product or service combine their total sales, this is said to show the total market value. An individual business can then express its own total sales as a percentage of this, and calculate its market share.

C Case study: Granada

Granada Group's Television Division made profits of £42.5 million and £55.5 million in 1993 and 1994. This enabled the company to buy (take over) one of its competitors – London Weekend Television – in 1994.

Granada also owned 10% of the shares in BSkyB, the satellite television company. The take-over will allow Granada to show London Weekend Television programmes on BSkyB. This will increase Granada's profits and market share.

A Comp-U-Clic's market share

Comp-U-Clic's annual sales turnover in 1995 was £750,000. The table below shows the main types of sales it made over the last three months of the year.

Table 1.2: Comp-U-Clic's sales turnover for 1995

Type of customer	Description of sale	Number of sales	Unit price
Local Health Authority	486 multi-media system	10	£ 1,000
Private engineering business	486 system	4	£ 700
Private individual customers, for home use	Pentium 75 Pentium 100 Compaq Notebook	15 10 11	£ 1,300 £ 1100 £ 1989
Local Educational Authority	486 DX 2-66 system	21	£ 700
Private businesses	486 system	10	£ 700
Private businesses	Training	3	£ 1,050
Local authority Private individuals Private businesses	Accessories; printers, modems, mice etc.	27 10 5	£ 2,500 £ 750 £ 450
Private individuals Local authority Private businesses	Consumables; disks, toner, paper etc.	195 10 65	£ 750 £ 125 £ 300
Private individuals Local authority Private businesses	Software	5 2 6	£ 1,200 £ 350 £ 1,700
Private individuals Local authority Private businesses	Repairs and upgrades	75 0 6	£ 4,500 £ 120

1 Present this information as graphs and pie charts which show:
   – the breakdown of different markets (types of customer)
   – the breakdown of different types of goods and services
   – the breakdown of sales.

2 The market value of the computer trade in the Wolverhampton area is £5 million per month.
   a Comment on Comp-U-Clic's market share.
   b From the information given in the business sections of the quality press, specialist computer magazines and the trade press, try to find out details of the national and international markets for computer products and services. Write a summary of your investigation, and comment on Comp-U-Clic's business activities in the light of your findings.

▶ Graphs and pie charts, page 44

Price

Buying and selling can only occur when a **price** is agreed for a given quantity In the market for CDs these are priced around £11.99. In the designer trainers market, shoes are priced at around £50–£100 per pair depending on the 'make' and how exclusive they are.

Read the article in the margin about beef prices. The price of beef went down as people stopped buying due to worries about BSE. In this case the 'mad cow disease' scare drastically reduced demand, as schools and colleges took beef off the menu and the public stopped buying. In addition international buyers of beef including Singapore, New Zealand and France put a ban on British beef.

The farmers at local markets who sell beef were unable to sell their livestock at the current price and were forced to reduce their prices to get a sale or not sell at all.

> An ICM poll of adults on Saturday 30 March and Sunday 31 March showed that the number of people prepared to eat beef has dropped from nearly two-thirds of the population to less than one-third.

Demand

If a business gets its marketing right, it should succeed in creating a **demand** among customers for its goods and services.

Demand: *the amount consumers want and are able to buy at a particular price in a given time period.*

▶ Market research, page 109

▶ Production, page 110

▶ Promotion, page 186

▶ Sales and after-sales service, page 111

Business success can depend on getting the right marketing mix

The business organisation then needs to be able to supply the right amount of goods or services to meet demand.

There is often a constant demand for some products. Food, for example, is bought on an everyday basis, soon eaten and replaced. People always demand food as it is a basic item for survival.

In contrast, some items would probably never be produced because they would destroy demand. For example, designing an 'ever-lasting light bulb' would not be in the best interests of light bulb manufacturers, as the constant demand for light bulbs would disappear and they would go out of business. However, if they designed longer-lasting light bulbs, they could compensate for the lower demand by charging higher prices.

A Chocolate bars and fizzy drinks

1. Conduct a survey in your group to find out how many chocolate bars and fizzy drinks they buy in the next week. Then ask them how many drinks and chocolate bars they would have bought if:
   a. the price went up by 4p, 8p, 10p or 20p
   b. the price came down by 4p, 8p, 10p, 12p or 20p.
2. Using a computer make a table like the one below. Record your answers as follows:

Name	Numbers demanded per week								
	Fizzy drinks					Chocolate bars			
	-20p	-12p	-8p	-4p	ACTUAL PRICE	+20p	+12p	+8p	+4p

3. Plot a graph for each of the people you have interviewed for their purchases of fizzy drinks. Each graph should plot *quantity demanded* on the horizontal x axis and price on the vertical y axis.
   Each graph should have the title 'The Individual Demand Curve for fizzy drinks during the week beginning...' Don't forget to put the name of the person to whom this relates.

Price (pence)	Quantity demanded per week	
	Fizzy drinks	Chocolate bars
-20		
-12		
-8		
-4		
ACTUAL PRICE		
+4		
+8		
+12		
+20		

4. Using a computer calculate how many fizzy drinks and chocolate bars would be demanded at each price for *all* the people you interviewed.
   Record your answers on a table like the one on the left.
5. Using the figures in 3 plot two *market demand curves* one for fizzy drinks and one for chocolate bars. Label the axes in the same way as 2 only this time you should refer to the *total* quantity demanded for:
   a. fizzy drinks
   b. chocolate bars
6. Why do you think people buy more fizzy drinks and chocolate bars as price falls?

Case study: Mud Monsters

Comp-U-Clic has a supplier of 'shareware'. These are disks of software, mainly games, which run on PCs. They have always been a popular line in the shop, selling mainly to people in the 12 to 18 age range. They usually sell for £4.99 per disk. The idea is that only part of a game can be played using a shareware disk. If people then want to play the complete game, they have to register with the writer of the software (or the distribution company), and pay for the full game.

A regular customer, Daljit, who is a student at the local college, designed a game called 'Mud Monsters' that he wanted to circulate as shareware. He approached Steve, and asked if Comp-U-Clic would sell the disks for him. Steve told Daljit to research the market and find out what the demand was.

Daljit started by carrying out a questionnaire with 100 people aged 12 to 18 attending local schools and colleges. He found out that:
- 35 students would buy the disk at £2.99
- 30 students would buy the disk at £3.99
- 20 students would buy the disk at £4.99
- 15 students did not want to buy the disk at all.

Market and demand

1. Calculate the mean price students are willing to pay for Daljit's disk. Remember to include the 15 students who would pay £0.
2. It costs Daljit 40p a disk to copy his game, and 25p to package it attractively. Steve would like to add a 20% mark-up to the cost of each disk. What price do you advise Daljit to set for the game? Explain your decision.

▶ Mean, page 56

▶ Percentages, page 32

Customer needs and wants

The goods and services we choose to spend our money on are either:
- to meet our needs – our basic requirements for food, shelter and so on
- to meet our wants – things which make our lives more comfortable, pleasant and enjoyable, such as sweets, magazines, televisions and CDs. Items which meet our wants often improve our standard of living, and fall into the category of luxury goods.

The same product can be a want to one customer, and a need to another. For example, one of Comp-U-Clic's customers is a student with a part-time job. He saved his earnings as he lived rent-free with his parents, and bought a computer because he wanted to play games in his spare time. Another customer bought the same product because he worked from home writing articles for publication, and needed a computer to earn his living.

Are these needs, wants, or both?

Needs and wants

1. Find out what your friends have spent their money on in the past seven days. List the items they have bought which are wants, and the items which are needs.
2. How much money did you have to spend over the past seven days?
   a. List what you spent your money on, grouping items as either needs or wants.
   b. Calculate what percentage of your total money you spent on needs.
   c. Calculate what percentage of your total money you spent on wants.
   d. What did you want to buy, but couldn't?

▶ Percentages, page 32

Ability to buy

As the last activity shows, the demand for goods and services not only depends on needs and wants, but also on ability to buy. A lot of people may want to buy a brand new Porsche, but will only be able to afford a second-hand Metro. **Effective demand** is the quantity the buyer is able and willing to buy

What determines the quantity of goods and services people are willing and able to buy? Or, as economists say, 'what makes up the **effective** demand for a product or service?' Economists have found that the link between price and the quantity demanded that you have discovered in the activity 'Fizzy drinks and chocolate bars' is similar for almost all products. The lower the price the more people will want to buy. Or, as economists say, a fall in price will lead to an **extension of demand** (or a rise) whereas a rise in price will lead to a **contraction of demand** (or a fall).

Extension of demand: increase in the quantity bought due to a fall in price.

Contraction of demand: reduction in the quantity bought due to a rise in price.

Using graphs

The table on the left shows the demand for trainers at Rackets and Runners during March 1996 based on a survey carried out by them which is similar to that done by you for fizzy drinks and chocolate bars. It assumes that factors such as income do not affect decisions as to whether the shoes should be bought or not. If we plot this, the result is shown on the left as a demand curve, illustrating how price and the quantity bought are related over time. If Rackets and Runners drop the price to £50 per pair there would be an extension of demand to 130 pairs of trainers. This is a movement *along* the demand curve.

Price per pair/£	No. of trainers sold/month
50	130
60	115
70	100
80	95
90	82

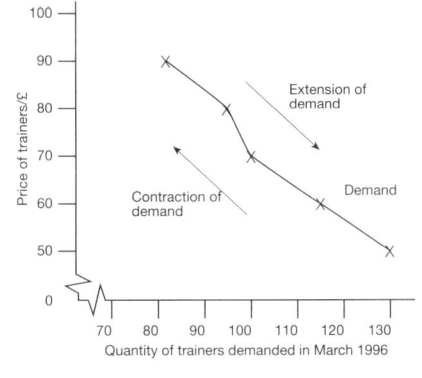

Note: we have skipped part of the x and y axes because the prices start at £50 per pair

A   Price rise

If prices rose to £90 how would the demand change? What would you call this – a contraction or expansion of demand?

If a customer is thinking of buying a pair of trainers at £70 but decides not to in the end because they are too expensive, this is *not* an example of effective demand. Why not?

There are two key stages in effective demand:
- wish to buy. A customer recognises a need or want, and has a 'wish to buy'
- ability to buy. The customer is able to pay for the product.

Ability to buy is often affected by what is happening in the economy at the time. For example, in times of high unemployment and high interest rates, the demand for luxury goods falls. In these circumstances, people have less money to spend and luxury items are not regarded as essential.

When you have a limited amount to spend you have to make choices. If you buy one product you have to give up the opportunity to buy something else.

Opportunity cost: what you have to give up in order to buy something else.

Business organisations and employment

> **A** **Buying vegetables**
>
> Find out what vegetables are bought for your family and where they are usually bought from. Keep a record on computer of the prices of the vegetables and the amount your family buys (preferably on the same day of the week) over a period of six months. Using the six months' evidence describe your findings. Draw a demand curve per week against each sort of vegetable. What problems did you face in collecting the evidence and analysing it

Consumer and customer demand

People who buy goods and services from businesses are usually referred to simply as 'customers'. However, they can be broken down further into consumers and customers.

Consumers: *people who actually use goods or services – the 'end users'. For example, children are the consumers of toys, but toy shops' customers tend to be older relatives buying presents.*

Customers: *people who buy goods or services, but don't necessarily use them.*

In most cases the consumer is also the customer – unless you are buying a present for someone, you will probably use most of the products you buy. Business organisations selling products need to create a demand among consumers and customers by considering:
- consumers' preferences, and the amount of money customers have to spend
- the price of a product or service
- the alternatives available
- any additional costs which result from a purchase.

A business' first step is to persuade consumers that they need or want products. For example, a jeans manufacturer may use advertising to try to convince consumers that they can't manage without a pair of its jeans.

Once the consumer wants the product, the business then has to persuade the customer – whether or not this is the same person as the consumer – that it sells the right products, at the right price, in a convenient way.

▶ Consumer demand, page 182

Products and customers

The output of business organisations can be classified in two main ways.

Consumables or durables
- **Consumables.** These are products which are 'used up', such as food, writing paper and computer disks. The demand for these types of goods is very high, because they constantly need to be replaced.
- **Durables.** These are products which are designed to last for a longer period of time, usually more than a year. Examples include cars, CD players, computers and washing machines.

Goods or services
- **Goods.** This is a broad term used to cover products which are made and sold. Goods can fall into two categories:
  – consumer goods, which are only used once, e.g. newspapers
  – capital or industrial goods, which are used by businesses, such as machinery.
- **Services.** This is a broad term used to describe products which are

▶ Tertiary sector, page 79

intangible and designed to make life easier or more enjoyable. Many services are part of the tertiary sector. Again, they can be divided into two categories:
– customer services, such as hairdressing
– industrial services, such as parcel delivery.

A — What type of product?

1. Go back to the list of what your friends spent their money on over the last week. Classify the items on the list as consumables, durables, goods or services.
2. Look at the products in the picture below, all of which are provided by Barnaby's Department Stores. How would you classify them?

> Needs and wants activity, page 105

Individual consumers

Individual consumers are people or organisations who buy goods and services for their own use. For example:
- as an individual person, you would buy a pair of shoes to wear yourself, not to share with your friends
- an individual family would buy a particular brand of breakfast cereal because all the family likes it
- an individual business would buy particular goods or services for use within the business, such as office furniture or a delivery service.

> Consumer and customer demand, page 182

Government

This includes national government departments and local authorities who place orders for goods and services.

Many of these goods and services used to be supplied by departments within government or the local authority. Now it is seen as more cost-effective to put them out to tender – to invite businesses to compete for a contract. For example, local authorities used to employ school cleaners, but now most use contract cleaning services.

Some of the products bought by government are likely to be highly specialised. For example, the Ministry of Defence might need a specially designed computer interface.

Other businesses

Often, other organisations have to buy goods and services for the day-to-day running of their business. For example, Steve Parker at Comp-U-Clic has to buy lots of electrical mains supply leads with a plug at one end and a socket at the other, so he can make up and supply computer systems to his customers. His supplier sells the same product to a range of different businesses, including a kettle manufacturer.

> ### A Comp-U-Clic's market, products and customers
>
> Include your work for this activity in your portfolio of evidence.
>   Look back at the table of Comp-U-Clic's sales figures over a three-month period.
>
> 1. What is Comp-U-Clic's market? Is it domestic or international? What is the demand for Comp-U-Clic's products? Do they meet customers' needs or wants? Are they regular or occasional purchases?
> 2. What types of products does Comp-U-Clic offer? Are they consumable, durable, goods or services? Comment on the existing and potential product range.
> 3. What types of customer buys products from Comp-U-Clic? Are they individuals, government bodies or other businesses? Comment on the existing customer market and the potential customer market.

▶ Comp-U-Clic's market share, page 102

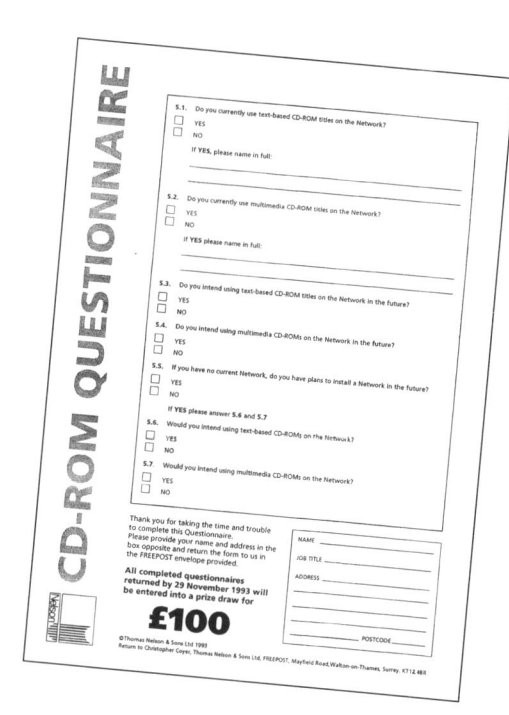

Business activities

Businesses are constantly trying to improve their market position by creating new products, improving existing products and promoting goods and services to customers. This involves a range of business activities.

Market research

Businesses carry out market research to find out as much information as they can about who their customers are and what their reasons are for buying.

To carry out market research, business organisations use desk and field research. Desk research involves going through existing information – for example, data on past sales or consumer trends – collected by the company or by marketing organisations. Field research involves going out to collect information by carrying out questionnaires, surveys and interviews.

The results of market research can help a business to evaluate:
- how well it is meeting its customers' needs
- whether it needs to design and produce new products
- whether its marketing communications (e.g. advertising and brochures) are reaching potential customers and giving the right messages
- how efficient its sales team and after-sales service are.

Businesses use market research to find out more about their customers

Design

Design is the process of planning, creating and testing products. It is used to:
- develop new products
- improve existing products, to make them more attractive, easier to use, safer, more efficient, or even taste better.

Some business organisations employ a design team, which is responsible for designing products to meet customers' needs in a cost-effective, efficient way. In smaller businesses, the production team may take on the design role. Sometimes, the designer may also be the owner or 'entrepreneur' of a small business. For example, the owner of a small arts and crafts shop which makes perfumed wax candles might make prototypes, specify the amount and type of wax to be used, and make sure that products meet safety requirement – all part of the design process.

What type of people do you think these packaging designs are aiming to attract?

Business organisations and employment

The design of packaging can play an important part in making products attractive to customers. For example, a business might decide to make packaging out of recyclable materials because it wants to attract customers who are concerned about green issues by showing that it cares about the environment.

Production

The main business activity of many businesses is production. This involves buying raw materials or other products, and making them into final, manufactured products. For example, chocolate manufacturers buy cocoa and other raw materials for their products, which they then mix, manufacture and package in their factories. In this process of manufacture, the business adds value to the raw materials. This allows it to sell at a profit.

Businesses involved in producing goods need to make sure that the production process is as efficient and cost effective as possible. Checks need to be in place to ensure that products meet specifications, quality standards and health and safety requirements.

▶ Health and safety requirements, pages 155, 257

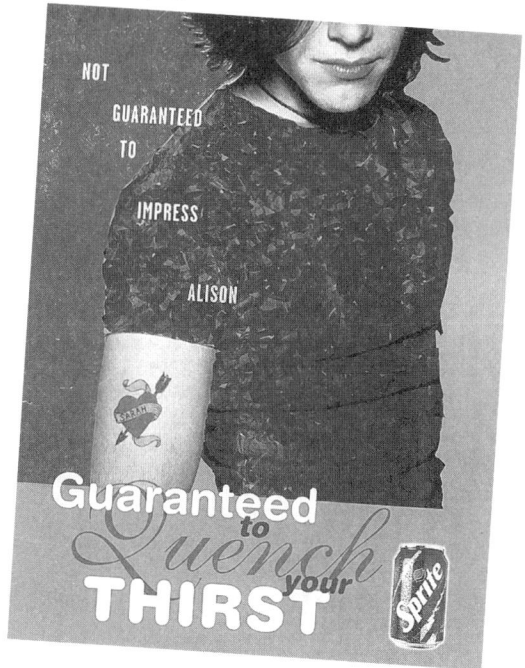

Marketing communications

Businesses use marketing communications to get information to their customers about their products and services.

One of the most obvious types of marketing communication is **advertising**. Businesses pay for space to advertise their products in local or national magazines, newspapers, trade press or even on the radio or television (although this is very expensive). Other forms of advertising include:

- tele-sales, when sales staff phone potential customers
- direct mail, when information is posted to potential customers
- leaflet drops, when leaflets are handed out in the area to target particular types of customer
- placing advertisements in shop windows, on bill boards, public transport, and so on.

What message do you think this advertisement is trying to communicate?

Advertising is part of overall **promotion** carried out by businesses. This is a general term which covers the ways in which a business organisation persuades its customers to buy from it. Often, this means launching promotional campaigns, combining advertising with special offers, coupons, discounts, competitions, free gifts, and so on.

▶ Advertising, page 185

Some organisations choose to promote their products through **sponsorship**. This involves the business contributing towards a particular event or charity in order to attract interest. For example, cigarette companies, which aren't allowed to advertise on television, often sponsor sports events.

▶ Promotional materials, page 186

All marketing communication involves producing and distributing **sales literature**, such as leaflets, brochures and posters. All sales literature should contain relevant information, be attractively presented and easy to read. It is usually aimed at attracting a particular type of customer or market.

▶ Sponsorship, page 188

C Case study: Comp-U-Clic's advertising

Comp-U-Clic advertises every week in the local free paper, placing a small advertisement which costs £6 per week. Every two months it also runs an advertising feature, which costs about £500. In the past the company tried advertising in national magazines, but the sales generated did not cover the cost of the advertisement. Most of Comp-U-Clic's advertising promotes its computer systems, a market in which there is considerable competition and profit margins are very low. With the company growing, Steve Parker is now prepared to invest 1% of the company's annual sales turnover (£750,000 in 1995) in promoting the business and improving its market position.

> ### A — Spending Steve's budget
>
> 1. In 1996 Steve spends 1% of Comp-U-Clic's annual turnover for 1995 (£750,000) on promoting the business. How much does he spend?
> 2. Advise Steve on the best way to spend this budget to improve the business' market position. Carry out research into the cost of different types of marketing communication, and decide which you think would be most effective in Comp-U-Clic's case. Draw up a marketing budget for the year, suggesting how much Steve should spend on different activities.

▶ Industrial sectors, page 80

▶ Types of business organisation, page 81

Sales and after-sales service

Sales activities are important to businesses, as without selling their goods and services they won't make a profit. Many companies employ people especially to sell – sales representatives. They are the link between the company and its customers, passing on information about customers to the company and helping the customer to use or sell on goods and services.

One of the main responsibilities of a sales team is to provide after-sales service. This enables customers or end users to remain in contact with the business for help, technical back-up or support after the sale has been made. Many companies selling domestic appliances, e.g. washing machines and cookers, use specialist contractors for after-sales service. After-sales service gives the business a good reputation, and encourages customers to buy more goods and services in the future.

> **HARRISON TOOLS IS OPENING A NEW WORKSHOP**
> and seeks workshop fitters. Must have a good technical background, preferably with tool hire experience, be committed to high standards and flexible. Good salary paid for 5½ day week.
> Further details: Mr Conran
> 0131 689 012

Investigating employment

Look around your local business community and think back to some of the businesses that you have already studied in this unit. Which do you think are successful? How can you decide?

One way to measure the success of a business is to see whether it has expanded – probably taking on new employees.

> ### A — Who is gaining employees?
>
> - Are there any businesses in your area which have taken on a significant number of new employees recently? For example, a branch of a large organisation opening in your area, or an existing business which is expanding its business activities.
> - What jobs have been advertised?
> - What sort of business activities are they involved in?
> - What sector are they in? How would you classify the business organisations which are taking on new employees?

> *An expanding national charity seeks*
> **2 NEW SUPPORT WORKERS**
> to provide a range of services for people with learning disabilities. For both posts you will need a minimum of one year's experience in the care profession and you must have good literacy, numeracy and communication skills.
> LTG offers a competitive package. For an application form, telephone 01317 24189

▶ Industrial sectors, page 80

▶ Types of business organisation, page 81

But as well as local businesses taking on new employees, you will probably have heard about organisations having to lose employees. This might be:
- to make financial savings
- because they are closing down the least profitable areas of the business and concentrating resources on the most profitable areas. For example,

Business organisations and employment

Recent years have seen an increase in technology which makes jobs easier

▶ Tertiary sector, page 79

A Who is losing employees?

- Are there any businesses in your area which have made employees redundant recently? You could talk to friends, family and people you know who work locally.
- What jobs have been lost?
- What sort of business activities are the organisations involved in?
- What sector are they in? How would you classify the business organisations which have made employees redundant?

Look back at the first activity in this section, 'Who is gaining employees?'. Can you notice any patterns in the information you are finding out?

▶ Industrial sectors, page 80

▶ Types of business organisations, page 81

Scottish Newcastle Breweries sold off a number of its pubs which weren't making enough profit and concentrated on its hotel, holiday and leisure activities like Center Parcs

- because they are streamlining the business, aiming to become more cost effective and efficient by introducing computerised equipment, machinery or robots to do jobs done by human beings in the past.

New technology has been one of the major reasons for businesses employing fewer people. Investing in up-to-date equipment, and training people to use it, is often very expensive in the short term. But in the long term it can mean reduced staff costs, fewer errors and improved efficiency.

C Case study: Rover car plant

The car industry has changed rapidly in recent years because of developments in new technology. The Rover plant in Birmingham now uses robots on the production line for jobs such as painting large panels, but still uses employees to hand paint areas such as wheel arches which the robots can't reach. This may lead to employees being given other tasks to do, or being made redundant. Rover needs fewer people on their production line now.

A Technology and employment

- List any businesses, locally or nationally, that you know have introduced computerised equipment or robots over the last few years.
- What sort of jobs do you think this equipment has replaced?
- What sort of skills, experience or qualifications will people need to operate this type of equipment?
- Do you know anyone whose job has changed, or who has lost their job, because of the introduction of new technology? How has it affected their life?

To help you with this activity, you could ask family, friends and people who work locally for their experiences.

When a business organisation has to lose employees, it can be very distressing for everyone concerned. It has an effect on family, friends, the company personnel who have to break the news and the employees that are left, as well as the people losing their jobs.

Sometimes, businesses are able to redeploy people within the workplace – giving them another type of job in place of their old one. This can mean extra training and learning new skills.

But often, business organisations are forced to make employees redundant. When this happens, jobs are lost permanently and people become unemployed, or are offered retirement at an early age. Depending on their age, how long they have worked for the business and company policy, some employees are offered money as compensation. Despite this, many people can't find another job, find it hard to adapt to having extra time on their hands, and can't cope with the loss of financial earnings.

Analysing information about employment

As you will probably have already realised, there are patterns – 'trends' – in the number of people employed and the types of jobs they are doing.

Recent years have seen the decline of many traditional industries, such as steel and coal. These industries, and the businesses which supported them, employed a large number of people in particular regions of the country.

Case study: Merseyside shipbuilding

In the past, people living on Merseyside relied heavily on the shipbuilding industry. The closure of shipbuilders has not only affected those who worked on the ships directly, but also those who worked for small engineering firms which supplied the shipbuilders with fixtures, fittings, welding equipment, security services and so on. It has also affected shops and stores in the community, where the workers spent their income.

At the same time, other industries, mainly in the tertiary sector, have been looking for new employees with particular types of skills. For example, there has been a significant increase in the number of people employed in the leisure industry in recent years, and lots of openings for people with customer service skills and experience.

Case study: Motorway services

The opening of new motorway services and facilities for road travellers has created new employment opportunities. Many motorway services provide shops, restaurants and cafes, indoor play areas for children, and overnight accommodation. In turn, these rely on other services, such as catering and cleaning. Granada Leisure, which includes motorway services, increased its number of employees from 4,619 in 1994 to 5,970 in 1995.

To get a clearer picture of employment trends we need to collect facts and figures about what is happening, and then analyse them by asking questions. A good place to start is to look at statistical tables of figures such as:
- how many people are employed
- whether employees are male or female
- how old employees are
- where people are employed
- which sector they are employed in
- what type of employment people are in.

By analysing information like this over a period of time and across different geographical areas (for example, locally, regionally, nationally and across the European Union), we can start to get a useful picture of employment trends.

Business organisations and employment

Year	Workforce	Workforce in employment	Male employees in employment	Female employees in employment	Self-employed persons	HM forces	Employees in employment
1990	28,761	27,206	12,046	10,872	3,562	303	22,893
1991	28,561	26,320	11,530	10,731	3,408	297	22,220
1992	28,461	25,783	11,240	10,698	3,230	290	21,904
1993	28,265	25,400	10,980	10,648	3,189	271	21,606
1994	27,998	25,413	10,913	10,651	3,298	250	21,547

Crown copyright. Reproduced with the permission of the controller of HMSO.

A Seeing is believing

Look at the table above, taken from *The Monthly Digest* magazine produced for the government by the Central Statistical Office.

Table 1.3: Distribution of the workforce

- All figures in the table are shown in thousands.
- Workforce consists of employees in employment and unemployment claimants.
- The workforce in employment comprises of employees in employment, the self-employed, HM Forces and participants in government training schemes.

▶ Bar charts, page 46

▶ Mean, page 56

▶ Rounding, page 25

1. Work out the number of unemployed. This will be the difference between the 'Workforce' column and the 'Workforce in employment' column.
2. Produce a simple bar chart showing the workforce in employment from 1991 to 1994.
3. Work out the average number of people in employment and show this on your graph.
4. Produce a bar chart which compares the number of men and women in employment over the five years. On the horizontal axis, put bars next to each other representing men and women for each year. On the vertical axis, put the number scale.
5. Compare male and female employment by rounding the figures for 1990 and 1994 to the nearest million, and showing the ratio of male employees : female employees in each year. What does this suggest?
6. What can you see happening to male and female employment over the five years?
7. What has happened to the workforce in general?
8. Look back at the table on page 80, which looks at the number of people employed in each sector. Produce a bar chart showing the growth or decline in employment in each sector for the years given. On the horizontal axis, group bars for each sector for each year. On the vertical axis, put the number scale.
9. What do you see happening in each sector over the years?

You can complete these tasks by hand, with a calculator or using a computer.

Looking at information for one region

The tables on the following two pages show information about employment in the Wolverhampton area in the West Midlands.

Table 1.4 shows:
the number of men and women employed in different industrial sectors
whether they are employed full time (F/T) or part time (P/T).

Table 1.5 shows:
- the total residents in the area – the total number of men and women in each age group
- the percentage of total residents in each age group who are economically active
- the percentage of economically active residents in each age group who are unemployed and on training schemes.

The information in these tables was taken from a census of employment carried out in 1991.

Economically active: people available for work. They might be working, on a government scheme, or unemployed.

Census of employment: a survey carried out every ten years to find out information about businesses, industrial sectors and employment.

Table 1.4: Employees grouped by gender, type of employment and industrial sectors for Wolverhampton, 1991

Industrial description	Males F/T	Males P/T	Females F/T	Females P/T	Total
Agriculture, energy, minerals, non metal products	1900	0	600	100	2600
Metal manufacture	2200	0	300	100	2600
Metal goods	4200	100	1300	300	5900
Mechanical engineering and vehicles	6600	100	1000	200	7900
Electrical, electronic instrument engineering	1100	0	400	100	1600
Other manufacturing	7800	100	2900	1000	11800
Construction	5600	100	800	300	6800
Wholesaling and distribution	3300	200	900	600	5000
Retailing	3100	500	2700	4100	10400
Hotels and catering	400	700	600	1900	3600
Repair of consumer goods and vehicles	500	0	100	100	700
Transport	2200	0	500	100	2800
Post and telecommunications	1700	0	900	300	2900
Banking and finance	700	0	1300	400	2400
Insurance	400	0	300	100	800
Business services	1400	200	1400	600	3600
Renting of movables	700	0	200	0	900
Owning and dealing in real estate	300	0	400	100	800
Public administration and defence	1900	0	1800	500	4200
Sanitary services	400	200	400	2600	3600
Education and research	2300	500	2700	1800	7300
Medical and health services	800	100	2200	3000	6100
Social and community services	300	100	1000	600	2000
Recreational and cultural services	400	100	400	500	1400
Other services	200	0	500	300	1000

Table 1.5: Employees grouped by age and gender, economically active, unemployment and training schemes

Gender	Age	Total residents	Economically active	%	Unemployed	%	On training schemes	%
Male	16-19	7039	4450	63.2	1298	29.2	551	12.4
Male	20-24	10015	8772	87.6	2060	23.5	205	2.3
Male	25-29	9315	8844	94.9	1631	18.4	144	1.6
Male	30-34	8249	7841	95.1	1174	15	127	1.6
Male	35-44	15067	14081	93.5	1816	12.9	209	1.5
Male	45-54	13396	12072	90.1	1478	12.2	117	1.0
Male	55-59	6444	5177	80.3	883	17.1	41	0.8
Male	60-64	6699	3871	57.8	848	21.9	2	0.1
Male	65+	15934	993	6.2	44	4.4	2	0.2
Female	16-19	6764	3639	53.8	755	20.7	484	13.3
Female	20-24	10292	6977	67.8	1085	15.6	160	2.3
Female	25-29	9633	6197	64.3	712	11.5	94	1.5
Female	30-34	8145	5133	63.0	449	8.7	46	0.9
Female	35-44	14801	10014	67.7	701	7.0	61	0.6
Female	45-54	13263	8923	67.3	637	7.1	50	0.6
Female	55-59	6452	3222	49.9	306	9.5	10	0.3
Female	60-64	6926	1319	19.0	26	2.0	1	0.1
Female	64+	22586	478	2.1	24	5.0	2	0.4

A Analysing employment in Wolverhampton

Look carefully at the tables of statistical information about employment in Wolverhampton.
1 Show the following information, as percentages, in graphs. Try to make your graphs as clear and visually interesting as possible, as you will need them for a presentation later on. For example, you could produce pictograms or pie charts with interesting keys.
   a Male and female employees in the primary, secondary and tertiary sectors, including both full-time and part-time workers. You will need to use Table 1.4, and decide whether each industrial description belongs in the primary, secondary or tertiary sector.
   b Unemployed people by age and by gender (Table 1.5).
   c People on training schemes by age and by gender (Table 1.5).

▶ Percentages, page 32

▶ Graphs, page 44

▶ Industrial sectors, page 78

2 Now that you have presented the information in a visual way, it should be much easier to analyse. Answer these questions by looking at your graphs:
   a Which sector employs most women?
   b Is unemployment higher among men or women?
   c Which gender group and age group have the least unemployment?
   d Which gender group show the greatest take-up of government training schemes?
   e What do the statistics show about the male and female population aged 16 to 19?
   f What do the statistics show about the male and female population over the age of 65? (You may need to look back at the tables for this information.)
3 Make a list of any factors (reasons) which you think might have contributed to the statistics. For example, looking at Table 1.5 you might think that more girls stay on at school or college than boys.
4 Research this type of information for your own area, and make a comparison with Wolverhampton. Do you notice any trends?

Carrying out independent research will help you with your GNVQ and in the future

Comparing information for different regions

As you will have seen in the last section, to get a broader picture of employment trends, you need to compare statistics for different regions. In this section you will look more closely at employment in the West Midlands and the Ile de France, the region of France which includes Paris.

The statistics about both regions are taken from Eurostats Regions 1994. The information included in the fact files is taken from Eurostat: Portrait of the Regions.

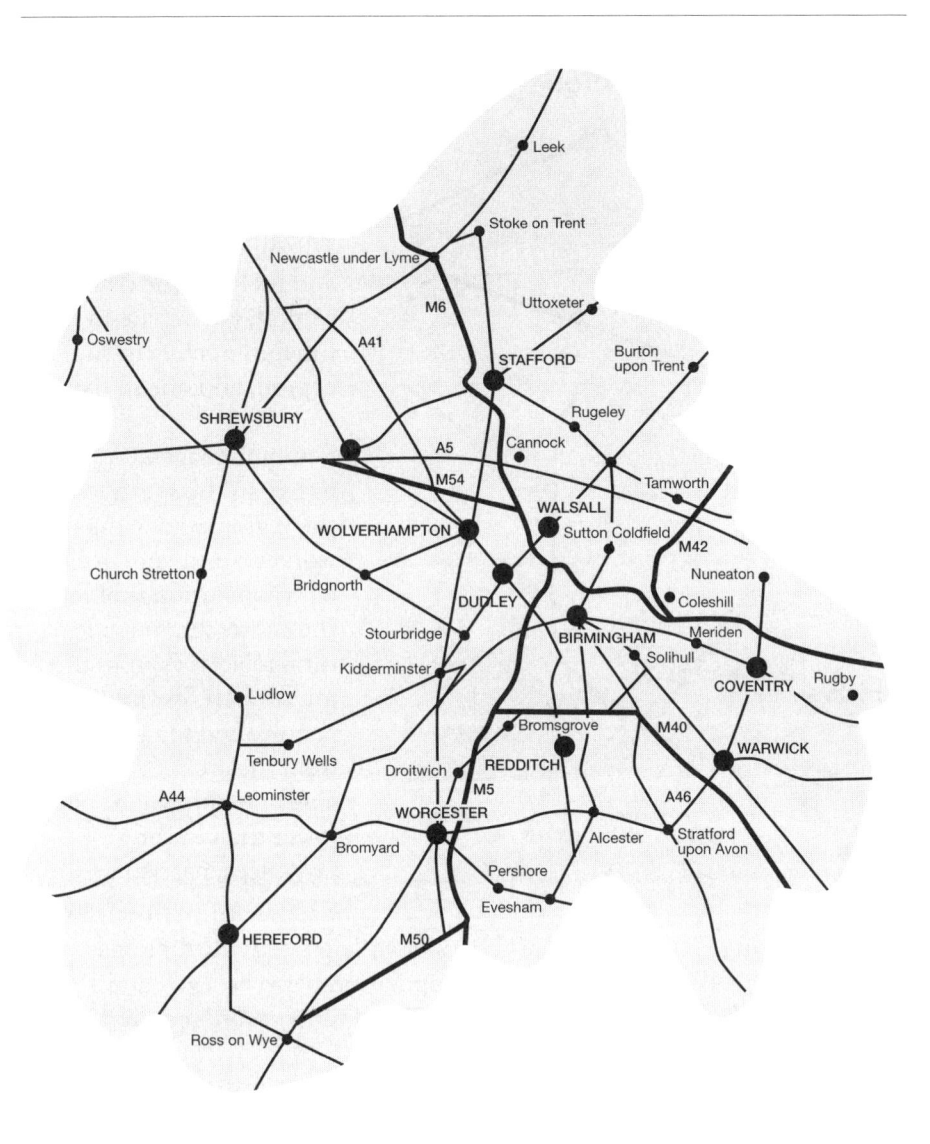

West Midlands fact file

- The West Midlands is less than 1000 km^2.
- It has a population of 2.6 million.
- The population has been falling in recent decades.
- Employment in manufacturing, while still important to the region, has been declining. Manufacturing employs half the workforce in areas like Sandwell, and one-fifth in Solihull.
- There is a high percentage of engineering companies because the region was once a centre for the production of iron. This led to specialisation in products such as locks and guns.
- The West Midlands' location in the centre of the country has led to it developing a good communications network.
- The National Exhibition Centre, close to Birmingham airport, has helped to bring more business and employment to the area.

Ile de France fact file:

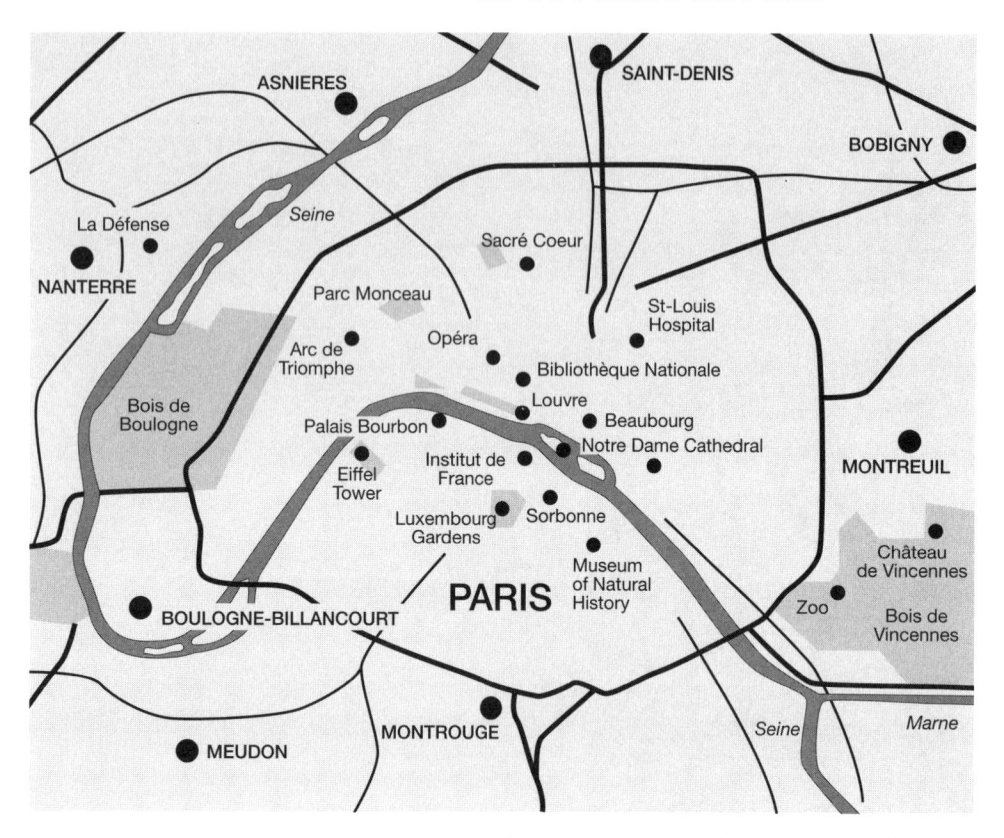

- The Ile de France has an area of over 12,000 km^2.
- It has a population of over 10 million inhabitants, and includes the country's capital, Paris. One in five inhabitants live in the capital, and one in three work there.
- Senior management tend to live in the south west of the region, and manual workers in the north east. The population is older in the centre and outside rural regions than in the middle belt. Retired people tend to move away from the area.
- The unemployment rate is lower than in the provinces, particularly for young people and women.
- Many young people stay on at school or college, studying diplomas. There was a 4% rise in the student population between 1989 and 1990.
- The Ile de France is more important to the French economy than any other region.
- Key industries in the area are electronics, cars, and printing, press and publishing. The region also leads in high technology, computers, pharmaceuticals and aircraft construction industries.
- Agricultural land growing cereal crops and several leisure parks, including Disneyland Paris, are found in the outer parts of the region.
- 75% of jobs created are in the market services sector.
- Manufacturing industries are moving out of the region into the provinces.
- The past 30 years have seen new motorways and an express rail system which links the provinces. This has encouraged the development of many new satellite towns, suburban shopping centres and housing estates. The city also has three major airports.

The following tables show employment statistics for the West Midlands and Ile de France, collected in 1991. They are taken from a book called *Eurostat*, which lists tables of information from across the European Union and is a good way to compare different regions of the EU.

Table 1.6: Statistics for the Ile de France region

- The figures given are in 1000s

Gender	Age	Total residents	Gender	Economically active	%	Unemployed	%
M+F	14-24	1617.1	Male	293	35.8	-	-
M+F	25-34	1869.5	Male	866	95	-	-
M+F	35-44	1738.4	Male	842	97.9	-	-
M+F	45-54	1190.8	Male	565	95.2	-	-
M+F	55-64	981.3	Male	221	50.2	-	-
M+F	65+	1166.6	Male	19	4.3	-	-
Males	-	-	Total	-	-	238.1	8.4
	14-24	-	Female	305	60.5	-	-
	25-34	-	Female	781	80.7	-	-
	35-44	-	Female	703	79.8	-	-
	45-54	-	Female	448	75	-	-
	55-64	-	Female	182	36.2	-	-
	65+	-	Female	12	1.6	-	-
Female	-	-	Total	-	-	232.3	9.3

Table 1.7: Statistics for the West Midlands region

- The figures given are in 1000s

Gender	Age	Total residents	Gender	Economically active	%	Unemployed	%
M+F	14-24	773.4	Male	290	72.4	-	-
M+F	25-34	787.0	Male	392	96.1	-	-
M+F	35-44	716.0	Male	352	96.2	-	-
M+F	45-54	615.5	Male	286	92.3	-	-
M+F	55-64	540.4	Male	181	68.6	-	-
M+F	65+	798.6	Male	27	8.5	-	-
Males	-	-	Total	-	-	198.8	12.6
	14-24	-	Female	234	60.5	-	-
	25-34	-	Female	275	69.6	-	-
	35-44	-	Female	265	74.8	-	-
	45-54	-	Female	222	73.4	-	-
	55-64	-	Female	103	38.6	-	-
	65+	-	Female	11	2.4	-	-
Female	-	-	Total	-	-	93.4	8.4

Business organisations and employment

Table 1.8: Labour force by age shown nationally in 1000s for 1991

Age	France Total M+F	UK Total M+F
14-24	3112	5636
25-34	7247	7366
35-44	7354	6771
45-54	4588	5376
55-64	1896	3046
65+	150	463
Total	24347	28658

Table 1.9: National unemployment figures shown in 1000s

Gender	France 1986	France 1993	UK 1986	UK 1993
Males	1105.3	1204.2	1952.9	2052.9
Females	1297.6	1346.0	1329.8	964.9
Total	2403.1	2550.2	3282.8	3017.8

Table 1.10: 'Employment by branch' for the Ile De France and West Midlands regions

Employment by branch	Ile de France 1983	Ile De France 1990	West Midlands 1983	West Midlands 1990
Agricultural, forestry and fishing products	28 000	24 000	48 000	46 000
Fuel and power products	72 000	68 000	47 000	40 000
Industrial products	1 035 000	876 000	819 000	692 000
Building and construction	306 000	312 000	included in the figure above	131 000
Market services	2355	2 686 000	785 000	1 311 000
Non-market services	921	977 000	404 000	included in the figure above
TOTAL	4 718 000	4 942 000	2 103 000	2 220 000

Branch: *another term for an industrial sector.*

▶ Graphs and charts, page 44

▶ Wolverhampton activity, page 117

▶ Percentages, page 32

The tertiary sector has grown rapidly in the Ile de France region

A Vive la difference

Include your work for this activity in your portfolio of evidence.

This activity is based on you using the statistics on West Midlands and Ile de France given here. If you prefer, you can research and analyse information comparing an area you have visited in the EU with your own area. Or you can focus on Ile de France and London, in order to compare two capital cities. If you do decide to carry out your own research, you should present and analyse the information in the way described in this activity.

Business organisations and employment

1. Using Tables 1.6 and 1.7, make two graphs comparing the percentages of different age groups in Ile de France and West Midlands that are 'economically active'. One graph should look at the male population, and the other at the female population. Prepare the information in the same way as you did for the Wolverhampton activity. Remember you should present the information as percentages, and try to make your graphs and charts in a variety of interesting ways.

2. Look at your graphs. What do they show about the male 14 to 24 age group in Ile de France and the West Midlands? What do you think is a factor causing the difference? (Look back at the information on page 120 for help.)

3. Using Table 1.10, make a graph which shows the number of employees in different 'branches' (industries), comparing Ile de France and the West Midlands. You will have to combine 'building and construction' and 'industrial products' as one sector, and 'market' and 'non-market' services as another.

4. Analyse the information by answering these questions:
   a Which sectors are growing?
   b Which sectors are declining?
   c What do the statistics show about the male and female population aged 16 to 19?
   d What do the statistics show about the male and female population aged over 50?

5. Using Tables 1.6, 1.7, 1.8 and 1.9, compare regional statistics with national statistics.
   a Find out the percentage of the French population living in the Ile de France and the percentage of the British population living in the West Midlands.
   b Comment on the national unemployment trends between 1986 and 1993.

6. What factors (reasons) might explain these statistics? You might find it helpful to read through the fact files for these two regions again.
   Make a copy of the chart on the right, filling a sheet of A4 paper so you have plenty of space to fill in information. Fill in your own comments.

7. Explain what you think are the contributing factors to the growth or decline of one manufacturing or service sector in the West Midlands or Ile de France. For example, you may choose to look at health services, catering or the car industry.

8. Compare your findings from the West Midlands and Ile de France with your work on Wolverhampton. What trends can you see?

© L. Daniel, J. Joslin, K. McCafferty, L. Porter, A. Thomas 1996. *Intermediate GNVQ Business.*

Facts	West Midlands	Ile de France
Size		
Population economically active		
Population unemployed		
Age statistics		
Gender statistics		
Numbers employed in primary sector		
Numbers employed in secondary sector		
Numbers employed in tertiary sector		
Significant factors affecting the region		

Business organisations and employment

Factors contributing to employment

There are many factors which affect the number of people employed and the type of employment available in different regions.

▶ Natural resources, page 94

▶ Incentives, page 96

Geographical factors often contribute to tourism in an area

Factors	Why does it influence employment?	Example
Historical	Some areas have a long tradition of people working in a particular type of industry or organisation.	Cadburys, originally a family business in Birmingham, has always been based in the West Midlands.
Geographical	Natural resources can affect the type of industry in an area. Some positions are particularly well positioned for transport links, which encourages industry.	South Wales and Yorkshire were rich in coal, and had flourishing mining industries. Industry grew up in ports like Liverpool and London.
Cultural	Some communities have been traditionally known for a particular type of business and have built up special skills.	Nottingham is famous for its lace making.
Industrial	Industries grow up to support one another. Often, related industries are based in one area where there is a ready supply of customers and resources.	Packaging and printing developed near Cadburys to support the main activities of chocolate production. Silicon Valley in California is the base for a large number of electronic companies.
Political	Special incentives are sometimes offered to encourage employment in a particular industry or region.	Government grants were given to new towns like Milton Keynes and Telford to encourage their development.
Economic	New businesses often move to an area to support existing organisations and to meet the needs of the workforce who live and spend their money there. This contributes to the prosperity of a region.	The financial services sector (banks, insurance etc.) has grown around areas where lots of people live, to offer services to businesses and individuals.

A Factors affecting your own region

Brainstorm the main types of business organisations or industries in your region. Then suggest as many factors as you can which explain why they are there (look at the chart above for ideas). You may also be able to think of other reasons of your own.

Types of employment

Many business organisations need a wide range of employees to meet their business needs. Comp-U-Clic is typical in employing people on a range of different terms, to do different jobs at different times of the week.

Case study: The Comp-U-Clic payroll

Simon is employed on what is called a casual basis. This means that he only works occasionally, when extra help is needed. In particular, he helps Steve install networks, which requires a lot of manual work in laying cables and moving equipment around.

Victoria is 16 and is on a YT course with the Chamber of Commerce. She is studying for an NVQ in Business Administration. She works Monday to Thursday, from 9 to 5, and receives training from the Chamber on Fridays. Steve pays a contribution to the Chamber towards her weekly allowance. She answers the phone, does filing, and sends out letters as part of her job.

Steve Parker, the owner of Comp-U-Clic, is self-employed. This means that he is responsible for paying his own National Insurance (NI) contributions, and the amount of income tax he pays will depend on the amount he earns.

Lawrence is 19 and a full-time, permanent employee. Working full time means that he spends at least 37 hours per week at work. Having permanent status means that his job will continue indefinitely. Once he has worked for the company for two years he will have certain rights, as defined in the Employment Act.

Fred is a retired BT engineer whose hobby is fixing computers. He works for Comp-U-Clic on a part-time, permanent basis. He spends three hours, three afternoons a week, helping with repairs and upgrades to machines.

Suki is 17 and works for Comp-U-Clic on Saturdays. He is studying for Intermediate GNVQ Business at a local college, and is using his part-time job to provide evidence. He types in data from purchases and sales invoices into an accounting software package and helps out in the shop when it is busy.

Steve has a mixture of skilled and unskilled workers helping him out in the business. Skilled employees usually have a qualification in the area in which they are employed, while unskilled workers do not. In some cases employees may have a lot of experience, but no qualifications. In this case, do you think they are skilled, or unskilled?

Business organisations and employment

Working conditions

One of the employment trends you will probably have discovered is the growth in information technology and communications. In the Ile de France region, many businesses have grown up, like Comp-U-Clic in England, which rely on computers and computer-related products.

Jean Herrault works for one of these, a French company called 'Le Signal'. Here we compare his working conditions with those of Lawrence Wood, who works full time for Comp-U-Clic.

Case study: Jean Herrault

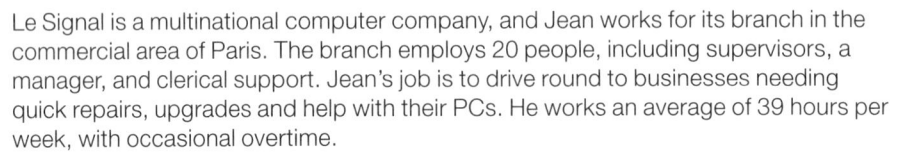

Le Signal is a multinational computer company, and Jean works for its branch in the commercial area of Paris. The branch employs 20 people, including supervisors, a manager, and clerical support. Jean's job is to drive round to businesses needing quick repairs, upgrades and help with their PCs. He works an average of 39 hours per week, with occasional overtime.

Jean was given a contract of employment when he started work for Le Signal, and has rights of employment. He earns an annual salary equivalent to Euro 16,600 (£13,280), and takes 25 days' leave a year. When necessary, he is given training on new equipment. The workplace meets health and safety legal requirements.

Jean is 18 years old and shares an apartment with two student friends during the week in the La Chapelle district. At weekends he returns to his parents' comfortable home in Rouen (about 140 km away). He travels there by train, as traffic is very heavy on the Paris ring road in the rush hour.

Jean chose to study technological subjects, and went to a vocational technical school where he took vocational courses similar to GNVQ and gained work experience. He achieved a Baccalaureat at 17, which enabled him to get a job or go on to higher education. He would like to continue his education by taking up an apprenticeship with the Academie de Paris. This would combine placements with study, and last for five years. He would study electronics and information technology, industrial systems and production.

Case study: Lawrence Wood

Lawrence is 19 and works at Comp-U-Clic for Steve. He works a minimum of 37 hours a week and has 20 days' annual leave, which includes public Bank Holidays. He works occasional Saturdays to replace Steve, and is given an extra day's pay for this. His weekly pay is £100 per week, but Steve only pays half of this as the Department of Employment and Education gives special project funding towards Lawrence's first year of employment as he was unemployed when taken on.

Lawrence's job is based at the Comp-U-Clic shop. He deals with customers, giving them advice and support when Steve is out, and referring them to Steve when he can't help. He makes sales, gives quotes, and orders stock. The safety in the workplace is regulated by legal requirements, as are his rights of employment.

Lawrence has a computer of his own, and software and games are his main hobby and interest. As a perk of the job, he is able to buy equipment and software at trade prices.

Lawrence lives at home with his parents, about 15 minutes drive away from the shop. He owns his own car. He attended a local comprehensive school and left at 16 with GCSEs grade C in Maths and English. He then went on a YT course with the local Chamber of Commerce, and achieved NVQ level 2 in Information Technology. He often goes on courses run by computer suppliers and manufacturers to learn about new products.

Lawrence is happy in this job, and does not want to take on extra responsibility.

A — Jean and Lawrence

Read through the two case studies and the regional fact files.

Prepare a short report which describes and compares the working conditions of Jean and Lawrence. Comment on:
- their hours of work
- physical working conditions
- rate of pay and any other benefits
- safety
- job security
- career opportunities
- training opportunities
- use of new technology.

You may choose to present this information as a table, saying which job you think is the best, giving reasons.

Collect job advertisements from the computer sector in your area, and also one from another country in the EU. You may prefer to research your own employment sector and EU regions. In this case, follow a similar format to the examples given, researching the particular job roles of two individuals from different EU regions.

▶ Regional fact files, page 118

▶ Reports, page 19

Summary questions

By answering these questions, you will put together your own summary of Unit 1. This will help you prepare for the unit test.

1. Name an example of a business you would find in the primary sector.
2. Name an example of a business you would find in the secondary sector.
3. Name an example of a business you would find in the tertiary sector.
4. Give two examples of recent developments within a named sector.
5. Give an example of growth within a sector.
6. Give an example of decline within a sector.
7. How might profit be used?
8. What is meant by market share?
9. What is meant by customer service? Give an example.
10. List seven different types of business ownership.
11. Give five purposes of business organisations.
12. Describe the difference between public and private sectors, and give an example of an organisation from each.
13. What is the difference between limited liability and unlimited liability?
14. Give six factors which would influence the location of a new business.
15. What is meant by an incentive? Describe three different sources of incentives.
16. List four ways the business environment can influence a business organisation. Give an example of each.
17. List four different types of products produced by business organisations, and give an example of each.
18. List six different activities which businesses carry out in order to improve their market share.
19. Name seven different types of employment.

Assignment

CHAMBER OF COMMERCE REPORT

Setting the scene

Steve at Comp-U-Clic has received help from his local Chamber of Commerce in making new business links and employing trained staff. Chambers of Commerce are local business networks set up to provide contacts, training and support to businesses in the area.

Your local Chamber of Commerce is carrying out research into business in your area. It has asked you to contribute to the research by:
- providing an overview of the primary, secondary and tertiary sectors
- presenting examples of local business organisations with different types of ownership
- reporting in detail on the operation of one local business organisation.

Doing this will give you good opportunities to work on your own and build up evidence towards a merit or distinction grade.

Task 1

Look back at the work on industrial sectors which you completed for the activity on page 80. Based on your findings:
- write a summary describing developments in the primary, secondary and tertiary sectors, explaining the current growth or decrease in each sector. (Include any answers and calculations in the activity. Word-process your summary and produce some graphics/charts using IT. You will need to input data into a spreadsheet or database first.)
- give examples of businesses in each sector, explaining their typical business activities.

Task 2

Look back at the work on the ownership of local business organisations which you completed for the activity on page 91.

Discuss with others in your group how each of you might present this information to the Chamber of Commerce in an attractive, accessible way. Could you produce a poster or design a leaflet? Or would you rather prepare a short talk? As a group, you could contact your local Chamber of Commerce and ask a representative to evaluate your materials or presentations.

However each individual decides to present the information, you need to explain:
- the ownership of each business
- whether it is in the public or private sector
- whether it is small, medium or large
- its main business purposes
- its type of liability
- its use of profit.

Task 3

Choose a business organisation in your area which you would like to research. You will find some information on carrying out research in the Toolkit.

Write a report along similar lines to the Comp-U-Clic case study. Use the following headings:
- Type of business
- Trends and location
- Products
- Links with other businesses
- Purposes
- Recommendations.

Remember to include an introductory background to the business organisation, similar to the Comp-U-Clic story. You may well be able to include support materials collected during your research as appendices to your report.

▶ Industrial sectors activity, page 80

▶ Classifying business organisations activity, page 91

▶ Comp-U-Clic case study, page 93

▶ Report, page 19

Opportunities to collect evidence
On completing these tasks you will have the opportunity to meet the following requirements for Intermediate GNVQ Business.
Unit 1
Element 1.1 PCs 1, 2, 3, 4

Core skills
Application of Number
Elements 2.2, 2.3
Communication
Elements 2.1, 2.2, 2.3, 2.4
Information Technology
Elements 2.1, 2.2, 2.3

▶ Core skills coverage grid, page 252

Business organisations and employment

Assignment

IN THE MARKET

Setting the scene
In this assignment you will examine business location, environment, markets and products by looking closely at one business organisation in your area. You might decide to focus on a business that you looked at for the last assignment, or to choose a different business that you are interested in.

Task 1
Give a short talk to your group on the location of the business you have chosen. Your talk should explain why you think the business is located where it is, including a description of:
- labour supply in the area
- any natural resources which might help the business
- other businesses in the area, including competition and suppliers
- the business' access to customers
- transport services in the area
- any incentives which might have encouraged the business to locate there.

▶ Preparing talks, page 11

▶ Business location, page 94

As part of your talk, produce a map – either as a handout or on an OHT – showing:
- the business' location
- natural resources
- other major businesses
- transport services.

Invite and respond to questions.

Task 2
Write a summary of how your chosen organisation is influenced by its business environment. Include an explanation of how it is affected by:
- competition
- legislation – describe any legislation it has to comply with
- environmental considerations – comment on whether any of the business' goods, services or practices might affect the environment
- public influences – comment on whether any of your chosen company's goods or services might be controversial or arouse public concern.

▶ Business environment, page 100

▶ Markets, page 101

▶ Marketing communications, page 110

▶ Report, page 19

Task 3
Prepare a report describing the market for your chosen company's goods or services. What products is it selling? Who are they bought by? Which markets are most successful? What activities does it carry out to improve its market position?

Include an analysis of the company's marketing communications (e.g. advertising and sales literature). How successful do you think they are? Do they have an impact on the business' market position?

Task 4
Present a design to your tutor, with sketches and notes, which either:
- improves one of your chosen company's existing product lines
- introduces a new product line.

For example, if you chose to look at a bakery, you might decide to redesign the way it packages its cakes and bread, or to design a completely new product for it to sell.

Get feedback on your ideas from a company in your area which provides similar products. For example, if you design products for a bakery, ask your local baker for an honest opinion and include this feedback in your portfolio.

▶ Design, page 109

Opportunities to collect evidence
On completing these tasks you will have the opportunity to meet the following requirements for Intermediate GNVQ Business.
Unit 1
Element 1.2 PCs 1, 2, 3, 4, 5, 6

Core skills
Application of Number
Element 2.3
Communication
Elements 2.1, 2.2, 2.3, 2.4

▶ Core skills coverage grid, page 252

Assignment

RESEARCH IN ACTION

Setting the scene
Having worked through all the activities and case studies in this section, you are now ready to make a presentation to the group on your findings. The graphs, charts and tables you have already produced will form a central part of your presentation. You may also be able to collect extra materials such as maps, photographs, news articles and so on to use as part of your presentation.

Task 1
Prepare, deliver and record (either on video or tape) a presentation, supported with visual aids, on either:
  a Percentages of people employed and employment opportunities across at least two European Union regions
     or
  b A comparison of the working conditions of two individuals across two regions of the European Union.

Task 2
Look back at the case study which describes the employees on the Comp-U-Clic payroll.

  a Write down one example of each of the following types of employment from the Comp-U-Clic payroll:
- full time
- part time
- permanent
- temporary
- skilled
- unskilled
- employed
- self-employed.

  b List the advantages and disadvantages of each type of employment, for both employer and employee.
  c Collect an example of a job advertisement to illustrate each category. Look in local and national newspapers.

▶ The Comp-U-Clic payroll case study, page 125

Opportunities to collect evidence
On completing these tasks you will have the opportunity to meet the following requirements for Intermediate GNVQ Business.
Unit 1
Element 1.3 PCs 1, 2, 3, 4

Core skills
Application of Number
Element 2.1
Communication
Elements 2.1, 2.2, 2.3

▶ Core skills coverage grid, page 252

Self-check questions

Each of the following questions shows four possible answers – **a**, **b**, **c** and **d**. Only one is correct.

1. A primary sector organisation:
   a. employs people in the 16 to 19 age group
   b. extracts raw materials or crops
   c. is in the leading sector of the economy
   d. has been growing in recent years in the UK.

2. A secondary sector organisation:
   a. adds a further stage of development to raw materials
   b. does not attract government funding
   c. concentrates on mainly farming activities
   d. provides the government with most revenue.

3. A tertiary sector organisation:
   a. concentrates mainly on farming activities
   b. has been declining in recent years
   c. employs mainly older people
   d. concentrates on providing services.

4. Employment in the primary sector in the UK:
   a. has declined in recent years
   b. has increased in recent years
   c. has remained the same in recent years
   d. is mainly for young people.

5. Employment in the secondary sector in the UK:
   a. has declined in recent years
   b. has increased in recent years
   c. has remained the same in recent years
   d. is mainly for people in the 30 to 50 age group.

6. Employment in the tertiary sector in the UK:
   a. has declined in recent years
   b. has increased in recent years
   c. has remained the same in recent years
   d. is mainly for people over the age of 50.

7. A public sector organisation:
   a. extracts raw materials and crops
   b. is owned and controlled by the government
   c. does not sell shares to private individuals
   d. has limited liability.

8. A private sector organisation:
   a. only sells shares on the stock market
   b. extracts raw materials or crops
   c. never publishes its accounts
   d. is owned by individuals rather than the government.

9. A sole trader:
   a. only sells one thing
   b. owns only one branch of a business
   c. is the only person employed in a business
   d. has unlimited liability.

10. A partnership:
    a. only employs two people
    b. has employees that work from home
    c. is usually a legal arrangement between up to 20 people
    d. is where all the employees share the workload equally.

11. A private limited company:
    a. has owners who do not lose all their personal assets if the business goes bankrupt
    b. has unlimited liability
    c. does not deal with members of the public
    d. does not pay tax.

12. A public limited company:
    a. has unlimited liability
    b. is owned by the government
    c. buys and sells shares on the stock market
    d. provides a public service.

13. A franchise:
    a. is always a fast-food service
    b. is owned by all the employees
    c. has shared ownership with an established, nationally recognised organisation
    d. deals with fresh fruit and vegetables.

14. A co-operative:
    a. is when everyone gets on well at work
    b. is when all the employees share in the ownership and control of the business
    c. sells shares on the stock exchange
    d. has unlimited liability.

15 A state-owned industry:
   a is owned and controlled by the government
   b is concerned with coal mining
   c sells shares on the stock exchange
   d extracts raw materials or crops.

16 Profit is:
   a how the government finances state industries
   b good for the economy
   c one of the main purposes of businesses
   d all the money received by a business.

17 Market share:
   a is a place where goods are sold
   b is about finding out who buys the business' products
   c is the percentage of total sales claimed by a business
   d is where profits are divided up.

18 Limited liability means:
   a the government has control of the business
   b the owners don't lose their personal assets if the business gets into difficulty
   c the owners do lose their personal assets if the business gets into difficulty
   d the owners share all the profits.

19 Unlimited liability means:
   a the government has control of the business
   b the owners don't lose their personal assets if the business gets into difficulty
   c the owners do lose their personal assets if the business gets into difficulty
   d the owners share all the profits.

20 A local labour supply is important to a business because:
   a a business needs a skilled and experienced workforce nearby
   b customers can find you easily
   c people rarely want to travel far to work
   d it means the work will always be done well.

21 Natural resources are:
   a often the reason for businesses being located where they are
   b a cheaper source of supplies
   c cheaper than employing labour
   d the main activities within the tertiary sector.

22 Having other businesses nearby is important because:
   a they may provide important supplies and services
   b they provide cheap labour
   c they prove there is a market in the area
   d they have limited liability.

23 Access to customers is important because:
   a businesses need to be able to sell goods to people who want them
   b businesses do not want to spend too much on advertising
   c businesses will be able to sell everything they make
   d customers keep coming back.

24 A business needs an efficient transport system:
   a to make sure their sales people do not have to travel far
   b to distribute goods to customers and receive supplies easily
   c to make good use of their company car scheme
   d so that people know where they are located.

25 Marketing research is about:
   a advertising goods and services
   b eliminating competition
   c links with the European Union
   d finding out what customers want.

26 Design involves:
   a keeping a close eye on competitors
   b making attractive window displays
   c making sure the business' products are attractive and useful
   d keeping customers informed.

27 Marketing communications enable a business to:
   a keep a close eye on competitors
   b make attractive window displays
   c plan improvements to the business, its goods or services
   d keep customers informed.

2 | People in business organisations

People are often said to be a business organisation's most important resource. Without employees with the right knowledge and skills, a business will fail.

This unit looks at different people who work in business – from machine operators to managing directors. By investigating organisational structures and the roles of employees within them, you will develop a broad knowledge of different types of employment.

You will also find out more about the responsibilities and rights of both employees and employers.

At the end of this unit you will use your new knowledge to explore the employment options open to you once you finish your Intermediate GNVQ Business course.

The Elements

Examine and compare structures and working arrangements in organisations
- describe organisational structures
- produce organisational charts showing departments
- describe the work and explain the interdependence of departments within business organisations
- identify and explain differences in working arrangements
- explain and give examples of reasons for change in working arrangements in one business organisation

In this element you will examine, and produce, organisational charts for business organisations. You will explore different business departments and how they rely on each other, and will compare working arrangements in two organisations.

▶ Investigating structures, working arrangements and job roles in organisations, page 136

Investigate employee and employer responsibilities and rights
- explain the benefits of employer and employee co-operation
- describe ways to resolve disagreements
- explain employer rights and responsibilities
- explain employee rights and responsibilities to their employers

This element focuses on the responsibilities and rights of both employees and employers. You will find out about legislation which affects employment, in particular equal opportunities legislation. You will also look at the benefits of co-operation between employers and employees, and how to resolve any disagreements which arise.

▶ Employee and employer responsibilities and rights, page 153

Present results of investigation into job roles
- identify and describe individual's job roles at different levels within organisations
- explain the benefits of team membership in performing job roles
- identify activities performed by individuals at different levels within organisations
- identify tasks in job roles
- present results of investigation into job roles

The third element looks at job roles at different levels within an organisation. You will explore the day-to-day activities of different employees, their tasks, and how team membership supports their work. To do this, you will carry out a detailed investigation of three people's job roles.

▶ Investigating structures, working arrangements and job roles in organisations, page 136

Prepare for employment or self-employment
- identify types of employment and self-employment
- identify opportunities for employment or self-employment
- select information from relevant sources which applies to identified employment opportunities
- analyse skills for employment or self-employment
- discuss own strengths and weaknesses in relation to skills for employment or self-employment

At the end of this unit, you will use the knowledge you have gained from the earlier elements to help you prepare for employment or self-

▶ Preparing for employment or self-employment, page 162

People in business organisations

employment after you complete your GNVQ course. You will investigate opportunities for employment and self-employment, and analyse the skills needed for different jobs. You will then consider your own strengths and weaknesses, and what type of employment might suit you.

Investigating structures, working arrangements and job roles in organisations

'Welcome to AL's! We manufacture mobile telephones which are sold throughout the UK and across the world. Mobile phone manufacturing is a fast-moving and sophisticated business environment. We don't connect directly into the telephone systems – this is done by companies like Vodaphone, Cellnet, Orange and Mercury.

The business was set up in the mid 1980s as a public limited company, and currently employs 500 people (350 full-time staff and 150 part-time). AL's is an equal opportunity employer and has an even distribution of male and female staff.

My name is Michael Roberts and I have just begun working in the sales and marketing department at AL's. I spent my first week meeting people and getting to know the layout of the company. Here are some of the key members of staff.'

▶ Public limited company, page 85

▶ Equal opportunities, page 156

Job roles

Managing director
Anne Harrison is AL's MD (Managing Director). She was appointed to the position by the board of directors. As the managing director, Anne is in charge of the company. Her **routine** tasks are to:
- plan the future of the company
- oversee financial decisions
- look after the shareholders and their interests
- ensure the company runs efficiently
- ensure the company makes a profit.

Human resources manager
This is Peter Shaw, the human resources manager (he is sometimes known as the 'personnel manager'). He reports to the human resources director. Peter Shaw's routine tasks are to:
- support staff in doing their jobs
- plan and organise staff training and development
- make sure that the human resources department runs smoothly
- work closely with other departmental managers
- ensure people in his department are achieving their work targets.

▶ Human resources department, page 148

Peter Shaw is also responsible for recruitment. The board of directors recently held a meeting and decided that the company needed to recruit a new customer services assistant. Anne, the MD, sent Peter the following memo asking him to advertise the position.

MEMO — *internal memorandum*

12 June 1996

To: Peter Shaw – Human Resources Manager

cc: Barbara Wilkinson

From: Anne Harrison – Managing Director

Subject: Customer Services assistant vacancy

With regard to our present success, the Board of Directors has given approval for the recruitment of a further customer service assistant.

AH

Recruitment, page 149

Supervisor

Paramjit Singh is a supervisor at AL's. Her routine tasks are to:
- give advice and help to people who work in the factory making mobile phones
- set **targets** for production operatives to achieve
- ensure that staff in her department meet their targets to assemble a certain number of mobile phones every day
- report to her manager on the progress of her department – whether there are any machinery problems, whether it is meeting its targets, and so on.

Production operatives

The components of AL's mobile phones are assembled on a production line. Production operatives are responsible for ensuring that the different components are fitted correctly.

People in business organisations

These are production operatives. They aim to achieve the hourly, daily, weekly or monthly targets set by their supervisor. The production operatives need to work together well as a team in order to achieve these targets. If one of the team members fails to reach his or her set target, this can affect the rest of the team.

Support staff

Anna Evans and Anita Martin are administrative assistants at AL's. Their **routine** tasks are to:
- word process documents for staff in different departments
- provide secretarial support
- keep filing up to date
- sort and open mail
- send faxes.

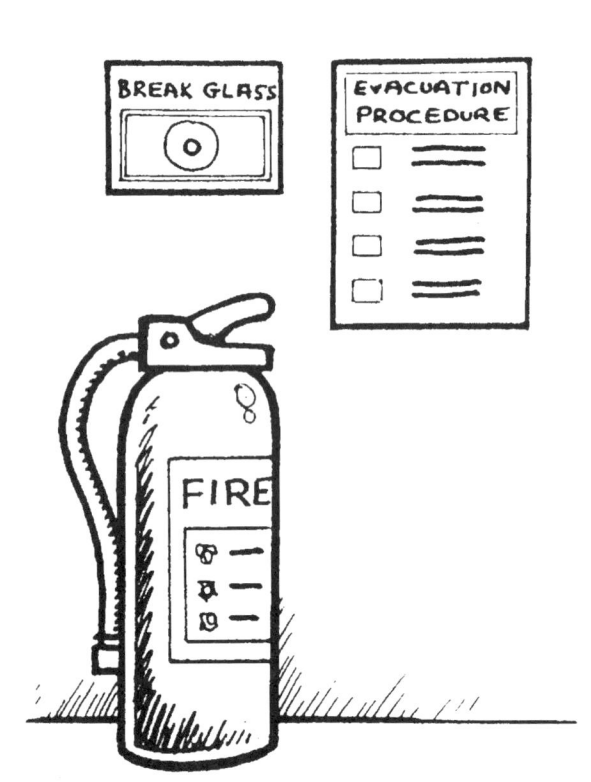

As well as carrying out routine tasks, employees at all levels have to be ready to deal with **non-routine** tasks. A special production run for Oman that has to be delivered this week is one such example. Accidents and emergencies are also non-routine tasks.

The fire alarm system at AL's has two different rings:
- an intermittent ringing sound (ring, ring, stop, ring, ring, stop) indicates a fire
- a continuous sound (the ringing doesn't stop) indicates a bomb threat.

A recent fire alarm practice showed serious problems with evacuation. People:
- were unsure what to do
- were unsure where to go
- remained in the building
- took their belongings with them.

> **A** **Emergency!**
>
> 1 Provide an actual plan for the layout of a small company, or your own organisation. Show the position of each door.
> 2 Design two posters, giving instructions for:
> a fire evacuation procedures
> b bomb evacuation procedures.
>   Your posters should include: the location of assembly points, the nearest fire exits and fire extinguishers; information on different types of fire extinguishers (water, foam and so on); and instructions on how to recognise alarms.
> 3 Carry out research to identify the dangers of not following these procedures.

Organisational structures

All organisations have a structure, which they display on a chart showing:
- who is in charge of the company
- different people working for the company
- people's job roles.

This chart helps employees to see who works where, and gives them a picture of their own position within the company.
There are three main types of organisational structures:
- hierarchical
- flat
- matrix.

Hierarchical structures

A **hierarchical structure** can be represented as a pyramid, with different levels of authority from the top to the bottom. The most senior member of the organisation is at the top of the pyramid structure. People at higher levels have more authority and hold responsibility for what people at lower levels do.

AL's has a typical hierarchical structure, with Anne Harrison, the managing director, at one end of the chart and Michael Roberts, the new sales clerk, at other.

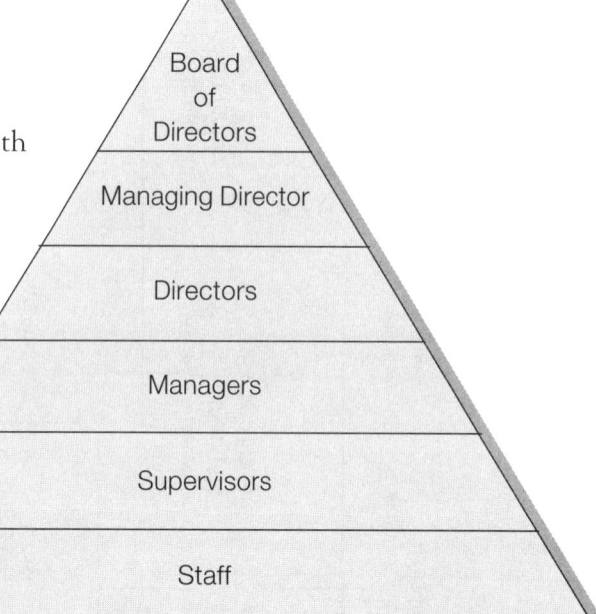

Pyramid (top to bottom): Board of Directors / Managing Director / Directors / Managers / Supervisors / Staff

People in business organisations

AL's hierarchical structure

Board of Directors (1)

Managing Director Anne Harrison (2)

Directors (3)
- Human Resources Director (3) — Barbara Wilkinson
- Sales & Marketing Director (3) — James McKintyre
- Purchasing Director (3) — Ken Hope
- Finance Director (3) — Charles Davies
- Administration Director (3) — Amanda Greenheld
- Production Director (3) — Harry Johnstone

Managers (4)
- Human Resources Manager (4) — Peter Shaw
- Sales Manager (4) — Roger McKenzie
- Marketing Manager (4) — Sue Ling
- Purchasing Manager (4) — Rhiannon Bartholomew
- Finance Manager (4) — Linda Holder
- Administration Manager (4) — Nicholas McDonald
- Production Manager (4) — Nicola Cromby

Supervisors (5)
- Office Supervisor (5) — Freya Reed
- Computer Technician (5) — Philip Buck
- Production Supervisor (5) — Paramjit Singh

Staff (6)
- Recruitment Officer (6) — Matthew Field
- Training Officer (6) — Vera Kidd
- Welfare Officer (6) — Sylvia Orpin
- Customer Service Assistant (6) — Sonia Spree
- Sales Clerk (6) — Michael Roberts
- Sales Representative (6) — Lorraine Handford
- Sales Representative (6) — Mark Jones
- Advertising Officer (6) — Rachel Friend
- Market Research Officer (6) — Don Parr
- Security Officer (6) — Malcolm Robinson
- Promotion Officer (6) — Joanne Crompton
- Buying Clerk (6) — Eric Thomas
- Wages Clerk (6) — Gareth Johns
- Trainee Accountant (6) — Paul Jones
- Invoice Clerk (6) — Ian Andrews
- Quality Control Officer (6) — Glynis Morrison
- Machine Operators (6)
- Storemen (6)
- Research Development Officer (6) — Richard Francis
- Receptionist (6) — Claire Glenister
- Admin Assistant (6) — Anna Evans
- Admin Assistant (6) — Anita Martin
- Photocopy Clerk (6) — Alice Johns

Key:
1 Board of Directors
2 MD
3 Directors
4 Managers
5 Supervisors
6 Staff

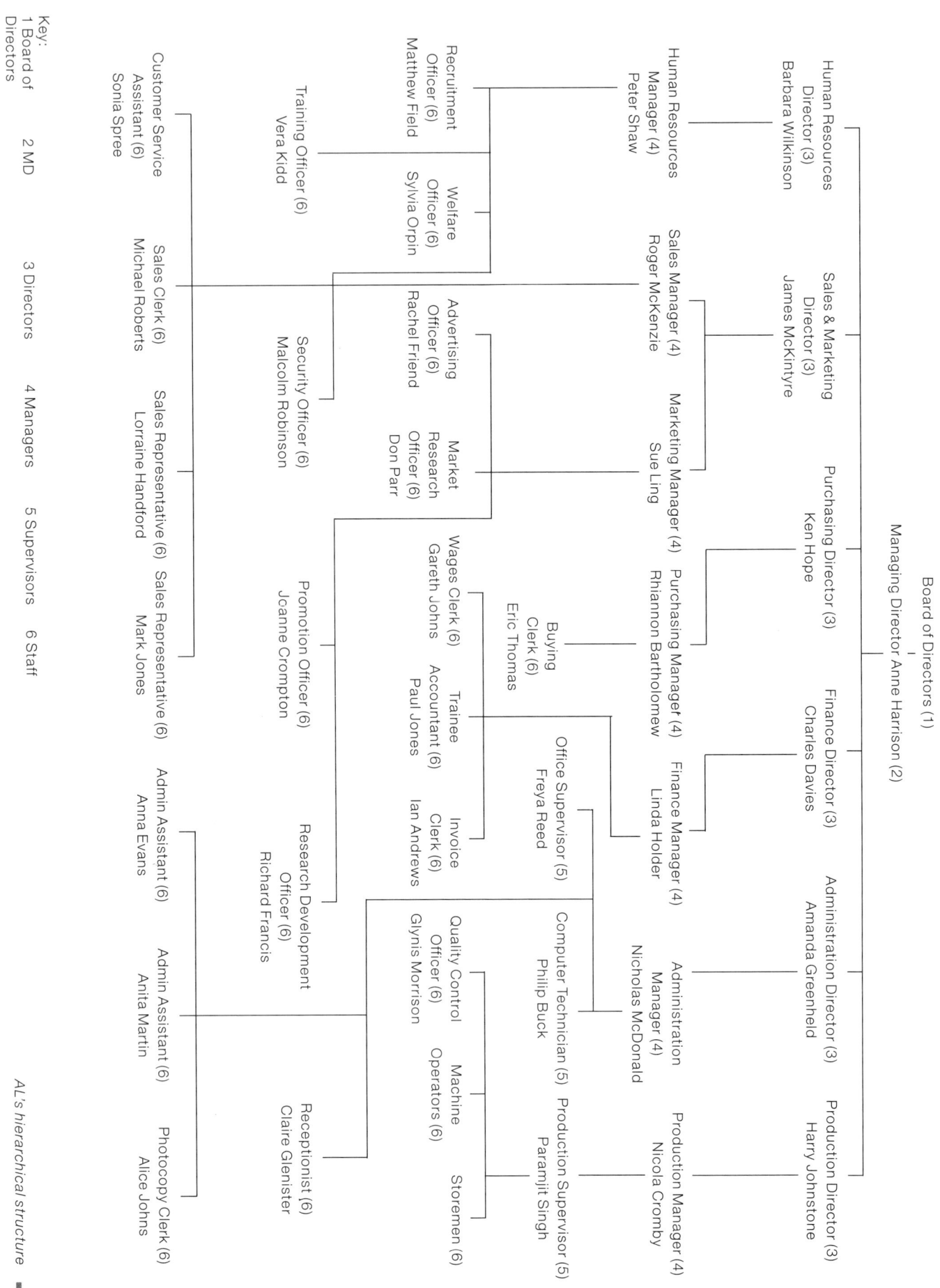

140

People in business organisations

As well as showing people's job roles and positions in the company, a chart like this shows the organisation's:
- chain of command
- span of control
- decision-making process.

Chain of command

An organisation's chain of command is shown by the vertical lines on the organisational chart. These identify the relationships between different members of staff, and give employees a clear picture of who they report to, and who they are responsible for.

For example, the chart for AL's shows that Eric Thomas, the buying clerk, has to report to Rhiannon Bartholomew, the purchasing manager.

Span of control

A manager's 'span of control' is the number of employees that he or she is responsible for.

The chart below gives a detailed breakdown of the sales and marketing department at AL's.

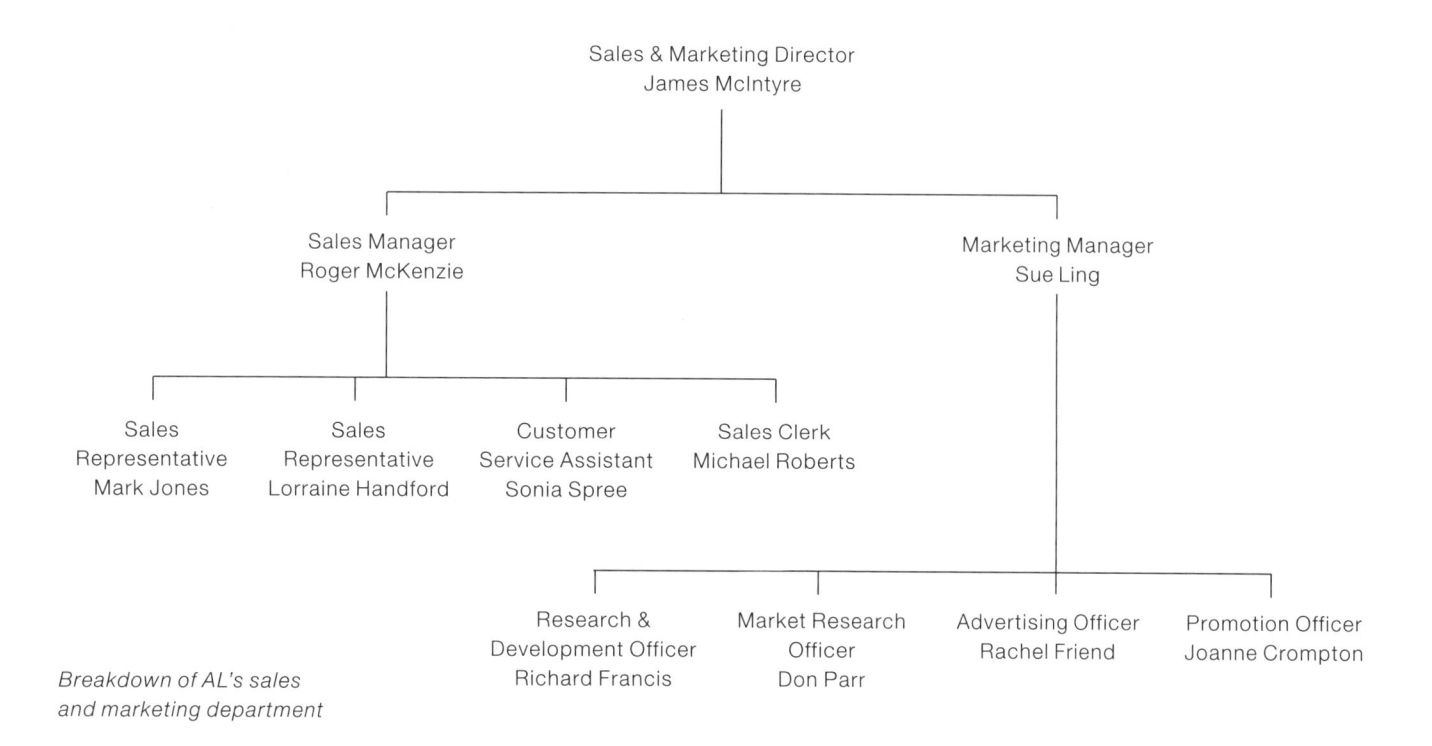

```
                    Sales & Marketing Director
                         James McIntyre
                    ┌─────────┴─────────┐
             Sales Manager        Marketing Manager
            Roger McKenzie             Sue Ling
     ┌──────┬───────┴────┬─────────┐   ┌──────┬──────┬──────┐
   Sales  Sales      Customer    Sales  R&D   Market  Advert. Promotion
   Rep.   Rep.       Service     Clerk  Officer Research Officer Officer
   Mark   Lorraine   Assistant   Michael Richard Officer Rachel Joanne
   Jones  Handford   Sonia Spree Roberts Francis Don Parr Friend Crompton
```

Breakdown of AL's sales and marketing department

A — Span of control

Look at the complete organisational chart for AL's opposite.

- Who is the marketing manager, Sue Ling, responsible for?
- What is her span of control?
- What is Roger McKenzie's span of control?

141

People in business organisations

MANAGING DIRECTOR
↓
HUMAN RESOURCES MANAGER
↓
RECRUITMENT OFFICER

Decision-making process

As you can see from AL's organisational structure, **decisions** are made by those at the top of the hierarchy (the managers) and passed down through the organisation ('**delegated**').

When the company decided to employ a new customer services assistant, the managing director, Anne Harrison, asked the human resources manager, Peter Shaw, to organise recruiting someone. In turn, Peter Shaw passed the task on to the recruitment officer, Matthew Field, who placed an advertisement in the local papers and notified the Job Centre.

A Hierarchical structures

Look at AL's organisational structure on page 140, and answer the following questions.
1. How many levels of authority are there in AL's business?
2. What do the vertical lines joining members of staff in the organisation show?
3. Who is responsible for the wages clerk? Who is responsible for Mark Jones?
4. Redraw AL's organisational chart, making the following changes:
   – Nicola Cromby, the production manager has left, and Paramjit Singh is promoted to her position
   – Andrew Longthorne joins the firm and becomes the new production supervisor.
5. What is Peter Shaw's span of control?
6. Give three reasons why AL's organisational chart is important to the company.

Flat structures

AL's new sales clerk, Michael Roberts, went with Mark Jones, the sales representative responsible for customers in the south-east of England, on a sales trip. They arranged to stay overnight in the San Clu Hotel in Ramsgate.

In the evening they spent time talking to the hotel's manager, Mr Edmunds, who showed them the San Clu Hotel's organisational chart.

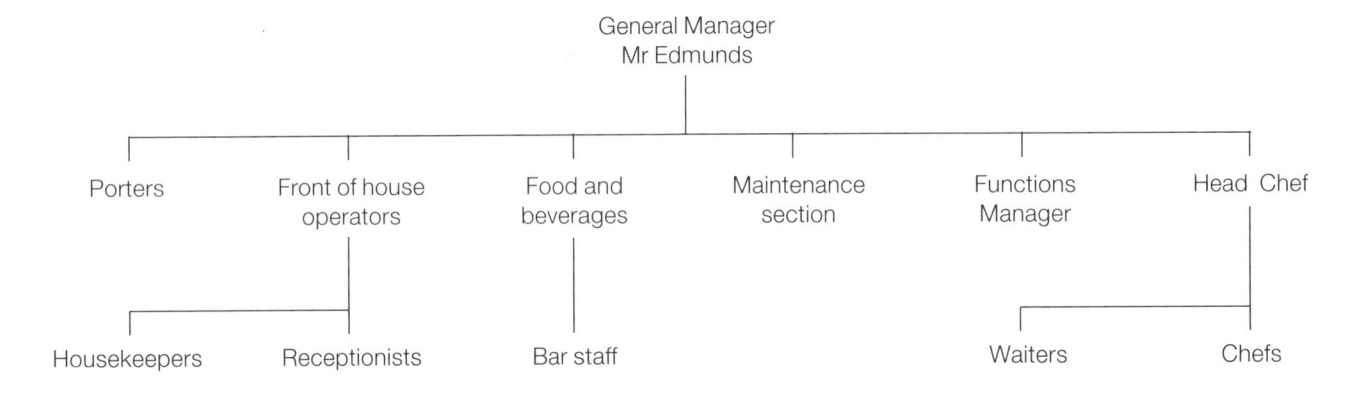

General Manager
Mr Edmunds
- Porters
- Front of house operators
  - Housekeepers
  - Receptionists
- Food and beverages
  - Bar staff
- Maintenance section
- Functions Manager
  - Waiters
- Head Chef
  - Chefs

The hotel's organisational structure is known as a **flat structure**, with fewer levels of authority than AL's. Mr Edmunds explained that this ensures that all staff feel part of the hotel's organisation, and can contribute to the decision-making process. This is possible in a small organisation like the San Clu Hotel, which doesn't have many staff.

Matrix structures

Sometimes, Mr Edmunds brings together a team of specialists to work on a particular project at the San Clu Hotel. This type of team is said to have a **matrix structure** In a matrix structure, groups of managers/teams report to different people for different functions.

For example, when planning a conference Mr Edmunds brings together people from across the organisation to discuss requirements, such as conference facilities and staff rotas. The project team reports to Mr Edmunds, the general manager, and not to each Head of Department.

> ### A Looking at your own organisation
>
> Investigate the organisational structure at your school or college. How many staff are senior or middle managers? How many are teachers or tutors? Try drawing an organisational chart for your school or college. Does it have a hierarchical structure, or a flat structure? Why do you think this is?

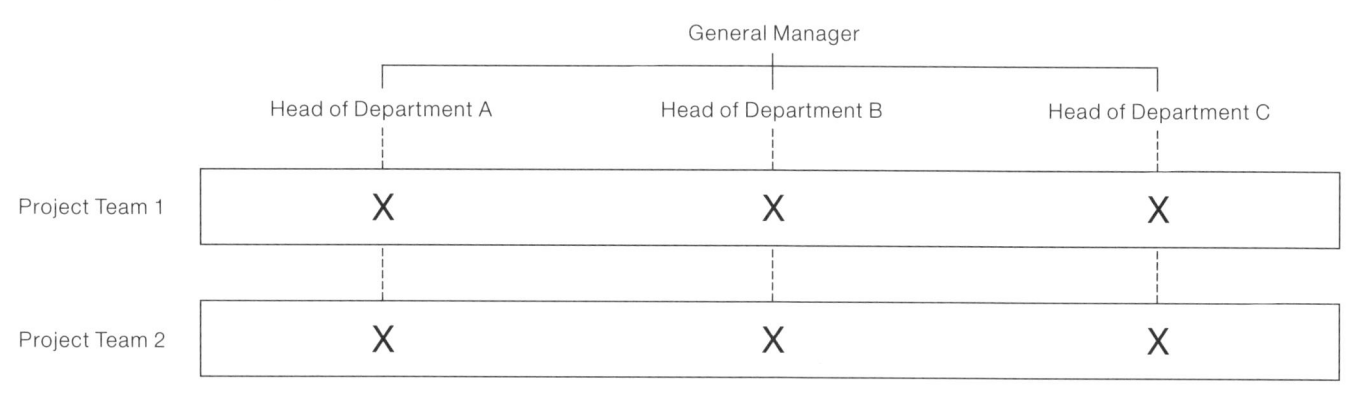

```
                          General Manager
                                 |
         ┌───────────────────────┼───────────────────────┐
   Head of Department A    Head of Department B    Head of Department C

Project Team 1      X                    X                    X

Project Team 2      X                    X                    X
```

X is a person from each department. The project team reports to the general manager and not to each Head of Department.

Working as a team

At both AL's and the San Clu Hotel, **teamwork** brings benefits to individuals and the organisation.

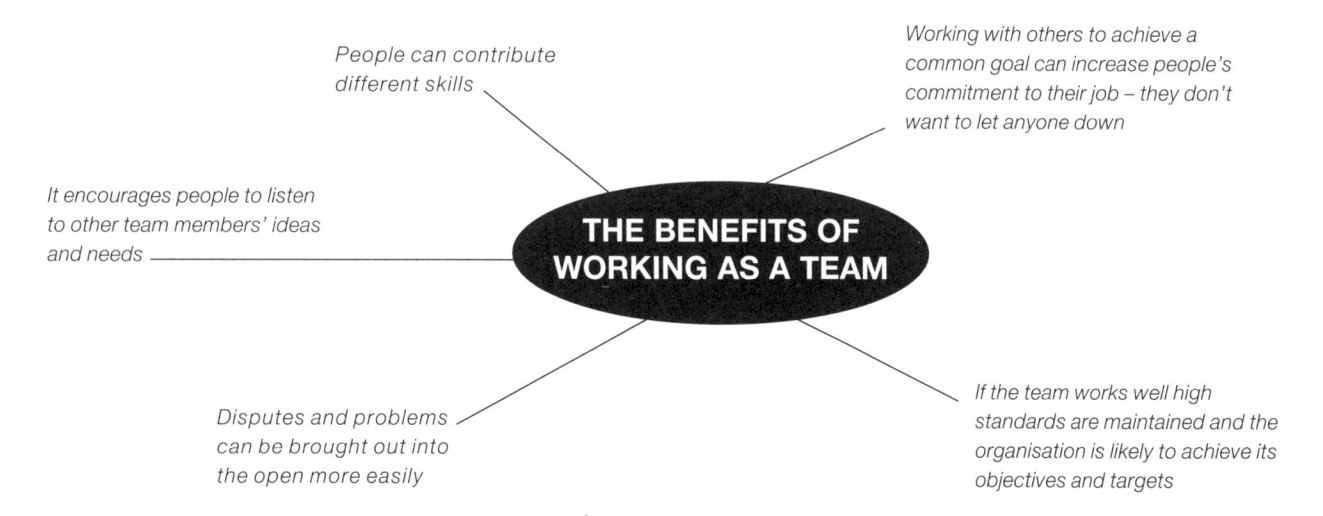

THE BENEFITS OF WORKING AS A TEAM

- People can contribute different skills
- Working with others to achieve a common goal can increase people's commitment to their job – they don't want to let anyone down
- It encourages people to listen to other team members' ideas and needs
- Disputes and problems can be brought out into the open more easily
- If the team works well high standards are maintained and the organisation is likely to achieve its objectives and targets

The San Clu Hotel's flat organisational structure encourages teamwork between staff in different departments on an everyday basis. For example, receptionists keep housekeepers informed of the number of guests arriving and leaving, so that rooms can be prepared.

In AL's hierarchical organisation, most teamwork takes place within departments. For example, the machine operators work together to achieve their production targets, but have little contact with staff in the sales and marketing department.

When the company feels that a particular project would benefit from teamwork across the organisation, it sets up a special team with a matrix structure. For example, when AL's wanted to change the design of one of its mobile phones, it brought together the following members of staff to work as a team:

Team member	Department
Richard Francis	Research and development
Paramjit Singh	Production
Don Parr	Marketing
Linda Holder	Finance
Eric Thomas	Purchasing

Don Parr explains the benefits of taking a team approach to the project:

'We met as a team regularly, to discuss ideas for improving the design of the mobile phone. We all contributed ideas and listened to each others suggestions. Working as a team ensured that research and development, production and marketing all liaised with the finance department, which often doesn't happen at an early enough stage of a project. As it was, we all knew our budget from the outset, so we didn't overspend when planning and implementing the project.'

Departments within organisations

Large organisations like AL's are usually divided into departments, as you can see from its organisational chart.

Each of AL's departments covers a particular area of work and has its own responsibilities.

Research and development department

The research and development department – often shortened to 'R&D' – is responsible for developing ideas for new products and expanding the organisation's product range. Consumers constantly demand more from AL's mobile phones, and it is the responsibility of the R&D department to make sure that they get what they want.

To do this, the department:
- works with the marketing department to find out what consumers need and want
- reviews the way the mobile phones work
- reviews the way the mobile phones look
- develops new designs to meet consumers' needs and wants.

For example, market research showed that consumers wanted a mobile phone that would fit into a handbag or pocket. The original mobile phone design was large and bulky, so the R&D department researched and developed a new, compact phone design which met consumers' needs.

▶ Organisational chart, page 140

▶ Consumer needs and wants, pages 105 and 185

▶ Marketing department, page 146

Production department

The production department is responsible for manufacturing (making) AL's mobile phones.

Manufacturing companies usually use one of the following three production methods:

- **job production** – when items are made to order (for example, a piece of designer jewellery)
- **batch production** – when a group of identical items are made at once (for example, a batch of bread rolls)
- **mass/flow production** – when components are assembled on a production line to make the final product.

Most manufacturing companies use a production line to make products

AL's uses mass production. When production operatives make a mobile phone, computer components are added section by section until the final product is complete. Quality control checks are made to ensure that each phone is produced to the same standard – customers have a right to expect all their mobile phones to work when they are delivered.

Quality assurance, page 152

The production department at AL's has a variety of functions, including:
- deciding what machines and tools are required
- contributing to the layout and design of the factory
- producing goods
- ensuring the smooth operation of equipment on a day-to-day basis
- checking quality control
- checking the progress of work.

Purchasing department

The purchasing department at AL's is responsible for:
- buying the raw materials needed to make mobile phones (for example, micro chips for inside the phones and plastic for the casings)
- buying fixtures and fittings for the company (for example, machinery, desks, photocopiers and chairs)
- monitoring stock levels (for example, checking that there is enough plastic in stock to meet a customer's order for phones)
- negotiating price and delivery times with suppliers (for example, persuading a supplier to give AL's a reduced price for plastic as it buys large amounts).

People in business organisations

> ### A · What needs to be bought?
>
> McDonald's is a well-known multinational company, famous for selling fast food. Explain what you think the person in charge of purchasing at McDonald's would be responsible for.

▶ Preparing accounts, page 232

▶ Processing invoices, pages 220 and 222

▶ Paying wages, pages 228 and 229

▶ Petty cash, pages 224 and 225

▶ Credit control, page 227

▶ Statements of accounts, page 231

Finance department

The finance department (also known as the accounts department) is responsible for all financial aspects of the organisation. At AL's, the finance department uses both manual and computerised accounting systems to:
- prepare accounts
- process invoices
- pay wages
- handle petty cash
- carry out credit control
- issue statements of accounts.

Sales and marketing department

At AL's, as in many business organisations, sales and marketing are grouped together in one department. However, they have quite different roles.

Sales staff:
- sell the mobile phones to high street shops
- forecast future sales (how many people they think will buy a particular phone)
- monitor competitors, in order to keep ahead of other companies who manufacture mobile phones.

Marketing staff:
- carry out marketing research and advise the research and development department on what the public wants
- plan advertising and promotional campaigns
- monitor consumer trends.

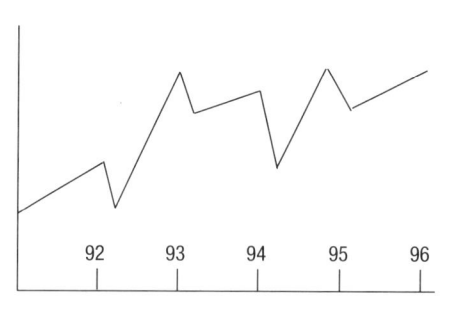

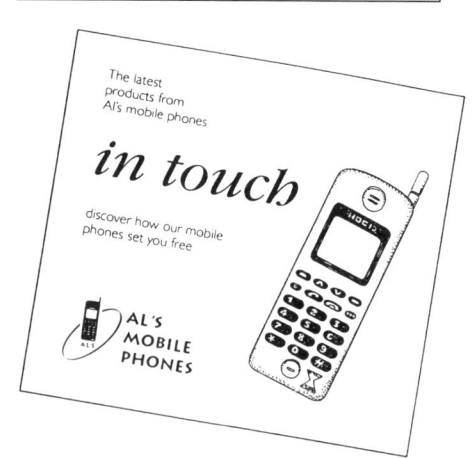

▶ Market research, pages 109 and 195

▶ Promotion, page 196

▶ Consumer trends, pages 182 and 183

Administration department

The administration department at AL's provides office support to other departments in the organisation. This includes:
- reprographics (photocopying)
- word processing
- secretarial support
- filing
- mail handling

146

- telecommunications (including telephone, telex and fax)
- reception
- insurance (all employers must be insured in case their employees injure themselves).

> Health and safety, page 155

A   Changes in administration

How do you think technology such as computers, faxes and photocopiers has changed job roles within administration departments? Look at the list of activities above, and consider how they would have been different 20 years ago. Talk to people you know who work in administrative jobs, to see what they think.

At AL's, administrative services such as photocopying are **centralised**. So when Ian Andrews in the finance department needed to photocopy the final accounts for a meeting of the board of directors, he asked Alice Johns to do the photocopying for him.

Centralised working arrangements: are controlled from one central point within the company. For example, photocopying and filing at AL's are controlled by the administration department.

Decentralised working arrangements: are not controlled centrally. For example, the different departments at the San Clu Hotel are each responsible for their own photocopying and filing.

Computer services department

AL's does not have its own computer services department. The service is contracted out. There is a technician working within the administration department to provide computer support for the company's own staff. His activities include:
- testing new software for the company
- buying new hardware
- maintaining existing computer equipment.

If the computer technician can't help with a problem, he calls in the help of an outside computer firm.

> After-sales service, page 111

> Customer services, page 147

Customer service department

The customer service department at AL's is part of the sales and marketing department. If customers ring up or write to the company wanting advice or information on mobile phones, customer service assistants are on hand to help. They:
- deal with complaints about phones not working properly
- organise refunds
- answer enquiries about products and prices
- provide an after-sales service. This is very important to AL's, because it helps them to keep existing customers and attract new ones.

The customer service department deals with customers over the phone, and staff need a good telephone manner

Distribution department

AL's needs to be able to deliver goods to its customers as quickly and cheaply as possible, and this is the responsibility of the distribution department. Like other large companies, AL's has its own lorries with its logo on the side. As they travel around the country, these provide the company with free advertising.

AL's mainly distributes its mobile phones by road. Organisations rely on a variety of different forms of transportation, such as couriers, and logistics companies like EXCEL logistics.

A   Delivering the goods

You work as a distribution manager for an engineering company. Your boss has asked you to find out the quickest and cheapest way of delivering the following:
- a large piece of machinery to Australia
- urgent documents to the USA
- documents to Companies House in Cardiff
- legal documents for a meeting that afternoon in a nearby town.

Carry out some research to find out what distribution method would be best in each case.

Human resources department

The human resources department at AL's – which used to be called the personnel department – deals with people working for the organisation. It is responsible for:
- maintaining staff records
- recruiting staff
- dismissing staff
- training and development
- staff welfare
- investigating employee and employer rights and responsibilities
- issuing contracts of employment.

▶ Employee and employer rights and responsibilities, page 153

AL's human resources manager, Peter Shaw, explains some of these functions in more detail:

'In the human resources department we deal with all of AL's employees. At one end of the scale, recruitment is one of our major responsibilities. Whenever the company needs to appoint new staff we advertise the vacant position and assist in the interviewing and selection processes. At the other extreme, sometimes people lose their jobs and we have to terminate their contracts. This is often a long process, and we have to follow set guidelines closely.

On a day-to-day basis, we look after the welfare of our staff. We provide sport and recreational facilities, medical services, and offer counselling when needed. If new or existing employees need training to carry out their jobs more effectively or to gain promotion, our training officer either leads courses herself, or organises training with outside organisations.'

The human resources department at AL's also deals with:
- health and safety
- superannuation (pensions)
- sickness.

Cleaning at AL's is carried out by outside contractors engaged by the human resources department. They check in with the security officer, and are responsible for ensuring the building is cleaned every day.

Security
AL's has a security gate which is staffed by a security officer. When visitors arrive at the company, they need to sign in with the security officer and obtain a pass. The security department is also responsible for ensuring:
- that the building is safe
- that fire and burglar alarms are in good working order.

Working arrangements
Different employees at AL's have different working arrangements for:
- when they work
- their terms of employment
- where they work.

Flexible working hours
The office staff at AL's are allowed to work flexitime, as shown in the chart below:

Time	Flexible or core?
7 a.m. – 10 a.m.	Flexible
10 a.m. – 12 noon	Core
12 noon – 2 p.m.	Flexible
2 p.m. – 4 p.m.	Core
4 p.m. – 7 p.m.	Flexible

Flexible hours: are those when employees are able to start and finish work as they please within the hours stated.

CUSTOMER SERVICE ASSISTANT

required to join a busy mobile phone company. AL's currently requires a self-motivated and well-presented person who has an understanding of customer service.

You should have good communication skills, be willing to work as a part of a team, and possess GCSE grade C or above in English and Maths. Previous experience is not essential, as full training will be given in all aspects of the job.

Interested? Then apply in writing and enclose a CV to:
PETER SHAW · HUMAN RESOURCES MANAGER
AL'S COMMUNICATION SYSTEMS PLC

▶ Health and safety, page 155

▶ Dismissal, page 157

People in business organisations

Core hours: *are those when all employees must be working.*

Staff clock in and out using a flexi-card and machine.

Other organisations use a flexi-sheet instead, like the one shown here.

DATE	TIME IN AM	TIME OUT AM	TIME IN PM	TIME OUT PM	NO. OF HOURS WORKED
27/3	7.30	12.30	13.00	17.00	9.00
28/3	7.30	13.00	14.00	16.30	8.00
			HOURS B/F		
			TOTAL HOURS		
			WEEKLY HOURS EXPECTED		37
			ADDITIONAL HOURS C/F		
			DEFICIT HOURS C/F		

Most employees at AL's have to work a minimum of 148 hours a month (37 hours per week). If they work more than this, they are entitled to take off the extra hours as flexi-leave at a time which suits them and the company. For example, Anna Evans, an administrative assistant at AL's, worked 156 hours last month. Her contract states that she must work 148 hours a month (37 hours per week). Therefore Anna worked 8 extra hours last month, which she is entitled to take off as flexi-leave. She has talked to her supervisor about when to take the time, and they have agreed that she can have two afternoons off.

A Flexible working hours

Philip Buck worked the following hours last June:

Week 1:   32 hours
Week 2:   43 hours
Week 3:   45 hours
Week 4:   37 hours

Was Philip able to take any flexi-leave in July? If so, how many hours?

Shift work

Unlike the office staff, the factory workers at AL's work shifts. There are three teams of workers which each work at different times during the day:

- Team one: 6 a.m. to 2 p.m.
- Team two: 2 p.m. to 10 p.m.
- Team three: 10 p.m. to 6 a.m.

The teams rotate each week, so that they change shifts regularly. For two weeks in August the factory closes and the workers take their holiday. During this time the machines are cleaned and overhauled.

The San Clu Hotel also has a shift system, with three receptionists working a rota of 7 a.m. to 3 p.m., 3 p.m. to 11 p.m., and 11 p.m. to 7 a.m.

A Shift workers and flexi-time

The following chart gives examples of people who work shifts and flexi-time. Can you add to it?

Shifts
Police officers
Fire Brigade officers
Hospital workers
Factory workers

Flexi-time
Local government employees
Civil Service employees
Office employees

You may know people in your own family who work shifts or flexi-time. Discuss with them how these working arrangements affect their day-to-day lives.

Contracts

Like all organisations, AL's has a legal obligation to issue contracts of employment to new employees within two months of them starting work.

Contracts of employment can either be **permanent** or **fixed-term**. Fixed-term contracts are temporary, lasting for a limited length of time (such as three months, or a year). For example, when AL's is really busy it takes on temporary workers to help out on the production line. Alternatively workers are employed to complete a short-term task. These workers are given a temporary, fixed-term contract.

AL's employs both full-time and part-time staff. **Full-time** employees work between 37 and 42 hours per week. **Part-time** employees work up to 16 hours per week.

Workbase

Employees at AL's are based in different working environments – 'workbases'.

- Staff in departments like finance and administration work in offices.
- Production workers are based in the factory where they manufacture mobile phones.
- The company's sales representatives are mobile – they spend most of the time travelling around the country.

Rachel Friend from the sales and marketing department has just had a baby and does not want to come straight back to work full time. The marketing manager is keen to keep her and has agreed that she can **work from home** on a part-time basis. AL's has given Rachel a computer, with connection to an e-mail system and fax machine. Working in this way, she can write marketing materials at home using the computer, then either fax or e-mail them to her manager.

What are the advantages and disadvantages of working at home?

A Where are they based?

What is likely to be the workbase of each of these employees?
- A computer programmer.
- A sales assistant.
- A sailing instructor.
- A welder.
- A bus driver.
- A gardener.
- A novelist.

Reasons for changing working arrangements

In order to remain efficient and competitive, AL's regularly looks at, and if necessary changes, its working methods. In particular, it monitors:
- productivity
- quality assurance
- technology
- competition.

Productivity

The production department is given set targets for manufacturing a certain number of mobile phones within a time period, and needs to ensure that it has enough stock and workers to meet these targets. If the targets aren't met, it affects the profits AL's makes at the end of the year.

If productivity is below target, the company needs to consider how it could improve working arrangements to help it meet its targets.

Quality assurance

The quality of the mobile phones AL's makes has to be maintained. This is known as quality assurance. AL's needs to ensure all the phones work properly before they leave the company.

A retail company called Canadian Communications has ordered phones from AL's two years in a row. Having quality assurance systems in place helps to ensure that the company receives the same standard of service and quality of product.

▶ Technology and employment, page 112

Technology

It is vital for business organisations to keep up to date with technology so that they work as efficiently and cost-effectively as possible. Robots are doing jobs performed manually in the past. AL's is currently planning to increase the level of automation of the production line to 90%. This means that the company will be able to produce mobile phones more quickly and at a lower unit cost.

Competition

AL's must always be aware of its competitors, and make sure that its mobile phones are better than others on the market. To do this, the directors and managers at AL's:
- check the function and design of other mobile phones regularly
- keep up to date with advances in technology
- ensure that their phones are competitively priced
- look at how other company's are marketing mobile phones, and try to make their own promotional material stand out.

A growing number of manufacturers are investing in technology to increase efficiency

▶ Planning promotional materials, page 190

A   The competitive edge

With so many different brands of products on the market, what makes you buy one rather than another?

Choose two products that you or your family buy regularly, such as soap, shampoo, breakfast cereal or tea. Visit your local supermarket and compare the brand names, prices, quantities (weight and amount) and special offers of your chosen products. Design a table to record this information. Would you and your family now still choose the same brands as you have in the past?

Employee and employer responsibilities and rights

John Daniels has just started a new job on the production line at Metlink Ltd, a medium-sized engineering company with about 500 employees. Metlink manufactures tie-pins, tie-clips and high-quality pens for high-street shops.

On his first day John is shown around the firm and introduced to different members of staff. The production manager gives him a tour of the factory – John is going to start by learning the lathe cutter's job. He is then taken to meet the human resources manager.

The benefits of employers and employees co-operating

The human resources manager, Sara Khan, welcomes John to the company and gives him an overview of how the business works. She explains to him that the firm's directors think of the company as a family and encourage staff at all levels to work together. Regular meetings are held between production staff, their supervisors and management, at which everyone is encouraged to contribute to decisions about the way the company is run.

John is surprised by this – in his old company there was little contact between managers and staff. Sara explains that co-operation has benefits for both the company and its employees:

- it creates a friendly, positive working atmosphere
- staff feel valued as individuals, loyal to their employers, and are more committed to the company
- efficiency improves because employees enjoy their jobs and work harder
- the company's performance improves, and it is more likely to survive.

Employer and employee rights and responsibilities

To introduce him to the company, Sara gives John a staff handbook. This contains information about:

- the company's objectives
- contracts of employment
- remuneration
- training
- health and safety
- equal opportunities
- discipline.

It highlights Metlink's rights and responsibilities as an employer; and John's rights and responsibilities as an employee.

Business objectives

At the front of the staff handbook is Metlink's mission statement:

This summarises the company's business objectives – what it wants to achieve. Sara Khan talks to John about the mission statement in some detail, explaining exactly how Metlink fulfils its goals. She emphasises that all employees can contribute by trying to meet customers' needs at all times, and ensuring that standards of quality are maintained.

> METLINK'S AIM IS TO PROVIDE EXCELLENT QUALITY GOODS:
> - in the right place
> - at the right time
> - at as low a cost as possible

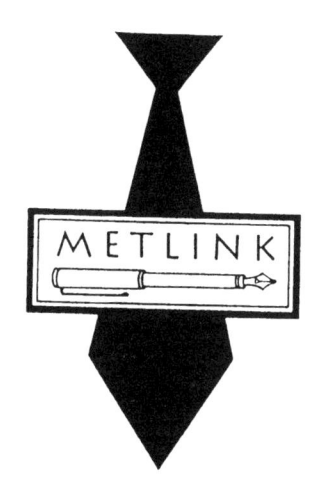

People in business organisations

- The **employer** is responsible for explaining business objectives clearly.
- The **employee** is responsible for helping to achieve business objectives by meeting customers' needs and maintaining quality standards.

Contracts of employment

The handbook explains that by law (under the Trade Union Reform and Employment Act 1993), all employees who work for eight hours or more a week and whose employment continues for at least one month must receive a written contract of employment within two months of starting work.

John's contract of employment should contain the following details:

- the employer's name and address
- the employee's name and address
- details of trade union membership
- grievance and disciplinary procedures
- likely length of employment
- remuneration (and when it is paid)
- working hours
- sick pay
- holiday entitlement and holiday pay
- length of notice by employer and employee
- job title
- place of work.

It also states the date employment began. This is important because some employment rights – for example, redundancy pay and being able to claim unfair dismissal – depend on a continuous period of employment of two years.

Once a contract of employment has been signed by the employer and employee, it is a legally-binding document, which can be enforced by either side through the civil courts. For example, John's contract states that he will work between 9 a.m. and 5 p.m. five days a week. If he fails to do this, Metlink can use the contract as evidence that John is not fulfilling his responsibilities.

- The **employer** has a right to expect the employee to comply with (keep to) the terms of contract.
- The **employee** has a responsibility to meet the terms of contract, and a right to expect the employer to comply with the contract.

Remuneration

John's contract includes details of how much Metlink will pay him – £9000 per annum. The company is going to pay him a salary on a monthly basis, and the money will go straight into his bank account around the 15th day of the month. John will receive a pay statement which gives details of his pay and deductions (money taken off).

The contract states that Metlink will deduct from his salary:

- income tax (PAYE, or Pay As You Earn). The company will send this money to the Inland Revenue
- National Insurance (to cover state benefits).

Sara explains to John that the company has its own pension scheme, and gives him a booklet to read. John already has a private pension plan, but

---

CONTRACT OF EMPLOYMENT

Name of employer: Metlink Ltd, Gas Road, Leeds, Yorkshire
Name of employee: John Daniels

1 Commencement of employment and continuous employment
Your employment with this company began on 4 January 1996

2 Job title
You are employed as a production operative.

3 Pay
Your rate of pay is £9,000 per annum.
You are paid at monthly intervals.
Income Tax and National Insurance will be deducted directly from your salary.

4 Hours of work
Your hours of work are 9 a.m. to 5 p.m., Monday to Friday.

5 Holidays
Your holiday entitlement is 20 days per annum.
Your holiday year begins on 1 January.
You are entitled to take all public holidays in addition to your holiday entitlement.
Your leave is to be taken at a time convenient to the employer.

6 Sickness
The standard statutory sick pay scheme applies. Notification of absence should be made on the first day of sickness, in writing or by telephone.

7 Notice
The length of notice for termination of employment required from employer or employee is four weeks.

8 Grievance procedures
In cases of dissatisfaction with disciplinary procedures, you are to apply in the first instance to the shift supervisor and thence the line manager. Further details are available from the Human Resources department.

9 Pension scheme
Details of the contributory company pension scheme for which you are eligible are available from the Human Resources department.

Signed (date): 4 January 1996
Human Resources officer: S. Khan
(on behalf of the company)
Employee: J. Daniels

Payslip, page 228

says he will look through the booklet and let her know whether he is going to join the company scheme. If he does, payments will be deducted from his monthly salary.

- The employer has a responsibility to organise an employee's remuneration.
- The **employee** has a right to expect remuneration, as agreed.

Training

Metlink encourages staff development, and allows each member of staff five days' training a year. Sara explains to John that some of these training days will be on-the-job (given within Metlink), and others will be off-the-job (organised by outside training companies). At first much of John's training is likely to be on-the-job, as he can learn basic skills from his colleagues. Sara arranges a time for him to meet the training officer, who will talk to him in detail about his needs for the future.

A good employer will make sure that staff receive training.

▶ Health and Safety at Work Act, page 257

Health and safety

Like all employers, Metlink has a statutory responsibility to protect the health and safety of its employees under the Health and Safety at Work Act 1974.

Statutory: enforced by law.

Metlink's staff handbook says that the company ensures the health, safety and welfare of its employees by:

- making sure machinery and equipment are safe
- ensuring the safe use, handling, storage and transportation of goods and substances
- providing information, instruction, training and supervision to employees on health and safety
- offering welfare services
- providing safety equipment, such as hard hats, goggles, boots and ear protectors.

The handbook shows the different personal safety equipment Metlink supplies to staff working in the factory.

Sara explains to John that if Metlink didn't provide this safety equipment, it could be taken to court for failing to follow health and safety laws and fined large sums of money. She also emphasises how important it is for employees to use the equipment provided and to follow health and safety procedures. Recently a member of staff had been dismissed for not wearing safety goggles when working in the factory and for fooling about near dangerous machinery on the production line.

- The **employer** has a responsibility to comply with health and safety regulations.
- The **employer** has a right to expect the employee to follow health and safety regulations.
- The employee has a responsibility to follow health and safety regulations.

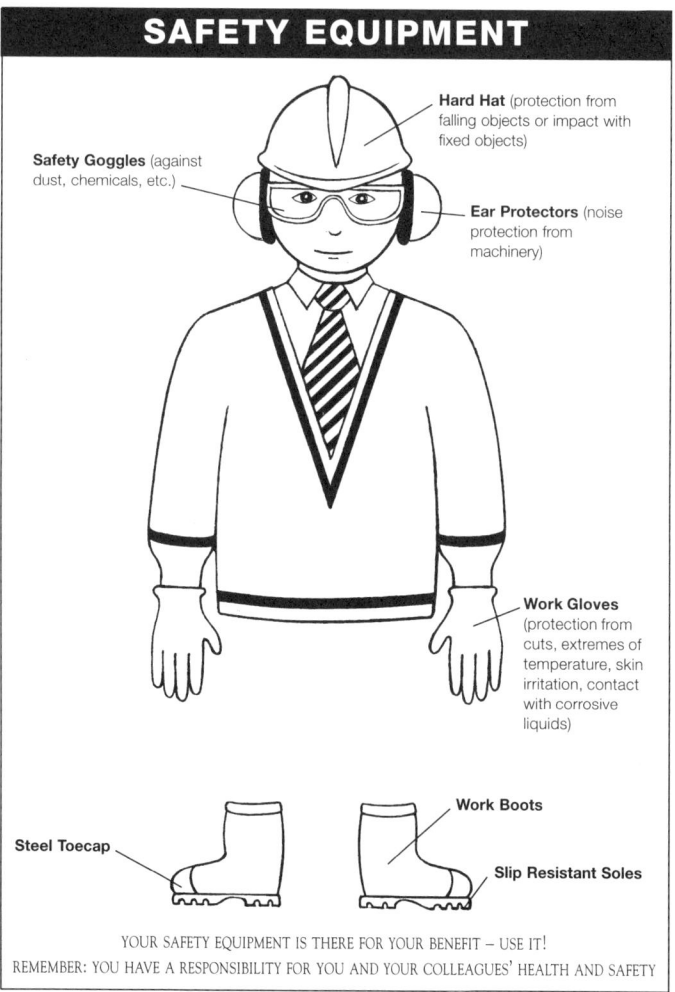

SAFETY EQUIPMENT

Hard Hat (protection from falling objects or impact with fixed objects)

Safety Goggles (against dust, chemicals, etc.)

Ear Protectors (noise protection from machinery)

Work Gloves (protection from cuts, extremes of temperature, skin irritation, contact with corrosive liquids)

Steel Toecap

Work Boots

Slip Resistant Soles

YOUR SAFETY EQUIPMENT IS THERE FOR YOUR BENEFIT – USE IT!
REMEMBER: YOU HAVE A RESPONSIBILITY FOR YOU AND YOUR COLLEAGUES' HEALTH AND SAFETY

People in business organisations

> ### A — Looking at health and safety
>
> Walk around your school or college looking for potential health and safety hazards. For example, you might consider:
> - safe use of VDUs
> - safe use of machinery
> - food hygiene
> - lighting and ventilation.
>
> Write a short report summarising your findings and suggesting how health and safety could be improved.

▶ Sex Discrimination Act, page 258

▶ Equal Pay Act, page 258

▶ Race Relations Act, page 257

Equal opportunities

All companies have a statutory responsibility to follow equal opportunities legislation, such as:
- the Sex Discrimination Act
- the Equal Pay Act
- the Race Relations Act.

Equal opportunities legislation aims to ensure that business organisations do not discriminate against anyone (treat them less favourably) because of their race, sex, marital status, disability or age. This includes:
- not discriminating against people directly by advertising for 'a male accountant', 'a single person', or 'whites only'
- not discriminating against people indirectly by putting conditions on a job which would make it difficult for some people to apply. For example, advertising for 'someone over six feet' would prevent most women applying.

Metlink has its own equal opportunities policy, which is included in the staff handbook. This states the company's equal opportunities policy for:
- recruiting and selecting staff
- training staff
- promoting staff
- paying staff.

Remember that:
- the **employer** has a responsibility to implement equal opportunities legislation at work.
- the **employee** has the right to expect equal opportunities at work.

People in business organisations

A Sex discrimination?

Read the information on the Sex Discrimination Act on page 258, then read the following article.

Do you think the landlord is being discriminatory? Discuss the issues involved.

Discipline

The last section of the staff handbook deals with discipline. It explains that Metlink has the right to take disciplinary action against staff for misconduct such as:
- poor time-keeping
- frequent absence
- not following health and safety procedures
- sexual or racial discrimination
- fighting
- stealing.

Sara explains to John that the usual disciplinary procedure followed is to give an employee:
- a first warning verbally (usually given by a supervisor on an informal basis)
- a formal warning (which is usually in writing)
- a final warning (which is usually verbal and in writing).

If these warnings have no effect, then the employee is dismissed with notice (as stated in the contract). This means that the working relationship between employer and employee is terminated.

Some forms of misconduct are so serious – for example, stealing or violence – that they result in instant dismissal. Sara says that in such cases Metlink usually suspends the employee without pay and carries out a full investigation before dismissing them.
- The **employer** has the right to take disciplinary action against staff.

Sex bias charge as women drink free
by Amit Roy

A PUBLICAN who dispenses free drinks to women has been warned that he faces prosecution under the Sex Discrimination Act because he is not equally generous to male customers.

Craig Pinches, who owns pubs called the Bushwacker in Worcester and in Walsall, says his marketing ploy is intended to build a regular clientele among women as well as boost the number of male customers.

But he had been told by the Equal Opportunities Commission to either stop giving free drinks to women or face prosecution.

On any Monday between 8pm and 10pm at the Bushwacker in Worcester, women can ask for anything they like, including champagne.

The cost to Mr Pinches is about £1,400 but this is quickly wiped out by the 300 men for whom the presence of so many women is an added attraction. The men pay for their drinks of course.

In Walsall, nearly 400 women turn up for free drinks on Wednesdays but the choice is limited to lager, martini and wine.

"I first came across the idea of holding free ladies' nights in America and introduced it here about three years ago," said Mr Pinches, 28. "Night clubs often let in women free so I cannot see why the commission is objecting."

Among his regular women customers, he does not lack enthusiastic supporters. Amanda White, a 21-year-old operations manager for an exhibition company, spends Wednesday evenings sipping brandy and lemonade – and none too slowly.

"I get through several," she said "If I had to pay it would be £2.60 a time. Women are generally on low wages and this is one evening when I don't have to worry about bringing my purse. The men are happy as well. After all what man would turn down a bar full of women?"

Rose Hatchard, a 23-year-old barmaid at Walsall's Bushwacker, said: "We get women of all ages. The pub has a really good atmosphere. It's good fun."

The Equal Opportunities Commission took up the case in response to a complaint from a man – Giovanni Mastrantone, a 47-year-old Open University lecturer.

He said: "I'm not a lager lout who is cheesed off because he can't have a free drink. I am interested in equality issues."

'I hope the owner will see that what he is doing is wrong and either offer free drinks to men as well – or scrap the promotion."

Tessa Gill, a barrister who won a famous victory in 1982 against the El Vino wine bar in Fleet Street because it barred women from buying drinks t the bar, backed the Equal Opportunities Commission's stance.

Miss Gill said the although the Bushwacker's breach did not appear to be serious, a significant legal principle was involved. "The commission must appear to be even handed," she said. 'You can't pick and choose, otherwise the law falls into disrepute. I am for equality of treatment, otherwise you cannot object if women are excluded from working men's clubs."

People in business organisations

Legal representation

John asks Sara what his legal rights are in the case of disciplinary procedures. If the dispute is not settled within the business, then the company and John could seek outside help. It is possible that they could go to the Advisory Conciliation and Arbitration Service (ACAS) or an Industrial Tribunal. In very extreme cases their dispute could be considered by the European Court of Justice.

John asks if he can have more information about these, and Sara gives him the following fact sheets.

- The **employer** has a right to legal representation in the case of disputes.
- The **employee** has a right to legal representation in the case of disputes.

ACAS: FACT SHEET

ACAS stands for the Advisory Conciliation and Arbitration Service. It is an independent body, set up by the Government in 1975, to help trade unions and employers settle industrial disputes. It offers:

- advice – guidance to employers/trade unions on industrial relations matters
- conciliation – an ACAS official tries to to establish common ground between employers and trade unions
- mediation – proposing the basis for a settlement if it is not possible to settle the dispute by negotiation or conciliation
- arbitration – an official hears the dispute and makes a decision which parties must agree to accept
- makes enquiries into industrial relations in particular industries and organisations
- publishes advisory handbooks on industrial relations matters.

THE EUROPEAN COURT OF JUSTICE: FACT SHEET

The UK became a member of the European Economic Community, and European law must now be followed by all countries who are members.

The European Court of Justice sits in Luxembourg and is composed of judges from each member state. Much of the law is in treaties and there are a number of articles and regulations dealing with employment law. For example, Article 119 states that there should be equal pay for equal work. All employees, whether in the public or private sector, can rely on this. If employees feel that the law has been broken, they can go to the European Court if they cannot settle the matter in the UK courts.

INDUSTRIAL TRIBUNAL: FACT SHEET

Industrial Tribunals are independent judicial bodies made up of a panel of three people. They may be asked to resolve employment disagreements on a range of matters, including:

- equal pay
- maternity rights
- race relations
- redundancy
- sex discrimination
- unfair dismissal
- trade union membership/non-membership rights.

For example, an employee may bring a case claiming unfair dismissal to the tribunal. If the tribunal decides that the dismissal was unfair, it can:

- tell the employer to give the employee his or her job back
- order the employer to pay compensation.

If the tribunal decides that the dismissal was fair, the employee can appeal to an Appeal Court or to the European Court of Justice.

The role of trade unions

After his appointment with Sara Khan, John has a meeting with Steve Ackers, a member of the General and Municipal Boiler Makers Union (GMB). Steve is a day shift supervisor at Metlink and has been elected shop steward by other workers. This means that he is their union representative.

One of Steve's responsibilities is to make sure that new employees know about the union. He tells John that the union's main roles are to:
- improve conditions of employment (such as wages, holidays and hours of work)
- ensure jobs are secure (for example, monitoring the effect of new technology on the number of people the firm employs)
- improve the working environment (health and safety, heating, lighting, cleanliness and so on)
- encourage equal opportunities
- protect workers who are sick, ensuring they get sick pay
- protect workers threatened with redundancy.

A Trade unions

Interview someone you know who belongs to a trade union. Ask them:
- What union do they belong to?
- How many members are there?
- What type of jobs do union members have?
- Why do they belong to the union?
- What is the membership fee?

Ways to resolve disagreements

Steve explains to John that one of the trade union's most important roles is to help resolve disagreements between employers and workers.

Sometimes employees feel they have been badly treated by the company, for example if they:
- are discriminated against because of their gender or ethnic background
- have an accident at work
- are made redundant
- are dismissed.

People in business organisations

Steve gives John the following chart summarising the steps he should take if he has a complaint.

```
Complain to your supervisor
           ↓ IF PROBLEM IS NOT RESOLVED
Take your complaint to the next level of management (your union representative will help you present your case)
           ↓ IF DISAGREEMENT IS NOT RESOLVED
See whether ACAS can help resolve the disagreement by talking to you and your management
           ↓ IF DISAGREEMENT IS NOT RESOLVED
Go to an industrial tribunal
           ↓ IF THEY RULE AGAINST YOU
Take your case to the European Court of Justice
```

▶ ACAS, page 158

▶ Industrial tribunals, page 158

▶ European Court of Justice, page 158

A Susan Edwards

Read the newspaper article on page 161.

Answer the following questions:
1. What was Susan Edwards' claim against London Underground?
2. Why was the introduction of new shift patterns discriminatory?
3. What was the outcome of her claim at the industrial tribunal?
4. If London Underground does decide to appeal, what will it do?

▶ Sex Discrimination Act, page 258

John says that he hopes he never has a disagreement with the company, as it all sounds a bit daunting. Steve reassures him that the trade union is always on hand to provide legal advice – between 1982 and 1992 the GMB recovered over £333 million in compensation for members who suffered accidents or illness at work.

Mother wins sex case over change in job hours

BY FRANCES GIBB AND JONATHAN PRYNN

A single mother who was forced to leave her train driver's job after new shift patterns prevented her caring for her son has won a sex discrimination claim against London Underground.

Susan Edwards, 37, who took her claim to an industrial tribunal with the backing of the Equal Opportunities Commission, was one of only 21 women drivers on the Underground out of 2,044.

Ms Edwards joined London Underground in 1983 and became a train driver in 1987, the year she gave birth to a son of whom she had sole care. She was able to carry on working for five years on day shifts.

But in 1992 – when she was being paid £17,000 a year – the company brought in a system that meant she would have to work early and late shifts and so would be unable to care for her son, then aged five. She said the management told her: "You can be a train driver or a mum."

Ms Edwards took voluntary severance despite wanting to continue working. She then sued London Underground, claiming loss of earnings and injury to her feelings.

She said yesterday: "I am delighted at the outcome but my victory shouldn't be lost in history. It should instigate change in working conditions for employees with family responsibilities."

What had happened was wrong, she added. " I was told by London Underground management that I could be a train driver or a mum and the kid was my problem. Three years later they now realise that this is not an appropriate attitude to take towards their employees."

London Underground argued at the tribunal in London that it had introduced the shift system to reduce costs and increase efficiency, but the tribunal found that the company could easily have accommodated Ms Edwards. The company said it was considering an appeal.

The level of compensation will be set at a later date.

Steve Ackers gives John the following list of disagreements he is currently dealing with:

- Ann Ashton has found out that her predecessor was paid more than her.
- Geoff Jones, a production worker, wants to leave his daughter in the company creche, but has been told it is only for female staff.
- John Richards, who works in the distribution depot, lost his driving licence for drink/driving. He has been told that he has to leave as he has to drive for his job and there was nothing else for him to do.
- Ranjit Singh works in the staff canteen. He has a beard which it is against his religion to shave off, and has been told that he has to wear a beard net when working in the kitchens. He thinks this is discriminatory.
- Brian Richards was injured when a pile of boxes fell on him in the loading bay. He says the boxes were stacked too high, and should have been tied down to prevent them toppling over. He is claiming compensation, but the management says he was careless.

A Legal positions

For each of the disagreements above, write a memo from Steve Ackers to the member of staff involved, explaining their legal position and advising them whether to take the case to an industrial tribunal.

▶ Legislation, page 258

▶ Memo, pages 17 and 237

People in business organisations

Preparing for employment or self-employment

Before you can prepare to get a job yourself, you need to find out more about different types of employment and self-employment in business.

Types of employment and self-employment

People's jobs can be divided into three main types:
- paid employment
- voluntary employment
- self-employment.

Paid employment

If you are in paid employment, it means that you work for someone else (an 'employer'). Employers are either business organisations in the:
- private sector – owned and controlled by one or more individuals
- public sector – owned by the government.

▶ The ownership of business organisations, page 63

Zoe Harris works for an employer in the private sector.

Case study: Zoe Harris, secretary to a legal executive

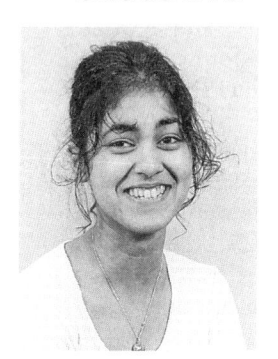

'In 1993 I completed a GNVQ Business course at Intermediate level. I have been employed as a secretary in Deal, Kent, for several years. My daily routine consists of filing, photocopying, making appointments for clients, dealing with correspondence (including mail), word processing, and making and receiving telephone calls. I need the following skills for my job.'

SKILLS NEEDED

- Meet deadlines
- Be organised
- Have good communication skills (oral and written)
- Have good computer skills
- Be able to deal with members of the public
- Be able to collate and file information
- Be reliable
- Be smart and presentable
- Be able to use my initiative
- Be able to work with other people

People in business organisations

A Private and public sector employers

National newspapers like *The Times*, *The Guardian* and *The Telegraph* advertise particular types of jobs on different days of the week (for example, marketing jobs one day, educational jobs the next). Look at the jobs sections of one of these newspapers every day for a week, and see whether most of the vacancies are with private or public sector employers. Cut out typical examples from each sector. What does this activity tell you about employment opportunities in the private sector, and in the public sector?

▶ The ownership of business organisations, page 83

Voluntary employment

If you do **voluntary work**, it means that you do not receive payment for your work. Most types of voluntary work are for the good of the community.

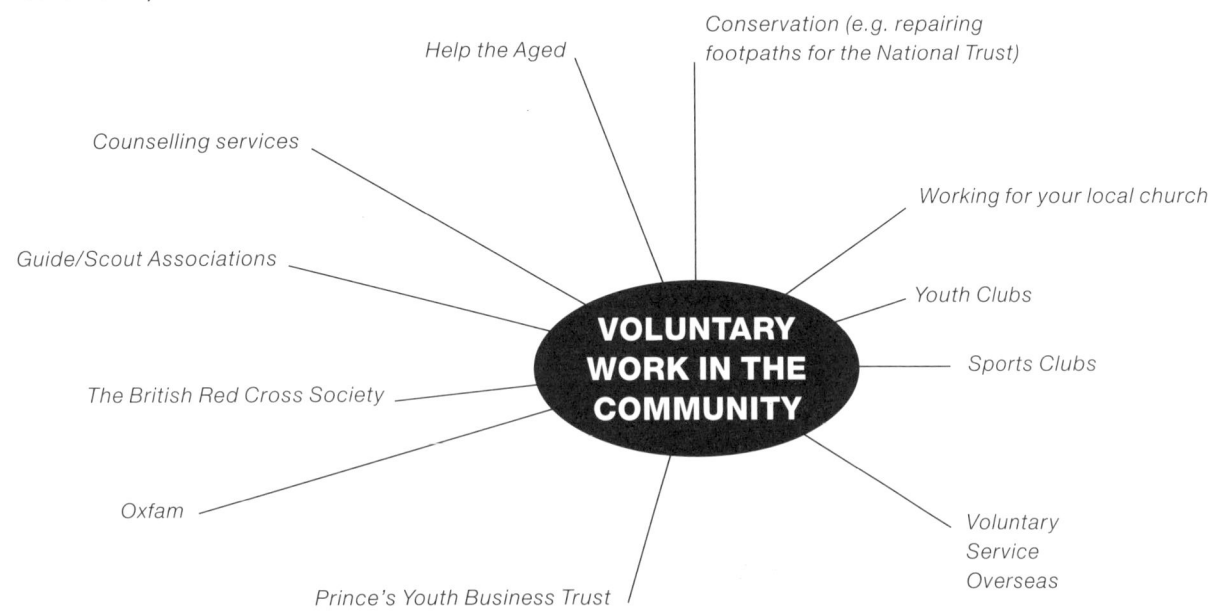

VOLUNTARY WORK IN THE COMMUNITY

- Help the Aged
- Conservation (e.g. repairing footpaths for the National Trust)
- Counselling services
- Working for your local church
- Youth Clubs
- Guide/Scout Associations
- Sports Clubs
- The British Red Cross Society
- Oxfam
- Voluntary Service Overseas
- Prince's Youth Business Trust

A Voluntary sector

1. Look in *The Thomson Local* Directory or visit your local library, and make a list of voluntary organisations in your area.
2. Investigate one of these organisations in detail. Find out what it does, where and when it meets, and obtain a contact name. Then present your findings to the rest of your GNVQ group.
3. As a group, collect together all the information you have found out about voluntary organisations and compile a database in the format shown below:

Organisation	Address	Telephone number	Contact name
St John Ambulance	Kent Road Canterbury CT4 6LH	01227 666424	Mr J Norris

163

People in business organisations

▶ Partnerships, page 84

▶ Franchises, page 86

Self-employment

If you work for yourself, you are **self-employed**. Therefore you are responsible for any risks involved and have to make decisions on your own – but any profit you make is yours.

There are several different ways of working for yourself:
- setting up **a small business** – for example, a painting and decorating business
- as a **partnership** – sharing the ownership of the business with other people
- as a **franchise** – buying into a large company which provides training, advertising, equipment and products.

C Case study: Les Spree, self-employed builder

'I have been in the building trade for 34 years. I began working for a large building company, then the opportunity arose for me to become self-employed. After careful thought and consideration, I took over my uncle's building business 20 years ago. My work involves general building work, for example house extensions and repairs. In addition, being self-employed means that I have to prepare my own quotations, keep my own financial records and order any materials I may need. The main advantages of being self-employed are being your own boss and making your own decisions. The biggest disadvantage is having to keep your own paperwork.'

A The Thomson Local

Look through *The Thomson Local* directory and try to find examples of:
- family businesses
- partnerships
- franchises.

How can you recognise them? What areas of work do they tend to be involved in?

What opportunities are there?

As you approach the end of your GNVQ course, the time will come when you need to think about what to do next. A number of options may be open to you, including:
- paid employment
- self-employment
- voluntary work
- higher education (HE)
- further education (FE).

If you want to start work, one of the first things you need to decide is where you would like to find a job. Different areas attract particular industries, and offer different employment opportunities. For example, if you are interested in agricultural work, you will probably need to look for employment opportunities in rural areas. If you want to work in the record industry, you will probably have to live in a large town.

Depending on what you want to do and where you live at the moment, you might decide to:

- stay in your **local** area (near your home)
- work somewhere else in the UK (look for **national** opportunities)
- work outside the UK (look for **international** opportunities).

If you want to find paid employment, the following might be useful sources of information.

Where you want to work	Sources of information

If you want to stay in your local area	- local Job Centres
	- media:
	  – local newspapers
	  – local radio
	- your careers officer
	- local employment agencies

If you want to work somewhere else in the UK (national)	- Job Centres around the country
	- media:
	  – national newspapers
	  – national television (Teletext)
	  – national radio
	- your careers officer

If you want to work outside the UK (international)	- Working Holidays – an organisation which gives advice and describes holiday jobs in other countries - *The Traveller's Survival Kit* – a book which gives information on employment in different countries - Commission of the European Communities – supplies information on the right for individuals to work in the European Union

Hoverspeed operates the fastest car carrying vessels across the English Channel. Our unique Hovercraft speed from Dover to Calais in just 35 minutes, and the revolutionary SeaCat carries up to 90 cars and 600 passengers between Folkestone and Boulogne in less than an hour.

Bought Ledger Clerk
Salary to £10,078 per annum

We have a vacancy in our Finance Department for a Bought Ledger Clerk.

Reporting to the Bought Ledger Supervisor the main duties are to process invoices and ensure suppliers' accounts are accurate. This work is carried out via the CODA accounting system. Assisting with desk sales reconciliations and monthly bank reconciliations (using the AFOS reservations system) will also be required.

The ideal candidate must be numerate, accurate and have attention to detail. Previous computer experience is essential although specific training can be provided. A good telephone manner is required to deal with internal departments and most importantly to assist suppliers with their queries.

— Skills required
— On-job training

For an Application Form please ring our 24 hour answering service on Dover (01304) 225448.

HOVERSPEED
FAST FERRIES

Police Officers
Throughout Kent

Are you looking for a career which can provide you with challenge, variety, job satisfaction and opportunities to progress? As a Police Constable you would combine these factors with the provision of an essential public service in seeking to reduce, disrupt and detect crime.

Kent County Constabulary has a well-deserved reputation as a pioneering and innovative force. We employ some 3,200 officers and 1,250 civilians, and use the most advanced techniques and technology to control crime and make the communities we serve safer. We are the only force to have land frontier with the continent of Europe, giving us the largest number of ports and the Channel Tunnel to police.

To join us you must be highly motivated, with drive, determination and total commitment. The role of the police officer is not for the faint-hearted but for those who take a pride in what they do, and want to do something that really matters.

You must be physically and medically fit, with basic keyboard skills, good eyesight and a full driving licence. You will need five GCSEs graded C or above (or equivalent), or be able to demonstrate exceptional achievement in other areas, e.g. 18 months service as a special constable.

Skills required
Qualifications

For further information and details on how to apply, please contact the Recruitment Section, Kent County Constabulary, Sutton Road, Maidstone, Kent ME15 9BZ. Telephone (01622) 653041.

Kent County Constabulary is an equal opportunities employer and particularly welcomes applications from under-represented groups.

KENT COUNTY CONSTABULARY

People in business organisations

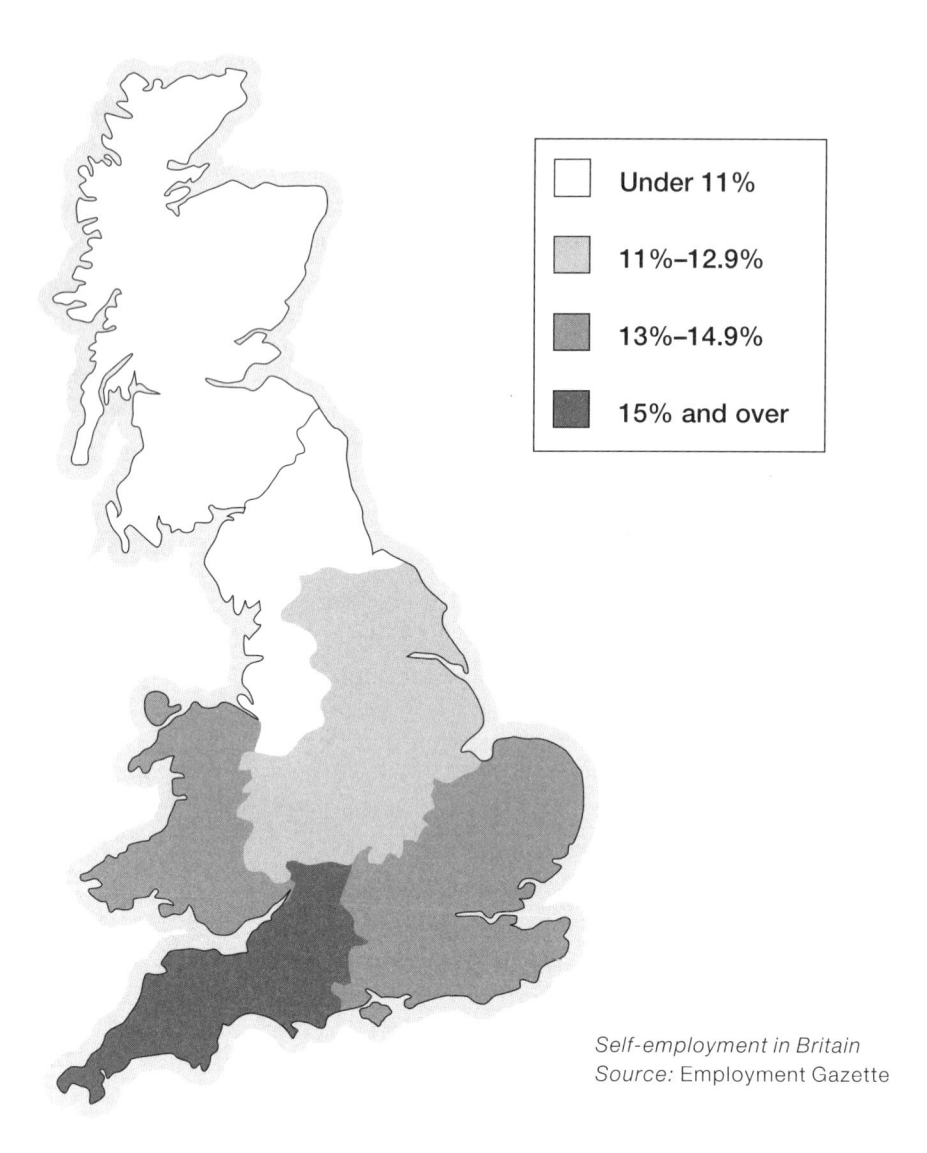

☐	Under 11%
▨	11%–12.9%
▨	13%–14.9%
■	15% and over

Self-employment in Britain
Source: Employment Gazette

Where you live can also make a difference if you want to be self-employed. You may need to be located near to a ready source of customers, with suppliers nearby and good transport links. As the map above shows, self-employment is more common in some regions of the Britain than in others.

A Finding out about self-employment

If you are interested in being self-employed, the following organisations may be able to give you useful guidance:
- Training and Enterprise Council (TEC)
- Federation of Self-Employed
- Chamber of Commerce
- banks.

Look up the addresses and phone numbers of your local organisations. Contact them, and ask for information about self-employment. What can they tell you about funding your own business, in particular:
- business start-up?
- enterprise schemes?

Carry out this activity as a group, so that only one person contacts each organisation.

People in business organisations

If you are interested in voluntary work, the following may be useful sources of information:
- charitable organisations
- your local volunteer bureau, which will co-ordinate voluntary work in your area
- advertisements asking for help in local papers.

Analysing skills needed

Before you can move forward into employment or self-employment, you need to:
- identify the skills you have now
- consider ways in which you could improve and develop these skills.

Don't forget that through your GNVQ course you are developing relevant and valuable skills for employment:

SOUTH KENT RELATE IS LOOKING TO RECRUIT VOLUNTEER COUNSELLORS

We are looking for people who have
- a minimum of 10 hours a week (mostly in the evening) to give to Relate (4 hours of which will be face to face counselling with clients)
- considerable life and family experience
- an interest in other people and couple problems
- good listening and communication skills
- a warm personality and a flexible and accepting attitude to people

We offer
- A two and a half year training leading to the Relate Certificate in Marital and Couple Counselling. This includes 6 Regional Training days and 6 two and a half day residential courses at Rugby
- High quality group and individual supervision
- The opportunity to work with clients in a safe and monitored setting
- The opportunity to be part of a leading National organisation working to improve the quality of family life

Relate is an Equal Opportunities Employer and welcome applications from all sections of the local community.

If you are interested in finding out more information about applying to be a Relate counsellor please write enclosing a large S.A.E to:

South Kent Relate, 9 West Cliff Gardens, Folkestone, Kent CT20 1SP.

Skills you are developing:
- Decision-making
- Communication
- Working with others
- Application of Number
- Information technology
- Working independently
- Evaluating
- Information seeking
- Time management
- Planning
- Problem-solving

A Developing skills

Make a copy of the following chart, and fill in:
- one example of when you have used each skill during your GNVQ
- one example of how this skill might be useful in a job.

People in business organisations

Skill	When have you used it in your GNVQ?	How might you use it in a job?
Working with others		
Working independently		
Time management		
Decision-making		
Problem-solving		
Planning		
Information seeking		
Evaluating		
Communication		
Application of Number		
Information Technology		

© L. Daniel, J. Joslin, K. McCafferty, L. Porter, A. Thomas 1996. Intermediate GNVQ Business.

▶ General skills for GNVQ Business, page 1

Occupational skills

The skills listed above, which you are developing during your GNVQ, are transferable skills – they will be useful whatever job you decide to do in the future. Once you start work you will also need to develop occupational skills – skills which are needed for a particular type of job.
Occupational skills vary from job to job:

A **secretary** or administrator may need occupational skills in:
- typing/keyboarding/word processing
- using computer packages
- filing
- organising meetings
- taking minutes
- organising mailings
- dealing with telephone enquiries.

An **accountant** may need occupational skills in:
- cash flow analysis
- providing financial advice
- using computer packages
- preparing end-of-year figures
- auditing clients' accounts
- budgeting.

You can develop some of these occupational skills by taking qualifications. For example:
- a secretary may develop occupational skills by taking vocational qualifications such as an NVQ or a GNVQ, City & Guilds, RSA or BTEC course, or going on other training courses
- a qualified accountant has to take professional accountancy exams, which may include a degree and/or NVQs in Accountancy.

However, in many cases occupational skills are developed on the job – learnt through experience.

A What skills do they have?

Talk to five people you know who work in different jobs. Ask them:
- what skills they need to do their job well
- how they developed these occupational skills
- how they aim to improve their occupational skills.

Produce a chart showing the information about occupational skills for each job.

These days 'lifelong learning' is encouraged and many individuals continue to receive education and training throughout their working lives. This could include professional updates to ensure knowledge is in line with current thinking. The workforce has to be flexible, as it needs to adapt to change. Technological change in a particular industry, for example, can lead to changes in the workforce requirements of that industry.

Summary questions

By answering these questions, you will put together your own summary of Unit 2. This will help you prepare for the unit test.

1. Explain the difference between a public limited company and a private limited company.
2. Describe the difference between a hierarchical structure and a flat structure.
3. Make a list of the functions carried out by the following departments:
   - sales
   - marketing
   - finance
   - human resources.
4. List three activities undertaken by a managing director, a manager and a supervisor.
5. Explain the difference between flexible working hours and shift work.
6. Why must an organisation be aware of its competition?
7. State what are an employer's responsibility is regarding health and safety.
8. Why should an employee receive a contract of employment? Within what time period must the employer issue it?
9. State three functions of a trade union.
10. Why might an employee go to an industrial tribunal?
11. Explain what funding is available to someone setting up their own business.
12. If you wanted to work in France, where would you look for information about jobs?
13. List five voluntary organisations.

People in business organisations

Assignment

INSIDE AN ORGANISATION

Setting the scene
In the first section of this Unit you found out about AL's mobile phone business and the San Clu Hotel. To carry out this assignment you should either use the information from these case studies, or collect information from two business organisations in your area. If you decide to research your own business organisations, you must make sure that you select one business with a hierarchical structure, and another with a flatter or matrix-type structure. Your organisations should include examples of staff who work as part of a team.

Task 1
Produce organisational charts showing the structures and departments of your two business organisations. Don't forget that their structures must be different (hierarchical, flat or matrix).

Describe the differences between the two organisational charts you have produced.

Check with your tutor that the organisations you have chosen, and the chart you have drawn, are appropriate, before moving on to the remaining tasks.

▶ Organisational structures, page 139

Task 2
Your charts will show departments within your two organisations. Describe the different work of these departments.

Some departments can be linked and are dependent on each other. Explain why this is, and give examples to support and illustrate your written work.

Task 3
All organisations have different working arrangements. Describe and compare the working arrangements within your two organisations. You should consider:
- the full-time: part-time staffing ratio
- the types of contracts that employees have
- the hours that staff work
- whether different activities are centralised or decentralised.

▶ Working arrangements, page 139

Task 4
Choose one of your organisations, and explain why it introduced team working. Summarise how teams operate within the business, and list the advantages and disadvantages of working in teams.

▶ Working as a team, page 143

Task 5
Choose one of your business organisations, and write a brief summary explaining:
- the effect that technology has had on the organisation
- why it is important for the business to remain competitive, and how it makes changes to achieve this.

▶ Reasons for changing working arrangements, page 151

Task 6
An organisational chart identifies people as well as departments. In order for a business to run smoothly, employees need to understand where they fit in, what their job roles are, and the tasks expected of them.

Look at one of your chosen businesses, and research three jobs at different levels – a director, a supervisor, and a clerk. Write a summary of each of the jobs, including:
- what activities the employee does on a day-to-day basis
- their specific tasks and responsibilities
- how team working helps them do their job.

Task 7
Choose one of the job roles you looked at in Task 6, and prepare a detailed presentation on this job role and the activities and tasks undertaken by the person carrying out this role. Your presentation should include a description of how the employee deals with:
- one routine problem-solving task.
- one non-routine task, such as an accident or emergency.

You might find it helpful to use the image of your organisational chart to support your presentation.

Make your presentation to your tutor and members of your group. Invite questions from the audience, and respond to them. Remember to play a positive role in responding to the presentations of others in your group.

▶ Job roles, page 136

▶ Routine tasks, pages 136, 137, 138

▶ Non-routine tasks, page 138

▶ Making presentations, page 11

Opportunities to collect evidence
On completing these tasks you will have the opportunity to meet the following requirements for Intermediate GNVQ Business.
Unit 2
Element 2.1 PCs 1, 2, 3, 4, 5
Element 2.3 PC 1, 2, 3, 4, 5

Core skills
Application of Number
Element 2.1

Communication
Elements 2.1, 2.2, 2.3

Information Technology
Element 2.4

▶ Core skills coverage grid, page 252

Assignment

EMPLOYMENT BOOKLET

Setting the scene
You work as a personnel assistant in The National Brand Paper Company. The company produces business paper – including copier paper and laser printing paper – from pulp shipped in from Scandinavia.

The personnel manager asks you to prepare a booklet to give to all new staff when they start work for the company. The booklet is to be called 'Your Rights and Responsibilities at Work', and is to deal with issues of employment law and what to do when disputes arise between employers and employees. The information should be divided into four main sections:
- the benefits gained by co-operation between employer and employees
- the rights and responsibilities of employers and employees in relation to health and safety at work
- the rights and responsibilities of employers and employees in relation to equal opportunities
- what to do in the case of disagreements.

Task 1
Decide how you are going to produce and lay out your booklet. It should be as user friendly as possible, and suitable for the audience (new employees). Find out if any employers in your area will give you copies of the materials they give their employees.

People in business organisations

▶ The benefits of employers and employees co-operating, page 153

▶ Health and safety, page 155

▶ Legislation, page 256

▶ Equal opportunities, page 156

▶ Legislation, page 256

▶ Resolving disagreements, page 159

Opportunities to collect evidence
On completing these tasks you will have the opportunity to meet the following requirements for Intermediate GNVQ Business.
Unit 2
Element 2.2 PCs 1, 2, 3, 4

Core skills
Communication
Elements 2.1, 2.2, 2.3, 2.4

▶ Core skills coverage grid, page 252

▶ Employment case studies, pages 162 and 164

Task 2
Call the first section of the booklet 'The Benefits of Co-operation'. Write a summary of the different ways The National Brand Paper Company, and its employees, would benefit from co-operating.

Task 3
Call the second section of the booklet 'Health and Safety: rights and responsibilities'. Explain:
- the rights and responsibilities of employers
- the rights and responsibilities of employees
- the legislation which deals with health and safety at work.

Task 4
Call the third section of the booklet 'Equal Opportunities: rights and responsibilities'. This should cover employees' rights to fair treatment regardless of race, sex, age or disability. Explain: the rights and responsibilities of employers
- the rights and responsibilities of employees
- the legislation which deals with equal opportunities in the workplace.

Task 5
Call the fourth section of the booklet 'Disagreements and How to Resolve Them'. Summarise the different ways in which employers and employees can try to resolve disagreements, including ACAS, industrial tribunals and the European Court of Justice.

Assignment

JUST THE JOB

Setting the scene
In this assignment you will find out about different jobs and the skills you need to do them well.

Task 1
Choose three people:
- one person who works in the voluntary sector
- one person who is self-employed
- one person in paid employment.

Interview them to find out:
- their name
- what type of employment they are in
- how they came to be in their current employment the skills required for the type of job they do.

With their permission, write a summary of the interviews.

Task 2
Collect job advertisements, articles and careers information on 15 different jobs. Include information on at least three voluntary jobs, three opportunities for self-employment, and three opportunities for paid employment. You should also ensure that you have a variety of local, national and international job opportunities.

You may find the following sources of information helpful:
- local and national newspapers
- your careers adviser
- your local Job Centre
- employment agencies
- the Federation of Self-Employed
- banks
- your local Training and Enterprise Council (TEC)
- charitable organisations.

Keep a detailed record of all your information sources.

Task 3

Divide the job opportunities you have collected into the following categories:
- local
- national
- international.

Draw a pie chart to show the proportion of jobs which are in each category.

Display the information on a poster, explaining the different opportunities for employment and self-employment.

Task 4

Decide which sector the job opportunities you have identified can be placed in. Are they:
- public sector
- private sector
- charity
- voluntary.

What fraction of the job opportunities are in the public sector?

If your information was typical, what is the probability that the next job opportunity you find will be in the private sector?

Task 5

Use a computer to produce a table like the one below, displaying the information you have collected in Tasks 2, 3 and 4.

Job	Location	Company	Category	Sector	Source
Sales rep	Leeds	Uniprice	National	Private	Telegraph

Compare your table with another student's. Would the tables help you recommend an information source to someone seeking a particular type of job? If not, why not? Record a summary of your discussion.

▶ Sources of employment information, page 165

▶ Employment opportunities, page 165

▶ Pie charts, pages 44 and 51

▶ Types of business ownership, pages 83, 91 and 163

▶ Probability, page 55

Opportunities to collect evidence
On completing these tasks you will have the opportunity to meet the following requirements for Intermediate GNVQ Business.
Unit 2
Element 2.4 PCs 1, 2, 3, 4

Core skills
Application of Number
Elements 2.1, 2.3

Communication
Elements 2.1, 2.2, 2.3, 2.4

Information Technology
Elements 2.1, 2.2, 2.3

▶ Core skills coverage grid, page 252

People in business organisations

Assignment

YOUR SKILLS

Setting the scene
An important part of preparing for employment is analysing your skills. You may be surprised just how many you already have!

Task 1
Make a copy of the following skills analysis form and complete the yes/no box. This will help you discover your strengths and weaknesses.

	Yes	No
I am well organised	☐	☐
I am punctual	☐	☐
I am reliable	☐	☐
I am prepared to work unsociable hours	☐	☐
I am sociable	☐	☐
I like working with figures	☐	☐
I like talking to people	☐	☐
I like using a computer	☐	☐
I can plan my time	☐	☐
I can keep to deadlines	☐	☐
I can research information	☐	☐
I can make decisions	☐	☐
I can work as part of a team	☐	☐
I prefer to work on my own	☐	☐
I can solve problems	☐	☐

Task 2
List any occupational skills you have – for example, typing/word processing, filing, using computer packages, operating a till.

Task 3
Write down brief suggestions of how you could develop your skills.

Task 4
Arrange a meeting with your careers adviser or tutor, and discuss your strengths and weaknesses in relation to skills for employment. Consider how your skills could prepare you for self-employment, paid employment, and working in the community.

Keep a record of:
- the date of this discussion
- who was present
- a summary of the discussion which took place.

Opportunities to collect evidence
On completing these tasks you will have the opportunity to meet the following requirements for Intermediate GNVQ Business.
Unit 2
Element 2.4 PCs 4, 5

Core skills
Communication
Elements 2.1, 2.2

▶ Core skills coverage grid, page 252

© L. Daniel, J. Joslin, K. McCafferty, L. Porter, A. Thomas 1996.
Intermediate GNVQ Business.

Self-check questions

Each of the following questions shows four possible answers – **a**, **b**, **c** and **d**. Only **one** is correct.

1. If an organisation has a flat structure, it has:
   a. four or five levels   c. five or six levels
   b. two or three levels   d. more than six levels.

2. An organisational chart shows:
   a. how a company organises its filing system
   b. what to do about unpaid bills
   c. who the shareholders are
   d. the people who work for a company.

3. A hierarchical structure can also be known as:
   a. a matrix structure   c. a pyramid structure
   b. a flat structure   d. a clover structure.

4. If customers have queries about products, they should contact:
   a. the human resource department
   b. the administration department
   c. the research and development department
   d. the customer service department.

5. Paying an invoice is the responsibility of:
   a. the sales and marketing department
   b. the human resource department
   c. the production department
   d. the finance department.

6. One responsibility of the human resources department is:
   a. buying machinery
   b. maintaining employee records
   c. producing customer accounts
   d. issuing new stock.

7. If Joe works from 10 a.m. until 6 p.m. one week, and then from 2 p.m. until 10 p.m. the next week, this is known as:
   a. flexi-time   c. standard week
   b. shift work   d. factory hours.

8. One benefit of working in a team is that the team members can:
   a. ignore each other
   b. think they are always right
   c. contribute to the decision-making process
   d. be selfish.

9. Quality assurance is important to a business because:
   a. it helps pay high wages
   b. it helps meet targets quickly
   c. it helps the product sell well
   d. it helps the business maintain standards.

10. Susan thinks she has been unfairly dismissed. Should she go to:
    a. her friend for help
    b. the customer service assistant
    c. her trade union representative
    d. the health and safety representative.

11. Under the Health and Safety at Work Act, employers have an obligation to:
    a. provide protective clothing
    b. provide regular tea breaks
    c. work to an agreed contract of employment
    d. let workers go home early on Friday.

12. An organisation has to issue a new employee with a contract of employment within:
    a. 3 months   c. 2 months
    b. 4 weeks   d. 1 week.

13. The employer is **not** responsible for:
    a. providing employees with a salary and an itemised pay slip
    b. providing employees with holidays
    c. training employees so they can be promoted
    d. supporting staff in the performance of their job.

14. Which of the following is an organisation that sometimes intervenes to help employers and unions settle industrial disputes?
    a. NUT   c. APEX
    b. ACAS   d. NUPE.

15. Who is responsible for ensuring that their section meets daily targets?
    a. a managing director   c. a supervisor
    b. a production operator   d. an office junior.

16. Who is most likely to be self-employed?
    a. a secretary   c. an electrician
    b. a sales assistant   d. a machine operative.

17. Who is most likely to be a voluntary worker?
    a. a builder   c. a care assistant
    b. a home help   d. an accountant.

18. If you want to set up your own business, you could approach:
    a. the Federation for the Institute of Bankers
    b. a local radio station
    c. the Training and Enterprise Council
    d. your finance department.

3 | Consumers and customers

Most of us like to buy clothes and CDs, watch the latest video or go out for the evening. Sometimes we have to visit the doctor or go to the local hospital. Whenever we do any of these things, we are consumers and customers. As such, we are an essential part of business organisations, and could be responsible for their overall success or failure.

This unit will make you realise what an important role you play as a customer, and will show how advertisements and special promotions can affect your choice. It will also show you the importance of providing good customer service – meeting customers' needs, communicating well, and following legislation. At the end of the unit you will look at customer service in one organisation in detail, and present proposals for how it might be monitored and improved.

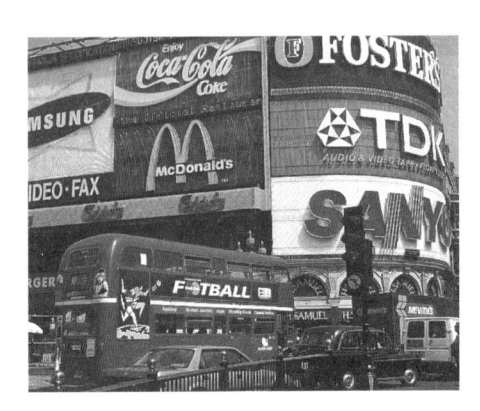

The Elements

Explain the importance of consumers and customers
- describe the effect of consumers on sales of goods and services
- identify and explain the buying habits of consumers with different characteristics
- identify trends on consumer demand
- produce graphics to illustrate the trend
- explain causes of change in consumer demand for consumer goods and services
- explain and give examples of the importance of customers to business organisations

This element describes how consumers and customers can affect the demand for, and stimulate the supply of, goods and services. You will look at the buying habits of consumers and how these have changed over the years. You will also explore the importance of customers to business organisations.

▶ The importance of consumers and customers, page 178

Plan, design and produce promotional material
- identify and give examples of types of promotions used in marketing goods and services
- describe constraints on the content of promotional materials
- plan to produce promotional materials to promote particular goods or services
- explain the purpose of the planned promotional materials
- design and produce promotional materials and use them to promote goods or services
- evaluate how successful the promotional materials were in achieving the stated purpose

In this element you will look at different types of promotions and see how they can affect a business. You will also design produce your own promotional materials.

▶ Planning, designing and producing promotional material, page 186

Providing customer service
- identify an organisation's customers and its customer needs
- identify and describe customer service in an organisation
- identify business communications which meet customer needs
- demonstrate business communications which meet customer needs
- describe procedures in one business organisation for dealing with customer complaints
- identify relevant legislation to protect customers

While the first two elements look at what attracts customers, the third focuses on the type of service which organisations provide to keep their customers happy. You will look at how businesses communicate with their customers, how they deal with complaints, and legislation in place to protect customers.

▶ Providing customer service, page 195

Present proposals for improvements to customer service
- explain the importance of customer service in business organisations
- identify how business organisations monitor customer satisfaction
- identify improvements to customer service
- present proposals for improvements to customer service in one organisation

▶ Improving customer service, page 200

177

Consumers and customers

We have all experienced good and bad customer service at some time. The last element in this unit looks at how organisations monitor customer satisfaction, and how improvements are made.

The importance of consumers and customers

From a very young age we are all consumers – people who use goods and services. Once we are older, and have money of our own, we also become customers – people who buy goods and services.

Have you ever stopped to consider how important you – the customer – are to a business? Without customers spending money, business organisations could not survive.

Customers:
- create income for a business by spending money on its goods and services
- contribute to profit
- bring repeat business to an organisation. If customers are satisfied with a product or service, they will probably buy it again and tell their friends. The more customers a business has, the more profit it is likely to make
- ensure the survival of a business, by bringing in the money it needs to pay rent, wages, buy stock and so on
- are a good source of information. By carrying out marketing research among their customers, businesses can find out what people need and want. They can then improve old products or create new ones, attract new customers, and increase their profitability.

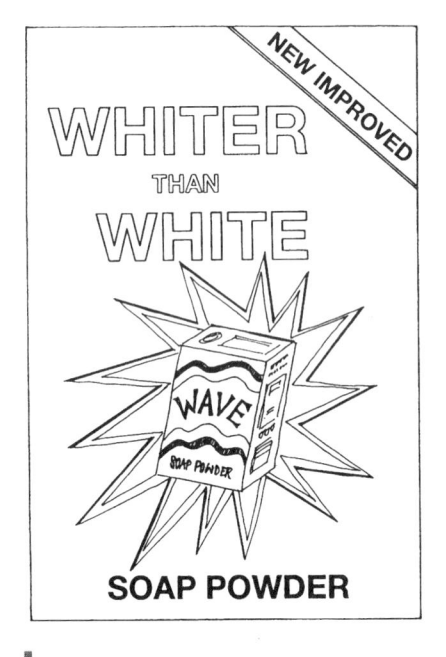

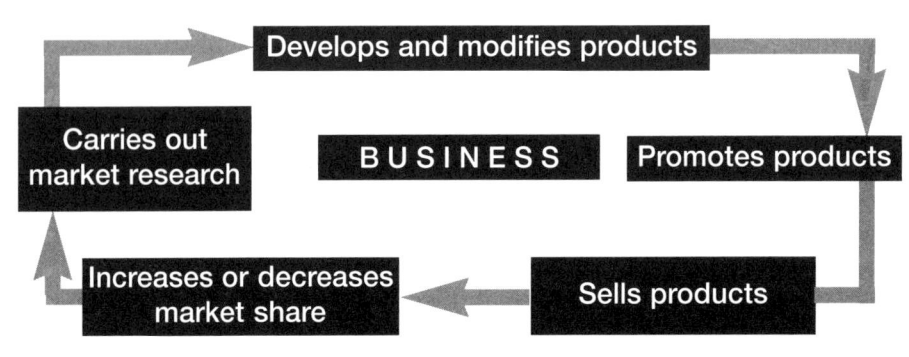

The effect of consumers on sales of goods and services

Every day, British consumers spend millions of pounds on goods and services. These goods and services can be divided into:
- **needs** – which are essential, such as a place to live, food to eat, clothes to wear
- **wants** – luxuries which improve the quality of our lives, such as designer label clothes, fast food, video players, CDs.

▶ Customer needs and wants, page 105

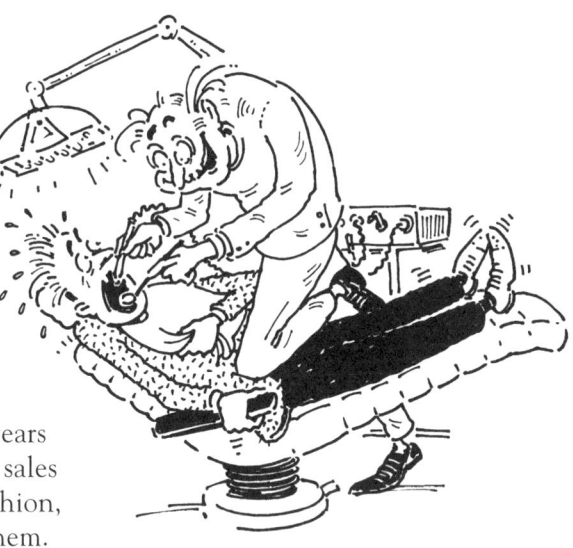

People's needs and wants depend on the society they live in. In the UK, we consider services such as healthcare, water, lighting and heating as essentials. In other societies, expectations and needs may be higher or lower.

In buying their needs and wants, consumers create demand for particular goods and services. Demand is reflected in the number of products sold.
- If sales are consistently high, it is because demand is **strong** or prices are low (lots of people want or need the product)
- If sales are falling, it is because demand is **weak** or the prices are high (fewer people want or need the product).

The demand for a product can change rapidly. For example, a few years ago shell suits were fashionable. Many people wanted to buy them, sales rose, and demand was strong. But shell suits quickly went out of fashion, and today demand is weak, with just a few people wanting to buy them.

'Just what I've always wanted...'

▶ Consumer and customer demand, page 107

Consumer demand for a product can change almost overnight

As well as fashion, the amount of money which people have to spend on goods and services can affect demand. People with a low income have low buying power, and are less likely to affect demand than people with a high income and high buying power. For example, someone with a low income may want a large house, expensive car and a yacht, but they are unable to buy them and will not affect actual demand.

Because of this, demand for goods and services changes at times of high unemployment. Consumers have less money or feel insecure in their jobs, do not spend as much money, and demand falls.

A Consumers and change in demand

What factors do you think would cause a change in demand for the following goods and services?
- CDs by a particular band
- private schooling
- dishwashers
- flared trousers

Consumers and customers

Manufacturers produce goods and services to meet consumer demand. Therefore:
- when demand is weak, fewer goods and services are supplied
- when demand is strong, more goods and services are supplied.

Sometimes, if demand rises very rapidly, manufacturers cannot produce products quickly enough to meet consumers' needs. This often happens with children's toys just before Christmas. There is a craze for a particular toy; thousands of children ask their parents for it; and the manufacturer cannot supply enough to meet the demand in shops. As a result there is a shortage and shops can take advantage of this and increase the price.

A Supply and demand

Can you think of occasions when you have wanted to buy a particular product and have not been able to? Do you think this has been because demand has been greater than supply? What other reasons might there be? What is likely to happen to the price of a product where demand is greater than supply?

The buying habits of consumers

You decide you want to buy a new pair of jeans. What will influence your choice?

Price?

Fashion?

Label?

Comfort?

Style?

Material?

Strength?

What your friends think?

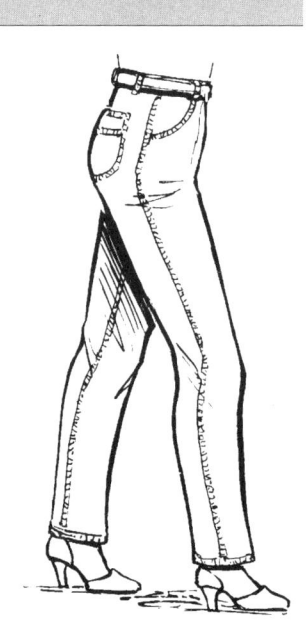

A Designer trainers

Would you buy the same pair of trainers as someone 25 years older than you, or as someone of the other sex? Explain your answer.

Many factors affect what consumers buy, including:
- age
- gender (whether they are male or female)
- where they live
- their lifestyle (fashion, tastes and preferences).

Manufacturers need to take these factors into account when designing and making products. For example, a company which manufactures trainers will target some pairs at a young market, and others at an older market. Young people are more interested in fashion and designer labels, and will probably be influenced by their friends (peer group pressure). Older people may be more concerned with price (value for money), comfort and style.

These factors also influence the way goods and services are marketed. For example, toy manufacturers try to catch the attention of children by producing bright, lively advertisements and screening them during children's television programmes. Although the children have no buying power, they then try to persuade adults to buy the toys for them. Catching the attention of a particular target market means:
- giving the right type of information in the right way
- placing the advertisement in the right magazine or newspaper, or at the right time on television or radio.

Children may not be customers, but they are a powerful consumer group

A Targeting advertising

In which magazines would you expect to find the following items advertised? Give reasons for your answers and try to find as many examples as you can.

- sports deodorant
- hair gel
- sanitary towels
- camping holidays
- suntan lotion
- remote control cars
- disposable nappies
- slimming foods
- family health cover
- cars
- building bricks

What does this activity show you about the buying habits of men and women of different ages and lifestyles?

Consumers and customers

Business organisations also need to think about regional differences when producing and marketing goods and services.

People living in different parts of the UK, and in different countries of the world, have varying needs and expectations. A large, international chain of stores like C&A carries out thorough marketing research to ensure its shops have suitable stock for its customers in every area. This is because:

- fashions vary from region to region
- customers who live in an area of high unemployment will spend less on luxury items of clothing and more on practical, everyday wear
- customers need different clothes depending on the climate.

So a shopping centre in Glasgow would probably sell different stock to a shopping centre in Brighton. The shops may be the same, but the stock will be different. If you visit a Marks & Spencer food hall in a provincial town, it will probably stock a smaller range of sandwiches than a major store in London.

A Geographical buying habits

Next time you visit a town or city in another part of the UK, or a different country, compare the types of products and services on sale to those which are available in your own home town. How do you think the differences reflect the needs and wants of consumers in each place?

As you will have seen, different types of consumers buy different types of goods and services. But they also have different levels and frequency of buying.

Some people will spend every penny they earn on goods and services, from food they buy regularly on a day-to-day basis, to major clothes shopping sprees once a month. Others will be much more careful, keeping track of how much they spend and how often they shop.

Trends in consumer demand

Consumer demand is constantly changing. Different products come in and out of fashion. New goods and services become available. The amount people spend on products rises and falls.

In many cases, what is fashionable and popular this year will be outdated and out of the shops by next year. These changes in consumer demand are known as trends. Business organisations need to monitor trends in consumer demand closely, so that they make sure they are producing the right products, at the right price, at the right time. For example, a record producer will look closely at patterns of sales for records, cassette tapes and CDs in general, and will monitor the sales of music by particular groups.

Consumers have different levels of buying

New technology has had a major effect on consumer demand this century

A generation ago, the pattern for most families was for the father to go to work and the mother to stay at home raising the children. She would walk to the local shops daily to stock up on fresh produce, and then go home to prepare the evening meal. She may have had a fridge, but would not have had a freezer or microwave. There were no superstores, and she probably did not have a car.

Today's family is completely different. Mothers often go out to work, and have less time for shopping. Nearly all family shopping is done just once or twice a week, in superstores on the outskirts of towns which people travel to by car or taxi. Freezers and microwave ovens mean that fresh food can be frozen, and people buy more convenience foods which can be cooked or re-heated in a microwave when required.

A Then and now

Interview someone born between 1920 and 1940, and ask them the following questions.
1 How have your food shopping patterns changed over the years?
2 What household appliances do you have today that you did not have when you were in your teens?
3 Are there any goods which were available in the past which aren't available today?
4 Has your standard of living improved? If so, how? Do you own more luxury items?

From the information they give you, write a list of examples of increasing consumer demand, and decreasing consumer demand.

Trends in consumer demand can either be:
- short-term (lasting for under six months)
- long-term (lasting for over two or three years).

Most of the trends you have identified so far will probably be long-term. Short-term trends are usually for fast-selling, short-life products such as concert tickets or computer games.

A Into the future

How do you think consumer trends might change in the future? Think of two short-term trends and two long-term trends you think are likely to happen.

Consumers and customers

Causes of change in demand

One of the major influences on consumer demand for goods and services is the amount of money people have to spend. This is affected by:
- the cost of living – how much people need to spend on essential items for everyday living
- earnings – how much money people earn from working
- discretionary income – how much money people have left after paying tax and national insurance.

The table below shows:
- the average amount people earned per week in 1993 and 1994
- the cost of living – the average amount people spent on needs such as food, gas and electricity
- discretionary income – the amount people had left to spend on luxury items and savings.

The cost of living and earnings

Year	Average weekly earnings (£)	Average weekly expenditure (£)	Average discretionary income (£)
1993	316.9	276.68	40.62
1994	325.7	283.58	42.12

Source: Annual Abstract of Statistics, Social Trends

As the table shows, although average weekly earnings rose from 1993 to 1994, so did the cost of living. In both years, people spent 87% of their earnings on basics, leaving just 13% for luxury items.

A Costs and consumer demand

From the figures given here, how do you think consumer demand has changed from 1993 to 1994? How might it have changed if:
- people's earnings had increased but the cost of living had fallen or remained the same?
- people's earnings had decreased but the cost of living had risen or remained the same?

Keep a record of what you spend money on each week. How much do you have available to spend? (This is your earnings.) How much do you spend on needs? (This is your cost of living.) How much do you have to spend in total? What is your discretionary income? If your earnings increased or prices were lower, how would it change your demand for goods and services?

As well as having money to spend, consumers need to have the confidence to spend it. At times of recession and high unemployment, people worry about the future and tend to save money rather than spending it on luxury goods and services. As a result, consumer demand falls.

At such times – when people have a limited amount of money to spend and are careful about how they use it – businesses need to invest extra time and money in analysing their customers' needs and wants. They will only attract customers if they provide the right products at the right price.

During a recession, consumers tend to think carefully about how they spend every penny

When people have a larger amount of discretionary income, and have the confidence to spend more freely, businesses can afford to advertise more to persuade customers to spend their money. A clever advertising campaign – such as those in recent years for ice-cream chocolate bars and air-cushioned running shoes – can increase consumer demand, or even create it from nothing.

A   Advertising campaigns

List ten recent advertising campaigns that have caught your attention (you don't necessarily have to like them). Alongside the name of the product or service, say whether you think the campaign increased demand. Explain your opinion.

Consumer demand is about meeting people's needs and wants. When these change, consumer demand changes. The most common reasons for needs and wants changing are:
- changing fashion
- new technology
- changing lifestyle.

The table below shows that the consumer demand for new technology grew enormously between 1981 and 1993. Businesses manufacturing goods like these have to constantly produce new and better products to keep up with consumer demand.

Percentage of households with consumer durables

	1981 (%)	1991 (%)	1993 (%)
Colour television	74	95	96
Black and white television only	23	4	3
Telephone	75	88	90
Washing machine	78	87	88
Deep-freezer/fridge freezer	49	83	87
Video recorder	-	68	73
Microwave	-	55	62
Tumble drier	23	48	49
Compact disc player	-	27	39
Dishwasher	4	14	16

Source: Social Trends

A   Trends in your group

Design a data collection sheet to find out the number of people in your group who have the different consumer goods listed above. Work out the percentage in each case.

Draw a composite bar chart to present your information and compare it to the figures for 1981, 1991 and 1993.

Does your graph indicate a change in trends? Or are trends continuing? Which items are increasing in popularity, and which are decreasing?

▶ Percentages, page 32

▶ Bar charts, page 46

Planning, designing and producing promotional material

Almost all businesses use promotional materials of some kind to market their organisation, goods and services. The main aims of promotion are to:
- create demand – make people want a product more
- create awareness – launch a new product
- raise awareness of an existing product – attract customers with special offers
- counter the competition – promote a product as better than others on the market
- increase sales – sell more of a product to customers
- increase distribution – encourage more outlets to sell a product.

Most business organisations use a range of different types of promotion to achieve these goals.

Types of promotion

Every day we are surrounded by promotional images – on the television, on commercial radio, in shops, on billboards, on the inside and outside of buses, in newspapers and magazines, even on footballers' shirts...

These can be divided into four different types of promotion:
- point-of-sale
- sponsorship
- advertisements
- competitions.

Point-of-sale

Point-of-sale promotions are any promotional materials on display at the place where goods and services are sold – usually in a shop. They may include:
- posters
- leaflets on goods and services
- displays on special offers
- free samples.

If you shop regularly in a supermarket, you will have noticed tempting items on display at the checkout – from confectionery and magazines to end-of-line bargains and special promotions. These are usually luxury items which you did not plan to buy, but which tempt you while you queue. Companies supplying these items may come to arrangements, such as a discount to the store, if their goods are displayed in a prime position. Many large supermarkets have responded to customer comments about displays encouraging children to eat sweets by removing all goods from the checkout area.

A — Point-of-sale promotion

Supermarket chains have a variety of point-of-sale promotions running at any one time. Visit your local supermarket and list as many special promotions, posters and displays as you can see. Be prepared to look closely – you may find that each checkout has its own display.

Advertisements

Advertising is the most popular way of promoting goods and services. Businesses can choose whether to advertise:
- in magazines and newspapers
- on posters and advertising billboards
- on radio or television.

Which method they choose to use will usually depend on what they are trying to promote, who they are trying to promote it to, and how much money they have to spend.

For example, advertisements in magazines and newspapers may be seen by a wide audience, and publications can be chosen to suit the content of the advertisement (a local paper to advertise a local event, a golf magazine to advertise golfing holidays, and so on). However, advertising in national magazines can be expensive, and people often flick through a paper or magazine without looking at the advertisements. Posters can be bright and eye-catching, but often get damaged. Advertising on radio is inexpensive, but people tend to forget radio advertisements quite quickly.

Consumers and customers

A — Spot the advertisement

Between getting out of bed and arriving at school or college tomorrow, count the number of advertisements you see or hear. Make a list of all the advertisements, stating what they were for and where you saw them. When an organisation chooses several different methods of advertising, you should mention them all.

Sponsorship

An effective way of advertising a product or organisation is to sponsor:
- a team. If you watch a football match, you will notice the players may have the name of an organisation printed on their football strip (team sponsorship). Formula One racing teams are sponsored by companies, and have logos painted on their cars, crash helmets and clothing
- a person – some businesses choose to sponsor an individual, such as a tennis or badminton player, rather than a team
- an event – from local, community-based events, to national sporting events
- a television or radio programme – from drama and films to the weather forecast.

A — Sponsorship

Draw a table like the one below. In groups, brainstorm as many television sponsorship deals as you can think of, to complete the table.

Television programme	Sponsor
Weather forecast	Powergen

Competitions

Have you ever been tempted to buy things you do not want or need simply to be eligible for a competition? Many organisations use competitions to promote their products and increase sales. Competitions attract customers, particularly if they have a chance of winning the holiday of a lifetime or a dream car. Often, customers have to buy several of the same product to collect enough tokens to enter a competition.

Competitions do not have to be on a large scale to attract customers, and might only target certain customer groups. For example, a high street chemist might hold a children's colouring competition. The child would have fun colouring the picture, and the adult would be made aware of the business.

Direct mail

Many businesses use large databases containing information about their customers as a basis for promotion. Leaflets and individual letters can be sent to customers' home addresses as a means of promoting the products and services offered by businesses. These direct mail techniques, used by banks, insurance companies and retailers allows the business to get direct access to people who are interested in their products and services.

General publicity

This can help to promote products. For example, when a band release a new single, they may play on prime time television shows. They could also be interviewed on television and radio chat shows. Paul Newman's salad dressing was promoted on a chat show where Paul was the guest. Sales increased from less than 1% of the UK market to about 20% at the time. Press releases, newspaper and television stories all help to promote particular products.

Constraints on promotional materials

Companies cannot advertise exactly as they may wish to – there are constraints placed on them in the form of legislation (laws) and standards.

The main legislation which affects advertising is:
- Trades Description Act
- Sale of Goods Act
- Consumer Protection Act.

▶ Legislation, page 256

As well as legislation, there are standards authorities set up to protect the public from offensive and misleading advertisements.

Every local authority has a Trading Standards Office which ensures that consumer legislation is not being broken. The work of a Trading Standards Officer may range from checking that a market trader is not selling counterfeit goods, to sampling spirits in a pub to ensure they have not been diluted with water. All goods offered for sale should have an accurate label – the description should be correct and the weight on the label should match the actual contents in the packaging.

The Advertising Standards Authority exists to ensure that all advertisements conform to the British Code of Advertising Practice, which states that advertisements should be:
- legal
- decent
- honest
- truthful.

In addition, advertisements should not cause 'grave or widespread offence'. For example, the Advertising Standards Authority stopped a clothing company displaying posters showing a person dying from AIDS.

The Trading Standards Office checks that goods live up to their labels

A What you see is what you get

Look carefully at advertisements on television and in newspapers and magazines. Do any give a misleading impression? Might any cause offence to some people?

Consumers and customers

Planning, designing and producing materials

Promotion can be very expensive, and when an organisation decides to mount a promotional campaign it must take great care to plan every stage carefully. If a company has a marketing manager, he or she will have a promotional budget and be responsible for deciding what form promotion should take.

Case study: Welcome Weekends

The Rosetown Hotel decided to launch a new range of themed weekend breaks – Welcome Weekends – during the low season, when rooms tended to be empty. The management team came up with a range of ideas for weekends, including murder-mystery breaks, health and fitness weekends, and ballroom dancing specials. The marketing manager, Anna Crick, was then asked to promote the new product.

The purpose of promotion

Anna began by thinking about the purpose of the promotional campaign for Welcome Weekends. She decided that her main aims were to:
- communicate a message to an audience of potential holidaymakers
- sell the new weekend breaks
- improve the public's perception of the hotel
- provide information about the weekend breaks, so people knew what was on offer and how to book.

Planning promotional materials

Having looked at her promotional budget, Anna decided to promote the weekend breaks through:
- advertising in magazines and newspapers
- sponsorship of the local town's football team
- a competition for guests who visit the hotel.

She began by drawing up a chart of the different resources she would need.

Plan for promoting Welcome Weekends

Time	Welcome Weekends are to start in October. Advertising should begin in July or August. We'll need three months to design and produce advertisements, so should begin work after Easter. The advertising campaign should run right through the low season, to try to catch the impulse buyer. The competition will be for guests who visit the hotel between August and October, with winners announced in November. Sponsoring the town's football team will be good timing, as the football season starts at the end of August, just before the Welcome Weekend breaks.
People	I will manage the campaign, with help from Gita (marketing assistant). Gita will also deal with the competition. The advertisements will be designed by Graphic Studio, and printed by Ark Press. We will also ask Graphic Studio to design football strips for the football team.
Equipment	No special equipment will be needed for the promotion.
Materials	We will need to buy advertising space in magazines. At least 26 football strips will need to be bought and printed with the Welcome Weekends logo.

The advertisements were going to be the most expensive part of the promotional campaign, and Anna planned these particularly carefully. She began by thinking about:
- who the Welcome Weekends were aimed at (the target for advertising)
- how to reach this target audience.

She knew that she could either decide the target group for advertising by:
- demographic group – sex (gender), age and area (national or local)
- socio-economic group – upper (A); higher professional (B); lower professional (C1); skilled non-professional (C2); manual workers, unskilled labour (D); pensioners, low-waged, unemployed (E). The letters A, B, C1, C2, D and E are a short-hand way of describing certain jobs and the level of income people earn.

After talking to the rest of the management team, Anna decided that the target group for Welcome Weekends were middle-aged couples and families living in the south-east of England (within a 50-mile radius of the hotel).

A Target groups

Which demographic groups (sex, age, area) might you target if you wished to advertise:
- expensive perfume?
- a local college?
- a toy train set?
- draught beer?

Designing and producing promotional materials

Anna and her assistant, Gita, began working on the promotional campaign by writing an advertisement for Welcome Weekends. Anna explained to Gita that people don't want to spend long reading advertisements – they skim them to pick up the key messages. Therefore it is important to:
- keep words to a minimum
- make sure the advertisement is easy to understand
- attract attention with a good headline.

Anna drew a chart showing the different types of information that should be included in an advertisement:

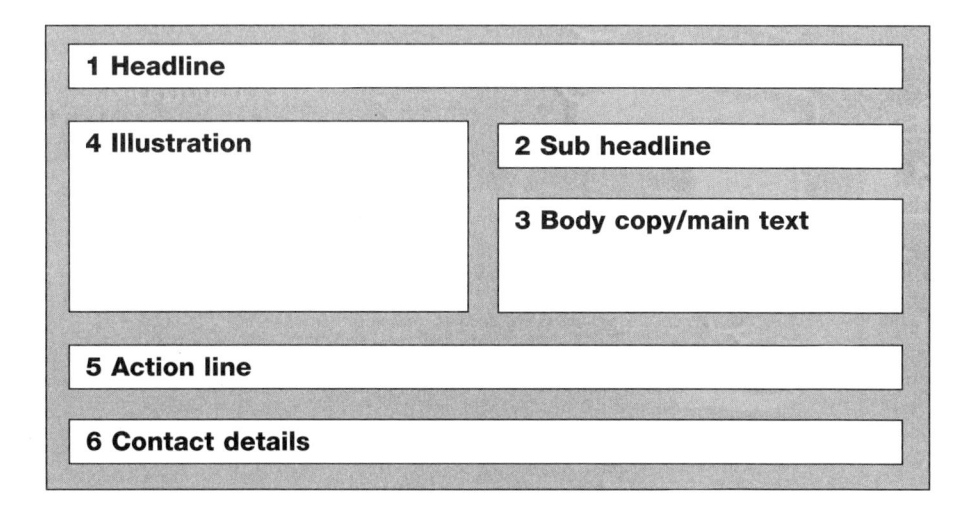

1 Headline	
4 Illustration	2 Sub headline
	3 Body copy/main text
5 Action line	
6 Contact details	

Consumers and customers

Gita looked at examples of advertisements in newspapers and magazines, to find out how different companies put the components of their advertisements together.

```
┌─ ─ ─ ─ ─ ─ ─ ─ ─ ─ ─ ─ ─ ─ ─ ─ ─ ─ ─ ─ ─┐
│          WHERE'S BASE?                   │
│                                          │
│   ╱╲         is bold, new and            │
│  ╱THE╲       innovative serving a        │
│ ╱BASEBAR╲    range of cocktails, beers   │
│  ╲    ╱     and wines from 5pm till     │
│   ╲  ╱       late 7 days a week.         │
│                                          │
│   ★★★★★★★★★★★★★★★★★★★★★★★★★★★★★★★★       │
│   ★       FREE BASEBAR FIZZ !       ★    │
│   ★         WITH THIS VOUCHER       ★    │
│   ★              WORTH £3.75        ★    │
│   ★ Offer closes 31 March 1996. Offer open only to persons over the age of 18 ★ │
│   ★★★★★★★★★★★★★★★★★★★★★★★★★★★★★★★★       │
│                                          │
│        The BaseBar is below Café Pasta,  │
│     8 The High Street, Wimbledon Village SW19 │
│              0181-944 6778               │
└─ ─ ─ ─ ─ ─ ─ ─ ─ ─ ─ ─ ─ ─ ─ ─ ─ ─ ─ ─ ─┘
```

Labels: Headline; Illustration; Sub-headline/bold copy; Action; Contact details

She then began drafting different versions of the advertisement for Welcome Weekends.

A Designing an advertisement

Design your own newspaper advertisement for Welcome Weekends. Don't forget to include:
- a bold headline
- brief, informative sub-headline and body copy
- an illustration (a photograph? cartoon? or just the Welcome Weekends logo?)
- an action line (what readers should do next)
- contact details (the address and phone number of the Rosetown Hotel – Main Street, Rosetown RT12 3DP. Tel: 01578 434098.)

Once they had written the words for their advertisement, Anna and Gita took it to a graphic design company which designed the layout (the way the advertisement would appear on the page). The designer decided to use a photograph of the hotel, and a blue headline to help catch readers' attention.

Anna and Gita then had to choose where to place their advertisement. They had already decided that their target audience was within a 50-mile radius of the hotel, so they got in touch with magazines and newspapers in this area to find out the cost of buying advertising space.

Advertising space in newspapers and magazines is usually sold in column widths. For example:
- three columns might represent 101 mm
- four columns might represent 136 mm
- five columns might represent 171 mm.

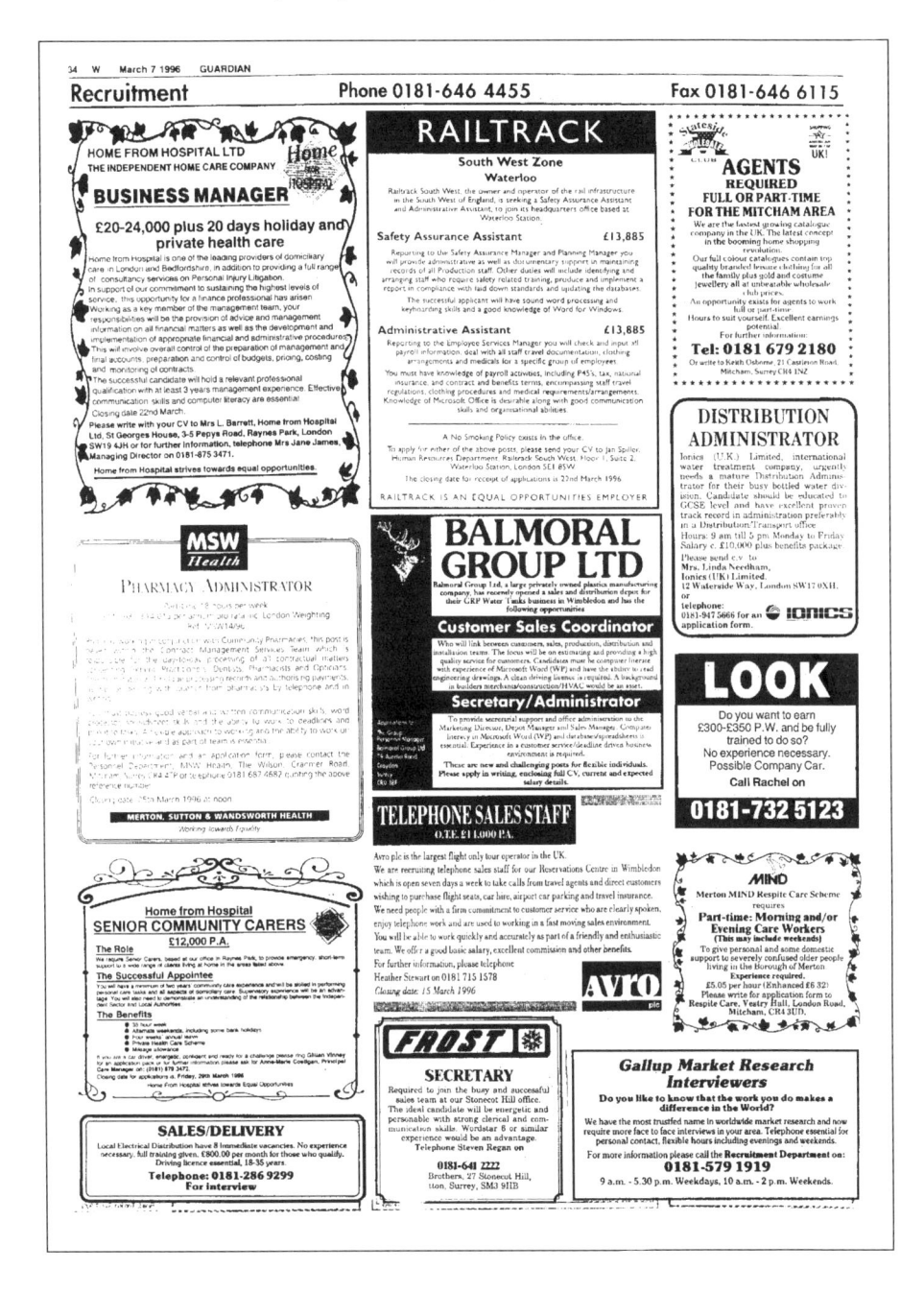

Each newspaper and magazine gave daily or weekly rates for advertising space. Anna and Gita worked out how much it would cost to place their advertisement by using the following formula:

$$\text{rate} \times \text{depth (cms)} \times \text{width (columns)} = \text{price}$$

For example, the daily rate for advertising in The Standard, a local paper, was £3.68. From this, Anna and Gita worked out that to place an advertisement which was 10 cm deep and 3 columns wide would cost:

3.68 x 10 x 3 = £101.40 for one day.

A Costing advertisements

Anna and Gita have asked you to work out how much it would cost to place an advertisement in The Standard for two days. They would like the advertisement to be 10 cm deep and 171 mm (five columns) wide. Calculate the cost using the formula above.

Designing and producing advertisements was the most complicated part of the Welcome Weekends' promotional campaign. The local football team had already approached the hotel to see if it would be interested in sponsorship, and Anna felt it would be a good way to promote the organisation and its products in the target area. The designer had already produced a logo for Welcome Weekends as part of the advertisement, and Anna arranged to have it printed on two sets of football strips for the football team.

The competition took more organising, and was Gita's responsibility. She decided that she needed to design a competition which would:
- be easy to judge
- be easy to enter
- offer a free Welcome Weekends break as a prize
- anyone staying at the hotel between August and October could enter.

Gita's competition involved answering three questions on the local area, with the winning entrant being drawn from a hat. To keep costs down, she decided to design a simple black and white leaflet on the hotel's computer, which could then be reproduced in the local print and copying shop.

A A competition leaflet

Design a leaflet for a Welcome Weekends competition in your area. Your leaflet should include:
- an explanation of the competition
- a description of the prize
- three questions about your local area, with space for entrants to answer them
- space for entrants to fill in their name and address, so you can contact the winner.

Evaluating the success of promotional materials

Business organisations need to evaluate promotional campaigns not only to find out how successful promotional materials have been, but also to learn lessons for future promotions.

Evaluation usually involves finding out:
- how effectively promotional materials are communicated to the target audience

- whether sales increased
- whether the campaign improved people's perception of the organisation and its products
- how well the materials provided information – do people know more about the organisation and its products as a result of the campaign?

To find out whether sales have increased, organisations can:
- look at sales figures
- talk to sales representatives and distributors, to find out whether interest in the product has increased since the campaign.

To find out people's response to the campaign, organisations need to talk to the target audience. They usually do this by carrying out marketing research – using surveys and questionnaires to find out what people think.

C Case study: McDonald's – Comments

McDonald's displays customer comment cards in every restaurant. Customers are encouraged to complete these, saying what they like and dislike about the restaurant and its service.

In addition, when McDonald's introduces a new product, it prepares specific questionnaires to find out customers' views and whether the product needs to be improved in any way.

A How is the new product going?

A chain of fast-food restaurants has just launched a new vege-burger, which it has promoted through:
- an advertising campaign in magazines and papers
- point-of-sale material promoting special offers
- posters on buses and billboards.

Design a questionnaire (up to ten questions long) to find out what the customers think:
- of the product
- of the promotional materials.

Providing customer service

Business organisations need to treat their customers well – provide good service – in order to keep their customers and attract new ones. To do this, they have to understand who their customers are, and meet their needs. Businesses have a responsibility towards other members of society, whether they are local residents, employers, customers or suppliers. This gives businesses the ethical responsibility to consider other people's views when deciding their own actions.

Customer needs

All customers have very specific needs. They may wish to:
- buy something
- get information about goods and services
- get a refund
- exchange goods

▶ Questionnaires, pages 20 and 21

Consumers and customers

- make a complaint.

In doing these things, they have a right to expect the business organisations they deal with to maintain certain ethical standards, and to meet any special needs they have.

For example, what are your needs when you go into a travel agency?

Your basic need is to buy a holiday. You will probably have a rough idea of your requirements. But you will need to ask the travel agent a range of questions before you choose and book your holiday:

How will I travel?
What sort of accommodation can I stay in?
Will I need to hire a car?
How much will it cost?

You may have special needs for the travel agent to take into account. For example, a person in a wheelchair may need help reaching brochures in the agency, and advice on facilities for people with disabilities at holiday resorts. Or a mother with young children may need information on creche facilities.

Whatever your needs, it is essential that the travel agent can answer your questions, and that the information he or she gives you is accurate and truthful. This means relying on the travel agent's ethical standards – being able to trust them not to send you to a half-built resort just because they will earn good commission. It is vital for customers to be able to rely on the personal honesty and integrity of the people meeting their needs.

A Obtaining information

List the different types of information a customer might need from the following organisations:
- a railway station
- a bank
- a restaurant
- a health centre
- a college.

If something goes wrong on your holiday and you want to complain, the travel agency should have systems in place to help staff handle your complaint. All organisations will face complaints from customers at some point. When there is a complaint, staff need to:
- take it seriously
- deal with it quickly and efficiently
- be courteous to the customer.

Unfortunately, you can't take a holiday back if something goes wrong. But organisations which sell goods such as clothes, books and electrical appliances need to be ready to exchange goods or offer a refund if there are problems.

▶ Dealing with customer complaints, page 199

A Exchange or refund?

Make a copy of the chart below, and list examples of occasions when you or a member of your family has exchanged a product or asked for a refund. Under the heading 'Experience', consider how easy it was to make the exchange or get the refund. For example, did you need a receipt? Were you offered a credit note? Was the exchange made without question?

Product	Retailer	Experience

Customer service

Have you ever stopped to consider what makes you choose to go to one shop rather than another? Or to one restaurant rather than another? Your first visit might be because of a friend's recommendation, a special promotion, or simply convenience. But what makes you go back again and again?

The quality of customer service you receive will probably play a part. If staff are polite, helpful and smart, you are more likely to return than if they are rude, can't give you the information you need and appear not to care about their customers.

C Case study: McDonald's customer service

Jack has recently become a McDonald's crew member. He works two evenings after college, and Saturday and Sunday. McDonald's aim is:

'100% Total Customer Satisfaction'

and all crew members are trained on-the-job in customer care. Jack will take part in McDonald's 'impressive service programme', and his progress will be monitored by a manager and recorded on an observation check list.

Before starting work at McDonald's, Jack helped his father in the family shop, and realised the importance of good customer care, although he was not given formal training.

Jack used to laugh at his father when he said 'serve as you would like to be served', and was surprised when he heard the same thing said during his training at McDonald's. Jack was also told the importance of meeting customers' special needs as efficiently as possible, whether this means helping:
- an adult to order food while keeping hold of three young children
- an elderly person with poor vision
- someone in a wheelchair
- a person who simply wants a Big Mac with extra tomato.

Crew members are encouraged to greet regular customers by name, to chat to them, and to have their orders waiting.

Consumers and customers

A Customer care

In Jack's position, what particular customer care would you provide to meet the special needs of the customers listed in the case study on page 197?

People who work for business organisations have to provide good customer service to both:

- external customers (people from outside the organisation who buy goods and services)
- internal customers (other people that they work with).

For example:

- when Jack started work at McDonald's, he was issued with a free uniform. When being issued with the uniform he was an internal, non-paying customer, and had the right to be treated with courtesy and respect
- when your tutors take photocopying to the print room in your school or college, they are internal customers.

A Customer charters

To show their commitment to good customer service, many organisations now have customer charters. How many customer charters do you know of? For example, does your college have a charter? can you get a copy of British Rail's customer charter? Ask your family and friends for help with this.

Business communications

Every time a business communicates with its customers, it is making an impression of some kind. Therefore, it is important that every piece of communication is polite, accurate and appropriate.

There are three main types of business communication:

- oral (face-to-face or over the telephone)
- written (for example, letters and memos)
- customer and product information (for example, statements of account, prices, guarantees and safety notices).

▶ Talking on the telephone, pages 10 and 11

▶ Letters, pages 15 and 16

▶ Memos, page 17

▶ Statement of account, pages 222 and 223

Most organisations communicate with their customers in a range of ways

Consumers and customers

A Looking for communications

The next time you go into a large shop, see how many different types of business communication you can identify. Look for:
- oral communications (staff talking to customers face-to-face and on the phone)
- product information (such as leaflets and brochures, price tickets, special offers, product guarantees)
- safety notices (for example, 'No Smoking' and 'Fire Exit').

It is important for business organisations to choose the most appropriate form of communication for different situations. Oral communication with a customer, either face-to-face or over the telephone, helps to build a relationship. Written communication is useful when a message is formal, and a record needs to be kept of what is being said.

C Case study: McDonald's – Communication

McDonald's uses all three types of information in different circumstances:

- Most communication with external customers is face-to-face.

- Occasionally, if a customer has a serious request or complaint, the organisation writes a letter. In addition, most behind-the-scenes communications are written. For example, staff communicate with each other by writing memos and sending faxes, and communicate with suppliers by letter, invoice, order form and so on.

- The organisation promotes new products, special offers and prices through posters, leaflets and price displays. It also produces safety notices for all its restaurants.

A Business communications

What would be the best form of communication for a shop to use in the following situations?
- When it needs to notify a customer that an urgent order has arrived.
- When it receives a serious complaint.
- When it is starting a 'buy one, get one free' promotion.
- When a customer has not paid an account.
- When staff are going to be given a bonus.

Dealing with customer complaints

As you have already seen, all business organisations should have procedures for dealing with customer complaints quickly and efficiently.

Organisations should always take customer complaints seriously...

Waiter, waiter! There's a fly in my soup.
Keep your voice down, Sir, or everyone will want one...

Consumers and customers

C Case study: McDonald's – Complaints procedure

McDonald's has a procedure which staff follow in the event of complaints. Jack has been trained to:

- listen carefully to the complaint
- respond with an apology
- ask relevant questions
- take action to resolve the complaint.

Crew members are allowed to deal with some complaints themselves – for example, if a customer complains that fries are cold. More serious complaints must always be referred to a manager.

A Dealing with complaints

Have you or your friends ever made a complaint in a restaurant or shop? Was it dealt with courteously and effectively?

Copy and complete the following table, giving as many examples as you can. An example is given to show you the type of information to include.

Nature of complaint	Name of organisation	How complaint was dealt with	Good customer care	Bad customer care
Stale sandwich	Joe's Cafe	Apology made, replacement given	Yes	–

Legislation to protect customers

A range of laws (legislation) are in place in the UK to protect customers. The most important of these are the:

- Trades Description Act
- Sale of Goods Act
- Consumer Protection Act
- Health and Safety at Work Act.

▶ Legislation, page 256

Improving customer service

Providing good customer service is important to business organisations for a number of reasons.

- Customers leave the organisation happy and satisfied.
- Satisfied customers are loyal. They come back again and again, and are less likely to switch to using a competitor's products or services.
- Satisfied customers attract new customers. They tell their family and friends, who tell their family and friends...
- Customers who receive good customer service take away a positive image of the organisation as a whole.

Business organisations constantly monitor the customer service they are providing, to make sure they keep their customers satisfied.

Some large organisations use external marketing research companies – such as the National Opinion Poll (NOP) – to carry out independent marketing research into customer satisfaction. The researchers question a number of people (a sample) to find out their views on a particular product or service. The organisation can then use this feedback to improve the quality of customer service and introduce new ideas.

Case study: McDonald's – Customer satisfaction

Jack has now been working at McDonald's for six months and has completed most of his training. His experience of customer service in this time has shown him that when customers feel they have received good service, they are more likely to return and recommend the restaurant to their friends. He has built up a good rapport with several groups of customers.

McDonald's relies on providing good customer service, and monitors customer satisfaction constantly. It keeps a check on numbers of customers by counting the number of meals sold in a given period, and identifying trends from month to month, season to season and year to year. Customers are asked to complete a customer comments card, to find out their views on the service and how often they use McDonald's restaurants. The organisation also keeps careful records of complaints, so it can act on them and make improvements whenever possible. For example, in one McDonald's restaurant, several customers complained about baby-changing facilities being on the upper floor. In response, the restaurant installed a baby-changing room and toilet on the ground floor.

Some businesses get useful feedback on customer satisfaction by monitoring the number of people who enter the shop or business, and the number of people who actually buy its goods or services. For example, many customers enter a clothes shop, browse, and then leave without making a purchase. By counting people as they enter the store, and comparing this with the number of customers actually buying goods, the store can see what proportion of people are tempted to spend. If it is a small proportion, they should investigate why and make changes to the products or services offered.

▶ Customer comments card, page 195

A Customer satisfaction

Choose an organisation you know well; for example, a shop, sports centre or cinema. Think of ten questions you could ask to monitor customer satisfaction in the organisation. How many people do you think you would need to question to get a useful amount of feedback? How often do you think the organisation would need to monitor customer satisfaction?

Once they have feedback on customer satisfaction, organisations need to act on it. Customers today expect a high standard of service from businesses, and constant improvements are needed to ensure:
- service is reliable, friendly and polite
- goods and services are always of a high quality and readily available
- goods and services are delivered quickly and on time
- customers are aware of policies for exchanges and refunds
- buildings and facilities are accessible to everyone (including people in wheelchairs and parents with children in pushchairs)
- the organisation is caring for the environment (keeping the area clean and free from rubbish)
- customers are safe at all times.

A Suggesting improvements

Look more closely at customer service in the organisation you chose for the last activity. Make a copy of the chart below, and comment on:
- the quality of each aspect of customer service
- how the organisation could improve each aspect of customer service.

Aspect of customer service	How good is it?	How could it be improved?
Reliability of service		
Friendliness of service		
Availability of goods and services		
Speed of delivery		
Published policy for exchanges or refunds		
Access to buildings		
Care for the environment		

© L. Daniel, J.Joslin, K. McCafferty,
L. Porter, A. Thomas 1996.
Intermediate GNVQ Business.

Summary questions

By answering these questions, you will put together your own summary of Unit 3. This will help you prepare for the unit test.

1. What is the difference between needs and wants?

2. Give three causes of change in consumer demand.

3. What are the main objectives of an advertising campaign?

4. How would you evaluate whether a promotional campaign had been successful?

5. Name three different types of promotion.

6. Explain the following legislation:

    – the Trades Description Act
    – the Sale of Goods Act
    – the Consumer Protection Act.

7. How can organisations monitor customer satisfaction?

Consumers and customers

▶ The importance of consumers and customers, page 178

▶ Memos, page 17

▶ Trends in consumer demand, page 182

Opportunities to collect evidence
On completing these tasks you will have the opportunity to meet the following requirements for Intermediate GNVQ Business.
Unit 3
Element 3.1 PCs 1, 2, 3, 4, 5, 6

Core skills
Application of Number
Element 2.3

Communication
Elements 2.2, 2.4

Information Technology
Elements 2.1, 2.2, 2.3

▶ Core skills coverage grid, page 252

Assignment

WHAT DO YOU KNOW ABOUT CONSUMERS AND CUSTOMERS?

Setting the scene
You are carrying out a work experience placement in the sales and marketing department of a local superstore. Your placement provider knows that you have been studying Intermediate GNVQ Business, and would like to test your understanding of consumers and customers before giving you tasks to perform in the office.

Task 1
Write a memo to Mrs R O'Connell, your supervisor, explaining:
a why consumers and customers are so important to a business
b how consumers can create demand for goods and services
c how consumers can cause changes in demand for goods and services.

Task 2
Consider the goods and services a large superstore would offer. Identify three goods or services which have changed over the last 25 years. For each, prepare detailed word processed notes to include the following:
a What would be the typical consumer for the goods or services?
b How has demand for the goods or services changed over the 25 years? The following books will give information on consumer demand:
   1 Social Trends
   2 Regional Trends
   3 Monthly Digest of Statistics
   4 National Income and Expenditure
   5 Annual Abstract of Statistics
c Suggest reasons for the changes which have occurred.
d Suggest how consumer demand will change over the next two to three years.
e Input relevant data into a spreadsheet and use this information to produce charts and graphs to illustrate the changing trends.

Assignment

NEW PROMOTIONS

Setting the scene
For this assignment, you will need to work in a group of two or three. Together, you are marketing representatives for a company which manufactures a fashion item (such as jeans or trainers). The company wishes to expand its product range, has designed a new product, and is looking for investors. You have been asked to prepare promotional materials for the new product idea, to present to potential investors.

Task 1
Decide on a name for your company, the product you are going to promote and the image you wish to portray. Who will be your target audience? Tape record your discussion.

Task 2
Make a list of all the suitable types of promotional activities you could use to promote your new product. Explain how you would use them.

Task 3
From the list you made in Task 3:
- a choose one promotional activity to develop and present to your potential investors
- b draft an advertisement for your product to appear in the local weekly paper
- c word process your advert and present it as it should appear in the newspaper
- d using the advertising costings on page 194, calculate the cost of placing your advertisement in the paper for two weeks.

Task 4
Prepare a plan which explains the purpose of your selected promotional activity. You have already calculated the cost of a newspaper advertisement, now estimate the time, people, materials and equipment you will need to prepare the whole promotion.

Task 5
What constraints must you consider when you are preparing your promotional campaign?

Task 6
Present your final proposal to the potential investors (students and tutors). You should use visual aids to make your presentation as clear and interesting as possible.

Task 7
Invite questions and feedback from your potential investors and use the information to prepare an evaluation of your promotion.

▶ Types of promotion, page 186

▶ Designing and producing promotional materials, page 190

▶ Constraints on promotional materials, page 189

▶ Making a presentation, pages 11 and 12

Opportunities to collect evidence
On completing these tasks you will have the opportunity to meet the following requirements for Intermediate GNVQ Business.
Unit 3
Element 3.2 PCs 1, 2, 3, 4, 5, 6

Core skills
Application of Number
Element 2.1, 2.2

Communication
Elements 2.1, 2.2, 2.3

Information Technology
Elements 2.1, 2.2, 2.3

▶ Core skills coverage grid, page 252

Assignment

SETTING UP A TRAVEL AGENCY

Setting the scene
Your school or college has decided to set up a temporary branch of a local travel agency in the reception area, to be open to both internal and external customers. You have been asked to find out what services it should offer, the type of customers who would use it, and how many hours it should be open each day.

Task 1
Visit some local travel agencies and make a list of all the services they offer. Establish which days and times are busiest, and whether the pattern is constant throughout the year. Ask, also, how they deal with customer complaints.

Task 2
Think of the different types of customer that would use the services of the travel agency based in your school or college. Prepare a table, identifying the services each type of customer might require, and whether they would be paying or non-paying.

For example:

Type of customer	Service	Paying or non-paying
Geography students	Field trip to Scotland	Paying
Business lecturer	Arrange travel to a GNVQ conference	Non-paying

Task 3
List all the business communications (oral and written) you would use when setting up the travel agency, giving examples of when you would use each one. List the different types of information you would need to use in the business (for example, brochures, notices and posters), and suggest ways in which you would display it.

Task 4
Write a ten-point plan for dealing with customer complaints at the travel agency. You may find the information you collected in Task 2 is useful here.

Task 5
Produce a table summarising the four Acts which protect customers. Your chart should list the main points covered by each piece of legislation, and give examples of how they may be used.

▶ Business communications, page 198

▶ Dealing with customer complaints, page 199

▶ Legislation, page 256

Task 6

In pairs, role play the following situations which might arise in a travel agency:

- A customer booking a holiday (as complicated as you like).
- A customer asking for information (think up your dream holiday).
- A customer demanding a refund (you have to cancel your holiday at the last minute).
- A customer making a complaint (the holiday was not what you expected).
- A customer having a special need (you cannot eat certain foods).

Take it in turns to act as customer and travel agent. At least one situation should be dealt with by telephone.

Tape record your conversations, and for each situation comment on how you dealt with your customer. Were you polite or rude? Was the customer satisfied?

Opportunities to collect evidence
On completing these tasks you will have the opportunity to meet the following requirements for Intermediate GNVQ Business.
Unit 3
Element 3.3 PCs 1, 2, 3, 4, 5, 6

Core skills
Application of Number
Element 2.1

Communication
Elements 2.1, 2.2, 2.3, 2.4

Core skills coverage grid, page 252

Assignment

WHAT IMPROVEMENTS CAN BE MADE?

Setting the scene

'I like the idea of a travel agency here, but it's a bit of a mess and it does not do much for the place. I nearly fell over a pile of brochures lying around on the floor.'

'The staff were very unhelpful and one girl seemed more interested in talking about her boyfriend than helping me.'

'I wanted to go to St Lucia but they only had one brochure available and could not offer me any other choices.'

'I think I'll keep using the travel agency in town. This one's far too small for people in wheelchairs.'

'I waited six months to get the refund from the holiday I had to cancel when I broke my leg. When I complained, they kept ignoring me.'

'They have so many brochures lying around – what a waste of paper!'

These comments came from a feedback questionnaire sent after the travel agency at your school or college had been running for nine months.

You have been asked to look into the findings, and propose improvements that could be made to customer service. Your headteacher/principal is keen to keep this project running, but needs some convincing.

Task 1

Write a memo to the chief executive of the project, explaining the situation and making suggestions for improvements that could be made to:

Consumers and customers

▶ Memos, page 17

▶ Questionnaires, pages 20 and 21

▶ Improving customer service, page 200

▶ Making a presentation, pages 11 and 12

▶ Reports, page 19

Opportunities to collect evidence
On completing these tasks you will have the opportunity to meet the following requirements for Intermediate GNVQ Business.
Unit 3
Element 3.4 PCs 1, 2, 3, 4

Core skills
Communication
Elements 2.1, 2.2, 2.3

▶ Core skills coverage grid, page 252

Note to the tutor:
This assignment has been developed to offer many opportunities to gather evidence for Application of Number core skills. You may prefer to develop individual activities from the tasks provided here.

- attract customers
- secure customer satisfaction and loyalty
- enhance the organisation's image.

In the memo, invite the chief executive to a presentation when you will propose the improvements in more detail.

Task 2
Design a short questionnaire (up to ten questions long) that you could hand out to customers of the travel agency to:
- monitor customer satisfaction more carefully
- find out what they feel about the service on offer (for example, friendliness of staff, waiting time, range of holiday destinations available, cleanliness).

Task 3
In groups of three, prepare a presentation on 'Improvements to customer service'. Your presentation should include examples of improvements to three of the following:
- friendliness
- availability of goods or services
- speed of delivery
- policies for exchanges or refunds
- access to buildings
- customer safety
- care of the environment.

Present your proposals to the headteacher/principal and the board of governors (students and tutors). Use visual aids to make your presentation as clear and interesting as possible.

Task 4
Write a short report recommending your proposals for improvements, and stating how the travel agency proposes to monitor its customer satisfaction on a regular basis.

Assignment

IMPROVING A RECEPTION AREA

Setting the scene
'Pity about the reception area; it gave a very bad impression of the hospital.'

'The reception area was far too hot. I nearly roasted while I waited.'

'Waiting in the reception area made a very bad start to my stay in your hospital.'

These comments about the reception area were three of many on the feedback questionnaire given by Safers Private Hospital. The senior management decided to redecorate and refurnish the reception area and decide on a suitable temperature.

You have been asked to plan and cost these changes. You must prepare a written report and present the main points of the report to your manager.

The reception area measures 5.4 metres by 6.2 metres. The height of the room is 3 metres. One short wall is one-third glass. One long wall has a double entrance door; the other has a single door into the hospital. Each single door measures 6'6" (6 feet 6 inches) by 2'6" (2 feet 6 inches). The reception area, a quarter circle of radius 2 metres, is in one corner of the room. The area must be organised to include at least 4 appropriate chairs and small tables for magazines.

You will probably find the Application of Number and Information Technology section of the Toolkit helpful as you work through this assignment.

Task 1
Using furniture catalogues, investigate the size and cost of various tables and chairs. Measure the space required for leg room for each chair.

Task 2
a Convert the door measurements into metres (use 12 inches = 1 foot = 30 centimetres).
b Use all the measurements to produce a sketch of the layout of the room – do not draw to scale at this stage. Discuss your plan with your manager (tutor), to ensure that it meets with approval.
c Once it has been approved, draw your plan to scale.

Task 3
Estimate the cost of furniture. To allow for variations in cost and quality, look at three different firms or three different styles/quality of furniture.
a What is the lowest price and the highest price you find? What is the range of prices for each item of furniture?
b Use the three prices to calculate the mean price for each piece of furniture. Use this mean price as your estimated price.
c If VAT is to be added to the furniture costs, show this information separately.
d Produce a list of items to be purchased, with each estimated cost.
e Set up a spreadsheet with this information. Date it using the insert function, print it out, and save it.

Task 4
Calculate the cost of carpeting.
a Look at the different prices of carpeting. Choose a hard-wearing carpet at a reasonable price, or choose three carpets, find the mean price, and use this value to estimate the cost. Decide whether you need underlay or not.
b What width of carpet will you need? What area (in square metres) will you need? What is the width of a roll of carpet? How does this affect the amount that you pay? In the case of your chosen carpet, what percentage of carpet will be wasted?
c The carpet will need to be fitted using grippers. Find the cost per metre of grippers, and the perimeter of the room. Do firms charge for fitting

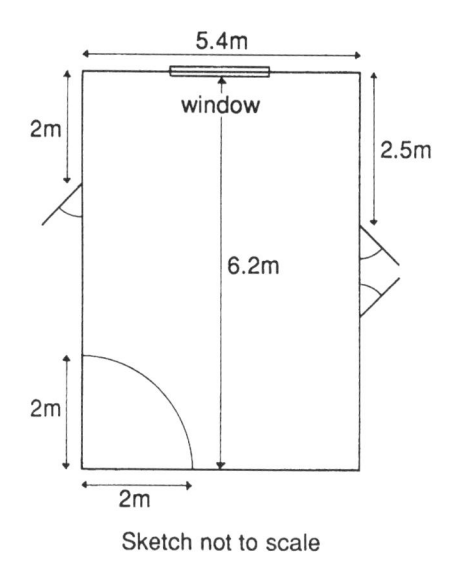

Sketch not to scale

Application of Number and Information Technology, page 25

carpets? If so, how much?
d   What will be the total cost of carpeting the room?

Task 5
Find the area of the ceiling and each wall (including the area behind the receptionist's desk). Remember to deduct the window and door areas. Find out how many square metres one litre of paint will cover. How many litres will you need to paint the room with two coats of emulsion paint? What colour do you recommend?

Task 6
a   Add the costs of carpeting and painting to your spreadsheet.
b   Find the total estimated costs.
c   Add an extra column to show the cost of the furniture, carpet and paint you would recommend to your manager.
d   Using appropriate formulae, add another column to show the variance (from estimated to actual).
e   Check the computer-generated date. Print a copy of the spreadsheet and save your updated file. Keep a back up copy of this file for security.

Task 7
Work out the best temperature for the reception area.
a   You are told that the official minimum office temperature is 61°F. Change this to °C by taking away 32°, dividing the answer by 9, and multiplying by 5. Round your answer to the nearest degree.
b   Check your own working environment by taking the temperature of your work area or classroom each day for two weeks. Record the information you collect on a bar chart (or line graph). At the same time, record whether the temperature was good to work in. Was it too warm, or too cold?
c   What was the temperature range over the two weeks?
d   What was the modal (most common) temperature over the two weeks? Was this too warm, or too cold? Draw a horizontal line on your graph to show the modal temperature.
e   On what fraction of the days did the temperature fall below the modal temperature? By how many degrees each time? What was the ratio of 'right days' : 'not right days'?
f   What do these facts tell you about your working area?
g   What would you recommend to your manager as the ideal temperature for the reception area?

Task 8
Present all your findings, including your workings, in a full report for your manager. You may find it helpful to break it into sections:
1   An explanation of why the reception area needs to be furnished.
2   Sketches and plans of the reception area, with a record of discussions you had with your manager (tutor).
3   Furniture costings, including how you worked out your estimated price (maximum, minimum, mean, range).
4   Carpet and painting costs, showing all workings.
5   Temperature analysis, including conversion of minimum temperature to °C, your graph with the modal line, and your preferred temperature (with reasons).

In each section, explain carefully what you did, where you got your information, and all your calculations.

Word process your report and include your spreadsheet at an appropriate point in the text.

Task 9
Prepare a short presentation for your manager (tutor) and your colleagues (your group). You may wish to use some of the diagrams, spreadsheets and graphs from your report. Would it be useful to put some of them on overhead projector transparencies?

Task 10
Each member of your group should give their presentations to the others. As a group, you must decide on the final design of the reception area and the amount to be spent on furnishing and decoration. How will you decide? Is a vote appropriate? Is cost a critical factor? You may need to ask the presenters for additional information to help you make the decision.

Opportunities to collect evidence
On completing these tasks you will have the opportunity to meet the following requirements for Intermediate GNVQ Business.
Unit 3
Element 3.4 PCs 1, 3, 4

Core skills
Application of Number
Element 2.1, 2.2, 2.3, 2.4

Communication
Elements 2.1, 2.2, 2.3, 2.4

Information Technology
Elements 2.1, 2.2, 2.3

▶ Core skills coverage grid, page 252

Self-check questions

Each of the following questions shows four possible answers – **a**, **b**, **c** and **d**. Only **one** is correct.

1. Which of the following publications would give a business most information on changing patterns of consumer demand?
   a the *Thomson Local* directory
   b a population census
   c *Social Trends*
   d the electoral register.

2. A new leisure centre has opened in your town. Which of the following characteristics would most interest the management?
   a gender
   b class
   c age
   d lifestyle.

3. Consumers would borrow less and save more if there were:
   a an increase in the cost of living
   b a decrease in the money they have to spend
   c an increase in interest rate
   d an increase in confidence to spend.

4. Jo plans to open a disco in her town. Which of the following consumer characteristics would be of *most* interest to her?
   a gender
   b nationality
   c age
   d number of people with children.

5. The *main* reason for a company sponsoring a sporting event is:
   a it is good for the company's image
   b it is a good way to get publicity via television
   c it is an inexpensive form of advertising
   d it persuades people the company produces high-quality goods.

6. Your local superstore would be *most* likely to promote a new product by:
   a an advert on television
   b money-off coupons beside the product
   c an advert on local radio
   d an advert in the local paper.

7. A family buys the same food each week. Their food bill would increase if there were:
   a a decrease in their needs
   b a decrease in their wants
   c a decrease in their confidence to spend
   d an increase in the cost of living.

8. The *main* advantage of distributing leaflets to promote a service is:
   a low cost
   b long production time
   c high cost
   d several colours could be used.

9. Some supermarkets offer a points collection card, which allows the customer to exchange points for goods. The main aim of this is:
   a to advertise goods
   b to encourage people to shop in the supermarket regularly
   c to make the supermarket's products seem better quality than the competition
   d to cut prices of products.

10. Which of the following products is not allowed to be advertised on TV?
    a organic food
    b foods with artificial preservatives
    c tobacco
    d alcohol.

11. For an advertisement to be approved by the Advertising Standards Authority it must be:
    a educational
    b honest
    c informative
    d exciting.

12. You bought a pair of boots marked 'genuine leather', and when you got home you discovered they were plastic. The shop has broken the:
    a Consumer Protection Act
    b Employment Protection Act
    c Trades Description Act
    d Health and Safety at Work Act.

13 If you buy a waterproof coat which leaks when you wear it in the rain, you are entitled to a refund under the:
   a Sale of Goods Act
   b Equal Opportunities Act
   c Consumer Protection Act
   d Trades Description Act.

14 You bought some designer perfume on a market stall, and later discovered that the packaging was genuine but the perfume was fake. You should refer the problem to the:
   a Trading Standards Office
   b Chamber of Commerce
   c Health and Safety Executive
   d Citizens Advice Bureau.

15 Sales literature meets a customer's need for:
   a assistance
   b after-sales service
   c information
   d care and attention.

16 The main advantage of recording and monitoring customer complaints is that it helps an organisation:
   a recognise troublesome customers
   b identify problems with products or services
   c prevent legal action against the company
   d improve staffing levels.

17 An organisation may implement voluntary codes of practice in promoting goods and services. These are an example of:
   a financial constraints
   b legal constraints
   c ethical constraints
   d financial constraints.

18 Some customers may prefer to use their 'corner shop' rather than an out-of-town supermarket because of:
   a higher prices
   b range of products
   c lower prices
   d personal customer service.

4 Financial and administrative support

We all have to learn to manage money in our everyday lives, although some of us are more successful at it than others. In the same way, business organisations need to manage money well in order to run smoothly and efficiently. This means setting up good financial and administrative practices, and completing documentation clearly and accurately.

Whatever job you are doing, it is important to understand business procedures and to learn to use them efficiently. This unit will help you do this, by looking at the documentation and procedures used by a small sports retail business, Rackets & Runners. It will describe the main documents the business uses, and give you plenty of practice in completing them correctly.

The Elements

Identify and explain financial transactions and documents
- explain financial transactions which take place regularly in an organisation and explain why records of transactions are kept
- explain and give examples of purchases and purchase documents
- explain and give examples of sales transactions and sales documents
- explain and give examples of payment methods and receipt documents
- explain the importance of security and security checks for receipts and payments

This first element explains the different financial documents a business needs and the basic language used in accounting. It also introduces you to security measures which businesses use.

▶ Financial transactions and documents, page 216

Complete financial documents and explain financial recording
- complete purchase and sales documents clearly and correctly and calculate totals
- complete payment and receipt documents clearly and correctly and calculate totals
- record income and expenditure over time periods
- explain why financial information must be recorded
- identify and give examples of information technology which businesses use to record and monitor financial information

You will put your knowledge into practice in this element, gaining experience in completing documentation. You will look at how business accounts are produced from financial documents, and how computers can help.

▶ Financial transactions and documents, page 216

Produce, evaluate and store business documents
- explain the purpose of routine business documents
- produce draft and final versions of business documents
- evaluate each business document produced
- compare the methods of processing business documents
- reference, correctly file and retrieve business documents
- identify and evaluate ways to send and ways to store business documents

The third element looks at all business documentation. It will give you practical experience in producing a range of documents, and will show you efficient ways to store and retrieve them. By the end of this element, you will understand how important it is for a business to produce good written documents.

▶ Producing, evaluating and storing business documents, page 236

Financial and administrative support

Financial transactions and documents

Have you ever run a business? Do you know anyone who does? However large or small an organisation is, it needs to keep financial records to:
- give an up-to-date picture of its financial position
- prevent fraud
- show if it is making a profit or a loss
- provide information to the Inland Revenue and HM Customs and Excise.

This means keeping records of all financial transactions.

Financial transaction: the exchange of goods and/or services for payment.

Inland Revenue: the government department responsible for collecting direct taxes, such as income tax.

HM Customs and Excise: the government department responsible for collecting and accounting for customs and excise revenue, including value added tax (VAT).

A   Financial transactions

List every financial transaction you made yesterday. Ask your family what transactions they made, and add them to your list. Remember to include transactions like paying the telephone bill, buying a magazine, and paying your bus fare.

If you found this activity hard, imagine how difficult it is for a business to remember thousands of transactions!

Rackets & Runners is a sports shop with two branches. It is run by three partners – Alan, Ian and Gemma – who share the profits equally. The business sells sports shoes, rackets, sports clothing and accessories. It also provides racket stringing and sports coaching services. The shops are open 12 hours a day and are staffed on a rota basis. Both shops are rented.

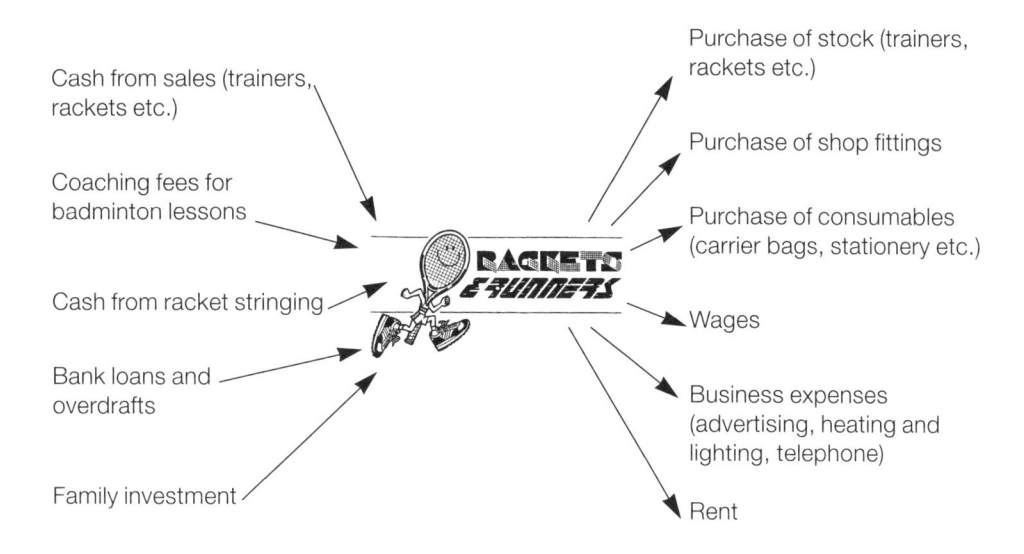

Financial and administrative support

Cash from sales (trainers, rackets etc.)

Coaching fees for badminton lessons

Cash from racket stringing

Bank loans and overdrafts

Family investment

Purchase of stock (trainers, rackets etc.)

Purchase of shop fittings

Purchase of consumables (carrier bags, stationery etc.)

Wages

Business expenses (advertising, heating and lighting, telephone)

Rent

A What do businesses spend their money on?

Gemma, one of Rackets & Runners' partners, is looking at ways to cut expenses and increase profits. At a partners' meeting, they agree to list all purchases made by the business, under the headings of materials, services and wages.

What purchases do you think the business makes? In groups of two or three, brainstorm ideas and produce a spider diagram to illustrate your findings.

▶ Toolkit, page 14

You may wish to use extra headings, but ask your tutor first to check that they are suitable.

Purchase documents

▶ Toolkit, pages 66–75

A Purchasing goods

Rackets & Runners wants to buy 5000 carrier bags printed with its logo and shop addresses from Foster Stationery Ltd. The transaction will involve the following documents:

- purchase invoice – a request for payment
- purchase order – a request for goods to be sent
- cheque – payment for goods received
- remittance advice – a summary of the invoice or statement, to be returned to the supplier with payment
- credit note – sent to the customer when goods are returned. This reduces the amount owed to the supplier
- statement – a list of purchases made, goods returned and payments made
- receipt – confirmation that the supplier has received a cheque
- advice note – informing the customer that the goods have been sent
- delivery note – sent with the goods. To be signed by the customer confirming safe arrival of the complete order, and returned to the supplier
- goods received note – similar to the delivery note, but kept by the customer to check the delivery against the invoice before paying.

217

Financial and administrative support

1. Can you arrange the documents above in the correct order? For example, (1) purchase order, (2) advice note...
2. Copy and complete the table below, to show the flow of documents between the customer (Rackets & Runners) and the supplier (Foster Stationery Ltd).

Customer (Rackets and Runners)	Supplier (Foster Sationery)
Purchase order ⟶	
	⟵ Advice note

Note: In most large companies purchase and sales documents are typed, word-processed or computer-generated.

As this activity shows, there are a large number of purchase documents involved in a financial transaction. Each document contains different information, and businesses must take care when completing them, as mistakes can waste a lot of time and money.

The transaction between Rackets & Runners and Foster Stationery Ltd involved five purchase documents:
- a purchase order
- advice note
- a goods received note
- a purchase invoice
- a credit note.

▶ Order received, page 221

Purchase order

Rackets & Runners has its own pre-printed order forms, which it uses to order goods from suppliers. It sent this purchase order to Foster Stationery Ltd, placing an order for 5000 carrier bags.

To Rackets & Runners, this is an **order placed**.

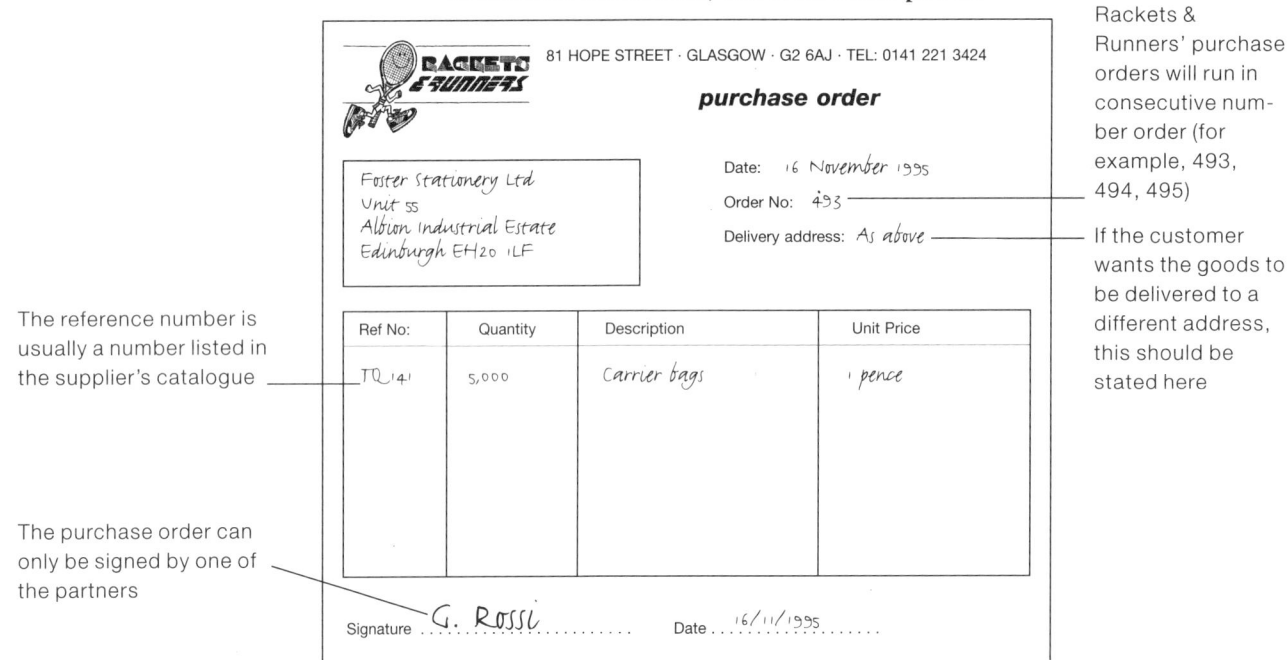

RACKETS & RUNNERS · 81 HOPE STREET · GLASGOW · G2 6AJ · TEL: 0141 221 3424

purchase order

Foster Stationery Ltd
Unit 55
Albion Industrial Estate
Edinburgh EH20 1LF

Date: 16 November 1995
Order No: 493
Delivery address: As above

Ref No	Quantity	Description	Unit Price
TQ 141	5,000	Carrier bags	1 pence

Signature: G. Rossi   Date: 16/11/1995

Rackets & Runners' purchase orders will run in consecutive number order (for example, 493, 494, 495)

If the customer wants the goods to be delivered to a different address, this should be stated here

The reference number is usually a number listed in the supplier's catalogue

The purchase order can only be signed by one of the partners

Financial and administrative support

A   Completing a purchase order

Rackets & Runners needs to buy 1000 sheets of headed paper, at a cost of £120, from Foster Stationery Ltd.

Photocopy a blank purchase order from the Toolkit, and order the headed paper.

▶ Toolkit, page 66

Advice note

Foster Stationery Ltd sent this advice note to Rackets & Runners when it sent out the goods. Rackets & Runners checked the advice note to make sure the right goods were on the way, and warned staff to expect the delivery.

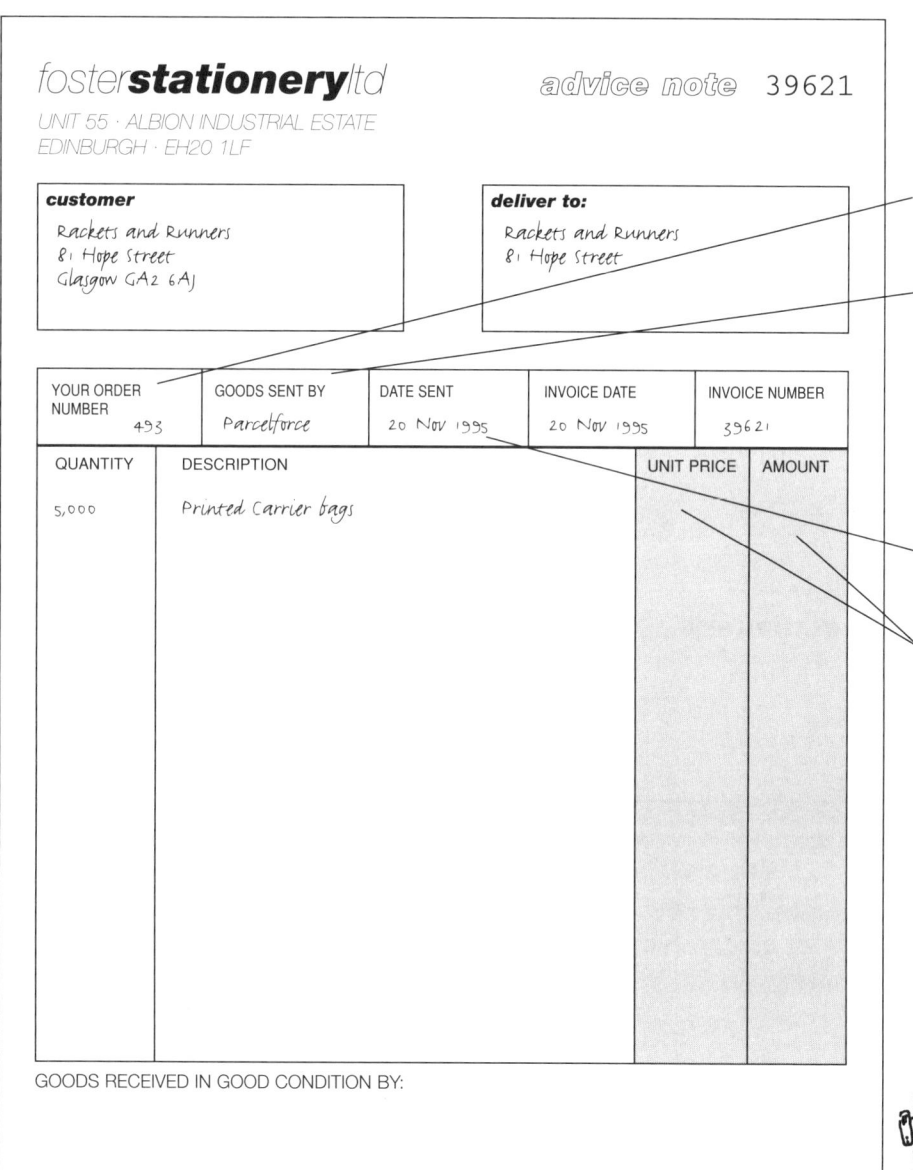

```
foster stationery ltd                advice note  39621
UNIT 55 · ALBION INDUSTRIAL ESTATE
EDINBURGH · EH20 1LF

customer                             deliver to:
Rackets and Runners                  Rackets and Runners
81 Hope Street                       81 Hope Street
Glasgow GA2 6AJ

YOUR ORDER    GOODS SENT BY   DATE SENT      INVOICE DATE   INVOICE NUMBER
NUMBER  493   Parcelforce     20 Nov 1995    20 Nov 1995    39621

QUANTITY      DESCRIPTION                    UNIT PRICE    AMOUNT
5,000         Printed Carrier bags

GOODS RECEIVED IN GOOD CONDITION BY:
```

The order number is taken from Rackets & Runners purchase order

'Goods sent by' refers to how the goods will be delivered (for example, carrier, post, Red Star)

This is the date when the goods were sent

The unit price and amount are not necessarily shown on the advice note. This is because warehouse checkers only need to check the quantity and description, not financial details

▶ Toolkit, page 67

Goods received note

The carrier bags arrived at Rackets & Runners with a delivery note saying exactly what goods were being delivered. Gemma checked the delivery against the delivery note, and then transferred the details onto the goods received note shown below.

▶ Delivery note, page 222

219

Financial and administrative support

▶ Toolkit, page 68

A Completing a goods received note

Rackets & Runners has received a delivery of 20 tennis rackets and 10 squash rackets from Dragon International, a sports equipment manufacturer. Photocopy and complete a goods received note from the Toolkit, showing details of the delivery. Why would you check this against the purchase order and purchase invoice before paying Dragon International?

▶ Sales invoice, page 222

▶ Toolkit, page 69

RACKETS & RUNNERS 81 HOPE STREET · GLASGOW · G2 6AJ · TEL: 0141 221 3424

goods received note

Supplier: FOSTER STATIONERY LTD
UNIT 55
ALBION INDUSTRIAL ESTATE
EDINBURGH · EH20 1LF

Date: 21 Nov 1995
Invoice No: 39621

Order No:	Description	Quantity
493	Printed Carrier bags	5000

Signature: G. Brown

Before paying Foster Stationery, Gemma checked this goods received note against the purchase order and purchase invoice.

Purchase invoice

Rackets & Runners received this purchase invoice from Foster Stationery for the carrier bags it was buying. This showed details of the goods bought and when payment was due.

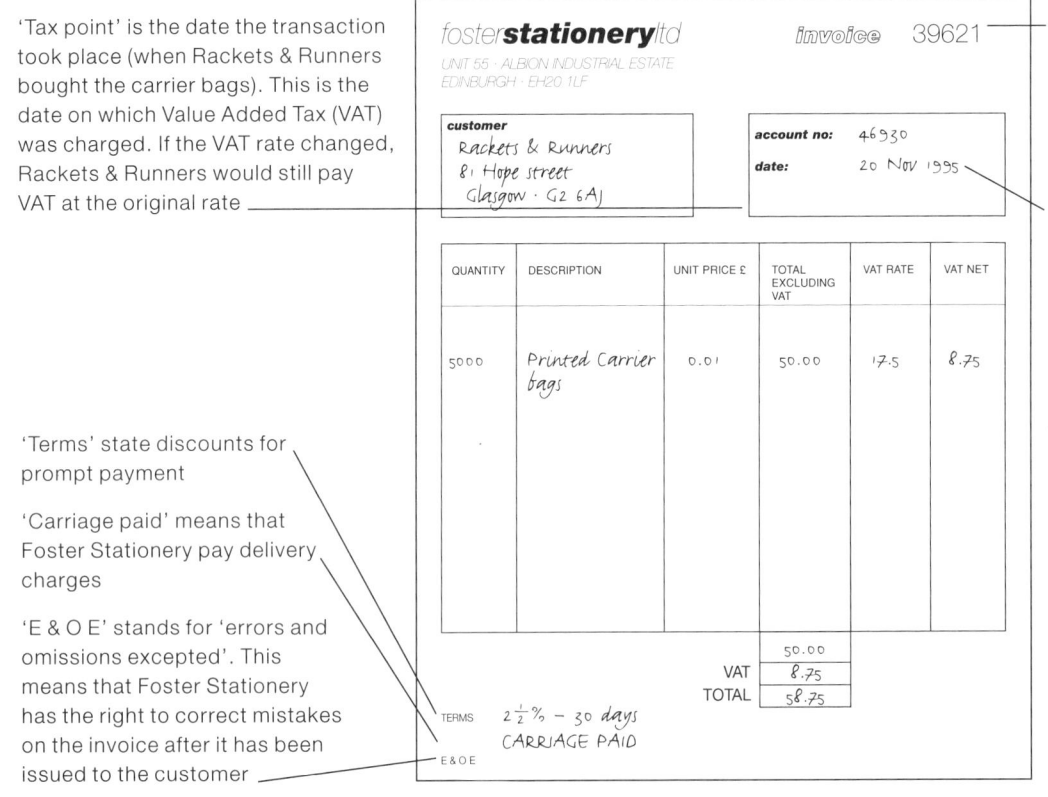

'Tax point' is the date the transaction took place (when Rackets & Runners bought the carrier bags). This is the date on which Value Added Tax (VAT) was charged. If the VAT rate changed, Rackets & Runners would still pay VAT at the original rate

'Terms' state discounts for prompt payment

'Carriage paid' means that Foster Stationery pay delivery charges

'E & O E' stands for 'errors and omissions excepted'. This means that Foster Stationery has the right to correct mistakes on the invoice after it has been issued to the customer

fosterstationeryltd **invoice** 39621
UNIT 55 · ALBION INDUSTRIAL ESTATE
EDINBURGH · EH20 1LF

customer: Rackets & Runners
81 Hope street
Glasgow · G2 6AJ

account no: 46930
date: 20 Nov 1995

QUANTITY	DESCRIPTION	UNIT PRICE £	TOTAL EXCLUDING VAT	VAT RATE	VAT NET
5000	Printed Carrier bags	0.01	50.00	17.5	8.75

TOTAL: 50.00
VAT: 8.75
TOTAL: 58.75

TERMS: 2½% – 30 days CARRIAGE PAID
E & O E

The invoice number is pre-printed on every invoice. This number also appears on the advice note

The invoice date is the date the invoice was raised (prepared). The date payment is due is worked out by adding the number of days allowed for payment (written next to 'Terms') to the invoice date

220

Credit note

Rackets & Runners had to return 1000 carrier bags because they had nothing printed on them! Foster Stationery Ltd sent a letter apologising for the mistake, with a credit note for the cost of 1000 bags. A credit note is a document informing a customer that their account has been credited. This could be because the customer returned faulty goods (like Rackets & Runners), or because they had been overcharged.

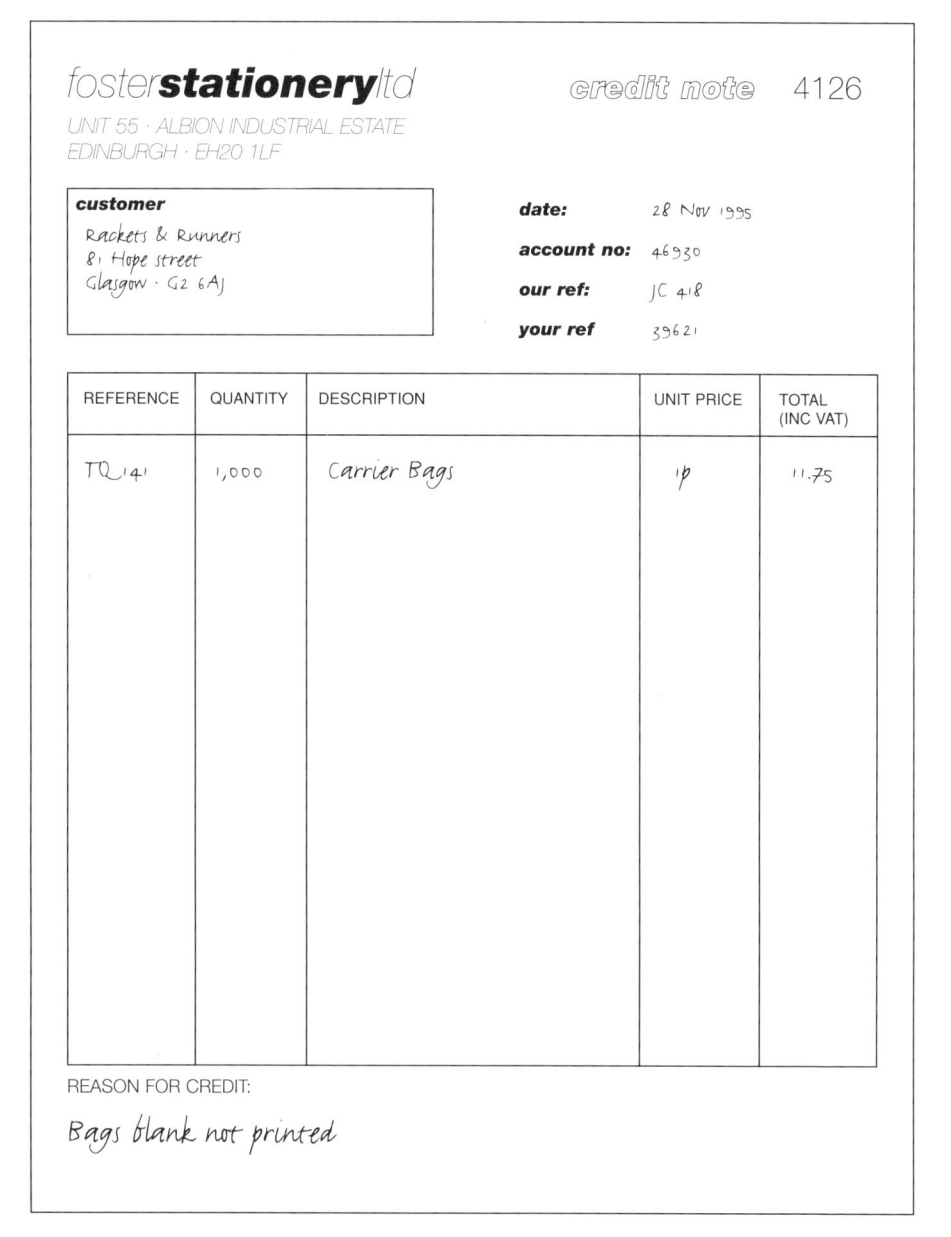

▶ Toolkit, page 70

foster stationery ltd
UNIT 55 · ALBION INDUSTRIAL ESTATE
EDINBURGH · EH20 1LF

credit note   4126

customer
Rackets & Runners
81 Hope street
Glasgow · G2 6AJ

date: 28 Nov 1995
account no: 46930
our ref: JC 418
your ref: 39621

REFERENCE	QUANTITY	DESCRIPTION	UNIT PRICE	TOTAL (INC VAT)
TQ 141	1,000	Carrier Bags	1p	11.75

REASON FOR CREDIT:
Bags blank not printed

Sales documents

The transaction between Rackets & Runners and Foster Stationery also involved a number of sales documents.

Order received

To order the carrier bags, Rackets & Runners completed the purchase order on page 218. When Foster Stationery received the order, it checked it carefully to make sure the information was correct, and then filed it as an order received.

Financial and administrative support

Toolkit, page 71

Delivery note
Foster Stationery sent this delivery note to Rackets & Runners with the delivery of carrier bags.

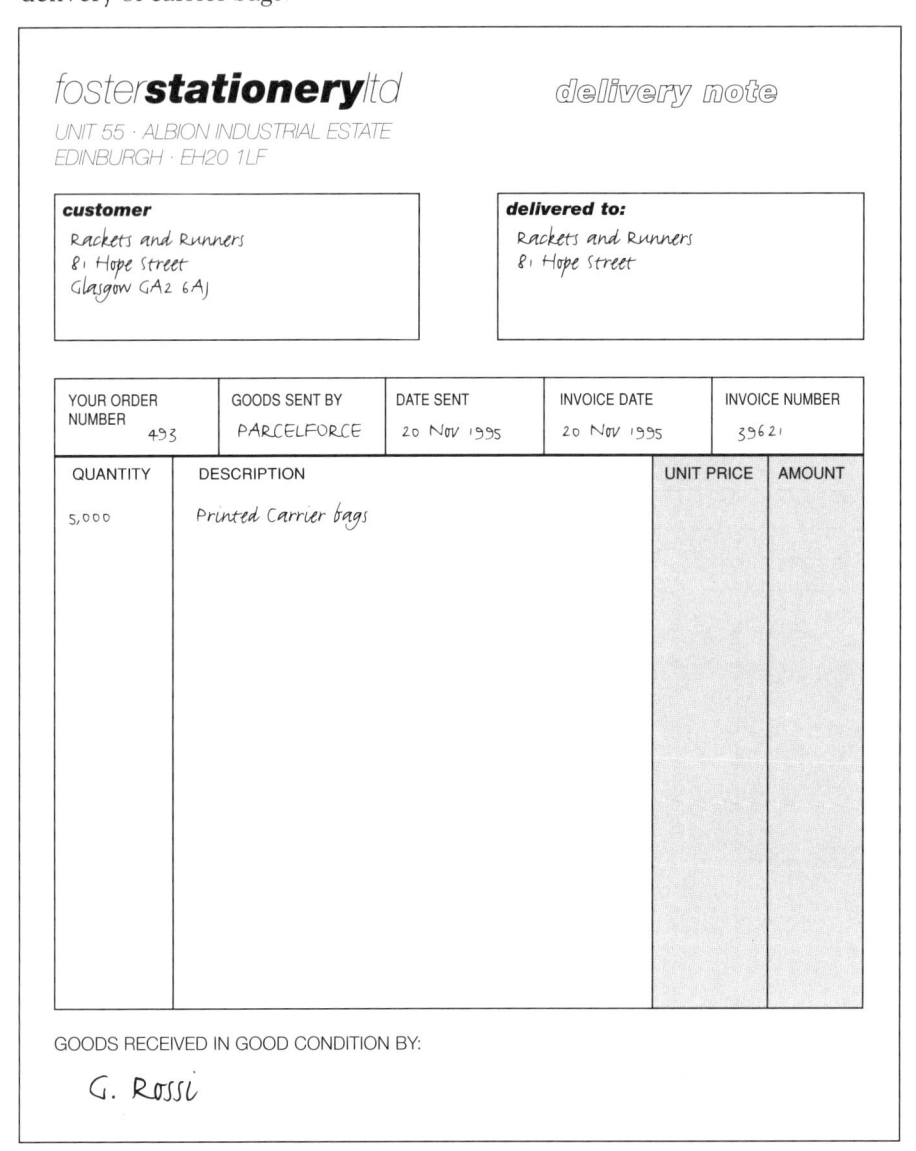

```
foster stationery ltd                    delivery note
UNIT 55 · ALBION INDUSTRIAL ESTATE
EDINBURGH · EH20 1LF

customer                          delivered to:
Rackets and Runners               Rackets and Runners
81 Hope Street                    81 Hope Street
Glasgow GA2 6AJ

YOUR ORDER   GOODS SENT BY   DATE SENT      INVOICE DATE    INVOICE NUMBER
NUMBER 493   PARCELFORCE     20 Nov 1995    20 Nov 1995     35621

QUANTITY     DESCRIPTION                    UNIT PRICE   AMOUNT
5,000        Printed Carrier bags

GOODS RECEIVED IN GOOD CONDITION BY:
G. Rossi
```

The customer signs the document after checking the delivery is correct

Sales invoice
Once it had delivered the carrier bags to Rackets & Runners, Foster Stationery completed an invoice for the transaction (see page 220). This was intended to remind Rackets & Runners when payment was due, and how much it owed.

To Foster Stationery, the invoice was a sales invoice, confirming a sale. To Rackets & Runners, the invoice was a purchase invoice, confirming a purchase.

Statement of account and remittance advice
Foster Stationery Ltd issues monthly statements to its customers. It sent this statement after it had given credit to Rackets & Runners for the faulty carrier bags, and before Rackets & Runners had paid the invoice. The remittance advice slip at the bottom of the statement is for Rackets & Runners to fill in and return when it pays the account. This then tells Foster Stationery that payment has been made.

Financial and administrative support

▶ Toolkit, page 72

fosterstationeryltd
UNIT 55 · ALBION INDUSTRIAL ESTATE
EDINBURGH · EH20 1LF

statement of account

customer
Rackets and Runners
81 Hope Street
Glasgow GA2 6AJ

account no: 46930
date: 30 November 1995
credit limit: £300
terms:

DATE	REFERENCE	DESCRIPTION	DEBIT	CREDIT	BALANCE
NOV		BAL B/F			28.20
20	39621	INVOICE	58.75		86.95
28	4126	CREDIT NOTE		11.75	75.20
			AMOUNT NOW DUE		75.20

- The balance owing at the beginning of the month
- This column shows any sales made (invoices sent)
- This column shows any payments received or goods returned (credit given)
- The outstanding balance (the amount owed to Foster Stationery) is shown clearly

remittance advice

account no:
cheque no:

DATE	DESCRIPTION	AMOUNT DUE

TOTAL CHEQUE ENCLOSED £

- Some companies have a remittance advice slip like this at the bottom of their statements. This should be torn off and returned to the supplier with a cheque

Completing sales documents

The partners of Rackets & Runners have a GNVQ Business student, Ismail, on work experience for three weeks. Ismail is keen to observe how Alan processes sales documents to back up transactions. He has learned the theory at college, but feels he doesn't have enough practical information. Ismail's college notes give him the following information:

Sales documents are similar to purchase documents. Organisations issue these sales documents to customers:

Sales order	an order sent to a supplier requesting goods
Sales invoice	a request for payment
Delivery note	sent by the supplier to the customer with the goods. When the customer checks the delivery, s/he signs the delivery note and returns it to the supplier via the carrier
Sales credit note	sent by the supplier to the customer when goods have been returned. This will be shown as a reduction in the amount owed on the statement of account (see below)
Statement of account	sent to the customer on a regular basis, usually monthly, showing purchases made, payments made and credit notes issued. It will clearly show the balance outstanding on the customer's account
Remittance advice	returned to the supplier with payment – often a tear-off portion of the statement

It is important to remember that businesses use sales documents when they sell both goods (like computers) and services (like catering). Sales can be to either individual customers, or to businesses. For example, a retail business such as a general store sells goods to individual customers. But a company which manufactures electronic components will sell these on to other businesses to make into computers, CD players etc.

223

Financial and administrative support

▶ Delivery note, page 222

▶ Invoice, pages 220 and 222

A Completing sales documents

Alan has received the following order from a local secondary school and has asked Ismail to complete the sales documents (an invoice and a delivery note).

QUEENSBOROUGH HIGH SCHOOL
DUMBARTON ROAD · GLASGOW · G69 4LQ

Rackets & Runners
81 Hope Street
Glasgow G2 6AJ

DATE: 3 May 1996
ORDER NO: 18462
DELIVERY ADDRESS: AS ABOVE

REF NO:	QUANTITY	DESCRIPTION	UNIT PRICE
624	30	Badminton Racket	£36.49

SIGNATURE C. Thompson   DATE 3 May 1996

▶ Credit note, page 221

▶ Toolkit, pages 69, 70, 71

▶ Statement of account, page 223

▶ Toolkit, page 72

When the school unpacked the badminton rackets, it found that one of them had a frayed handle grip, and returned it to Rackets & Runners. Alan asked Ismail to complete and issue a credit note.

How well do you understand the sales process? Photocopy a blank invoice, delivery note and credit note from the Toolkit, and complete them for Ismail.

At the end of the month, before the school had paid for the goods, Rackets & Runners wanted to send a statement of account showing the transactions that had taken place. Photocopy a blank statement of account from the Toolkit, and complete it to show the school's account.

Payment methods and documents

Rackets & Runners pays for transactions and receives money in several different ways, depending on the situation.

Petty cash

The business uses petty cash to buy inexpensive items, such as coffee, milk, window cleaning and bus fares. Staff buy these things out of their own money, and the business pays them back from petty cash.

Gemma is in charge of petty cash. She will not reimburse (pay back) any of the staff unless they have completed a petty cash voucher and attached a receipt.

Petty cash pays for the everyday expenses of running a business

Financial and administrative support

Petty cash: *cash businesses keep in the office to use for everyday expenses, such as coffee and flowers.*

A — Completing a petty cash voucher

Rackets & Runners has run out of milk, coffee and sugar, and Alan asks you to go to the shops to buy some. You come back with a receipt, and have to fill in a petty cash voucher to claim back the money.

Photocopy a blank petty cash voucher from the Toolkit, and complete it so Gemma can reimburse you.

PETTY CASH VOUCHER		Folio 321
		Date 4 May 1996

Date	Purpose	£	p
4/5/96	BUS FARES	1	34
	Total spent	1	34

Received by *Adam Burnside*   Approved by

▶ Toolkit, page 74

Cheque

Rackets & Runners makes most of its payments by business cheque.

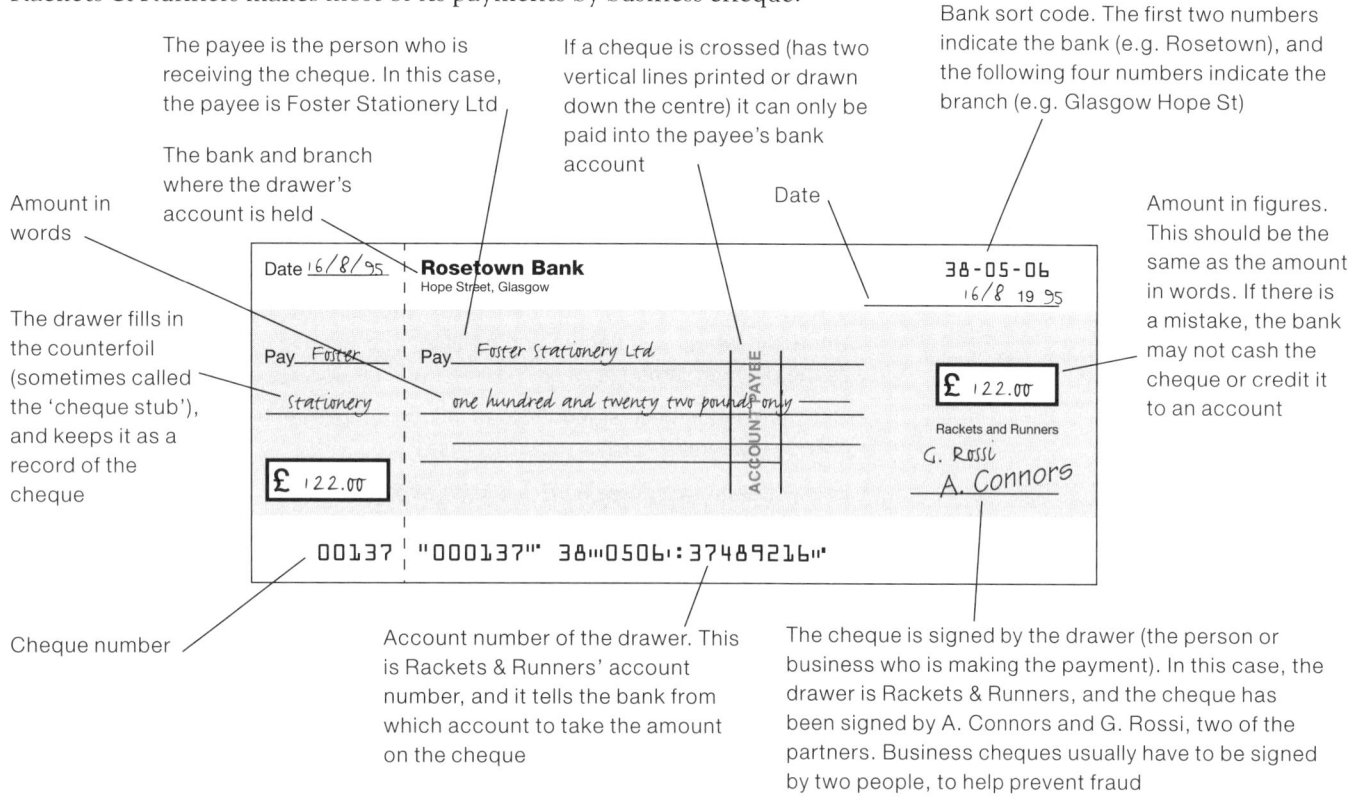

- The payee is the person who is receiving the cheque. In this case, the payee is Foster Stationery Ltd
- If a cheque is crossed (has two vertical lines printed or drawn down the centre) it can only be paid into the payee's bank account
- Bank sort code. The first two numbers indicate the bank (e.g. Rosetown), and the following four numbers indicate the branch (e.g. Glasgow Hope St)
- The bank and branch where the drawer's account is held
- Date
- Amount in words
- Amount in figures. This should be the same as the amount in words. If there is a mistake, the bank may not cash the cheque or credit it to an account
- The drawer fills in the counterfoil (sometimes called the 'cheque stub'), and keeps it as a record of the cheque
- Cheque number
- Account number of the drawer. This is Rackets & Runners' account number, and it tells the bank from which account to take the amount on the cheque
- The cheque is signed by the drawer (the person or business who is making the payment). In this case, the drawer is Rackets & Runners, and the cheque has been signed by A. Connors and G. Rossi, two of the partners. Business cheques usually have to be signed by two people, to help prevent fraud

Many of Rackets & Runners' customers also choose to pay by cheque. They have to show a cheque guarantee card to support their payment. The bank will honour a cheque up to the limit shown on the card (usually £50 or £100).

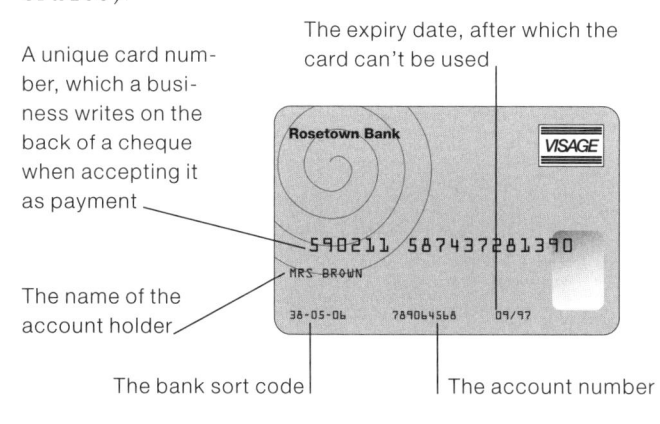

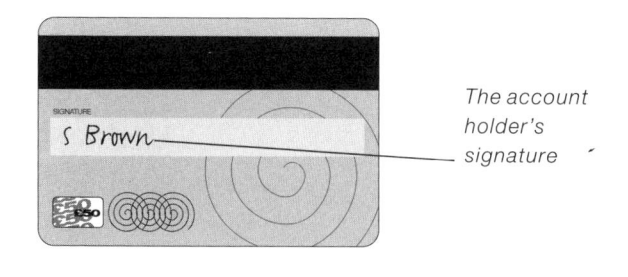

▶ Toolkit, page 73

- A unique card number, which a business writes on the back of a cheque when accepting it as payment
- The expiry date, after which the card can't be used
- The name of the account holder
- The bank sort code
- The account number
- The account holder's signature

225

Financial and administrative support

To help prevent fraud, account holders should sign the back of their cheque guarantee card as soon as they receive it from the bank. An unsigned cheque card is not valid, and could be found and used dishonestly by someone other than the account holder. A business accepting a cheque makes sure that the signature on the cheque matches that on the card.

Rackets & Runners' staff are given the following checklist to remind them what to do when receiving a cheque, with a cheque guarantee card, from a customer.

RACKETS & RUNNERS 81 HOPE STREET · GLASGOW · G2 6AJ · TEL: 0141 221 3424

CHECKING CHEQUES AND CARDS

- Is the date correct? A cheque more than six months old is 'stale', and will not be accepted by the bank. If the date is written *after* today's date, the cheque is 'post-dated' which means that we can't pay it into the bank until the date shown. It is not legally necessary for the customer to enter the date – we can do this for them.

- Do the amounts in words and figures match? If not, ask the customer to correct the mistake and sign the correction. The bank will accept a cheque where the words and figures don't match, and will use the amount in words as the payment amount.

- Has the cheque been signed? Does the signature match the one on the cheque guarantee card?

- Is the cheque guarantee card within its expiry date?

▶ Toolkit, page 73

A Completing a cheque

Photocopy a cheque from the Toolkit, and complete it to pay for Rackets & Runners' purchase of carrier bags from Foster Stationery Ltd (see page 223). Do not sign the cheque, as you are not an authorised signatory of the account.

Authorised signatory: *a person who is given the legal right to sign cheques for an account.*

Cash

Some of Rackets & Runners' customers who come into the shops pay by cash. Staff are told to check that notes aren't forgeries by looking for a metal strip running through them.

Every evening, Gemma's last task is to make sure that there is £30 in each shop's till, made up of a variety of coins and notes. She calls this the float.

The float: *an amount of money left in a shop's till to make sure that it always has enough cash to give customers change.*

For security reasons, any cash which is not needed for the float is stored in a locked safe, and only the three partners know the combination.

Debit cards and credit cards

Instead of paying by cash or cheque, more and more of Rackets & Runners' customers are now using:
- debit cards, such as Switch and Delta
- credit cards, such as Visa and Access.

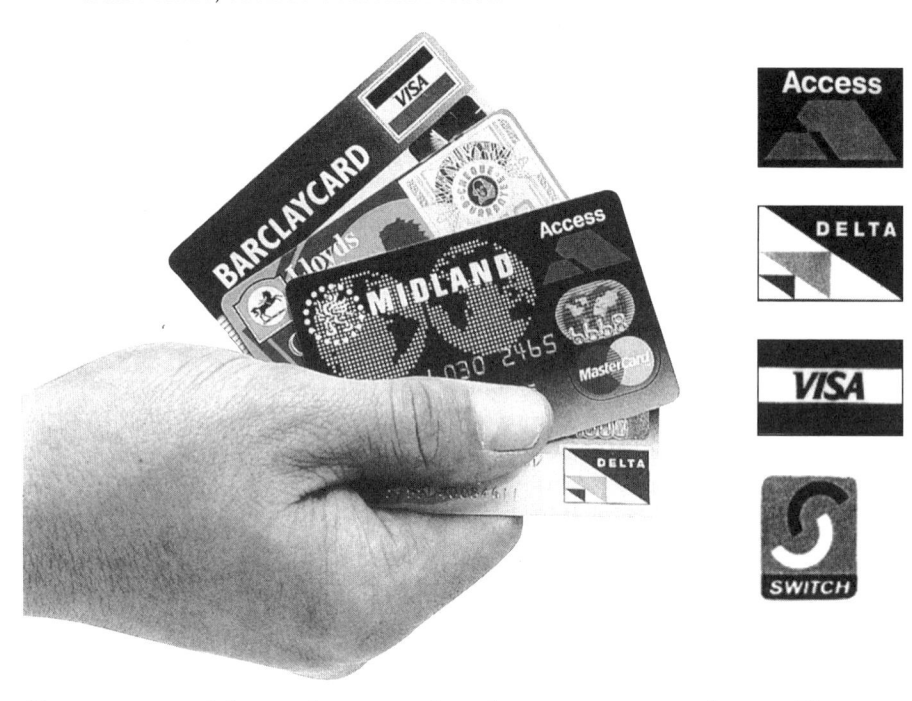

Customers use debit cards to save them having to write a cheque. The money is transferred from their account immediately by computer. This technology is called EFTPOS, which stands for Electronic Funds Transfer at Point of Sale.

Customers use credit cards to buy goods without having to pay for them immediately. When they use a credit card they borrow money from the credit card company, which gives them one month to pay before charging interest on the loan. Some people prefer to pay by credit card because of special offers given by credit card companies, such as Air Miles.

Interest: *a charge made for paying back money over a period of time. The amount of interest customers pay is a percentage of the total amount they owe.*

Banking Automated Clearing Services (BACS)

Rackets & Runners pays a few of its regular suppliers, and receives payment from some of its regular customers, by a system known as BACS – Bankers Automated Clearing Services.

BACS is a computerised system which involves money being transferred between bank accounts by a computer link.

When Rackets & Runners uses BACS to pay suppliers, it is called direct debit.

Direct debit: *an arrangement for payments to be made electronically from your bank account, usually once a month.*

Rackets & Runners decided to pay its gas bill by direct debit. British Gas sent the company a direct debit mandate, and the partners completed it to give British Gas authority to collect monthly payments from the business' account.

Financial and administrative support

British Gas now sends Rackets & Runners a monthly statement showing the amount being deducted. If the monthly payments don't cover the total bill, British Gas writes to Rackets & Runners suggesting an increase in monthly payments.

When customers use BACS to pay Rackets & Runners, it is called direct credit.

Direct credit: *an arrangement for payments to be made electronically into your bank account, usually once a month.*

Queensborough High School has a contract with Rackets & Runners for badminton coaching for its pupils. Each month the school pays an agreed amount as a direct credit into the company's bank account. The school then sends Rackets & Runners notification that the funds have been paid.

Electronic Data Interchange (EDI)

With the introduction of computer networks and the cost of new technology falling, small businesses are now able to take advantage of computerisation.

One system which more and more companies are using is Electronic Data Interchange (EDI). Foster Stationery Ltd has recently had a computer installed, and is going to use EDI to:
- authorise its bank to make payments directly to suppliers' banks.
- transfer documents to its customers and suppliers. For example, it is going to send invoices directly to Rackets & Runners using EDI.

Buying on credit

At a recent partners' meeting, Ian asked Alan and Gemma to consider buying new display racks for the shops. As this was going to be a major expense which they had not budgeted for, they agreed to investigate the possibility of buying the display racks on credit. They found out that a local shopfitter, Hillhead Shopfittings, offered a hire purchase option on purchases over £1000. Its terms were 10% flat rate, which meant that Rackets & Runners would have to pay £100 interest a year on a purchase worth £1000.

A — Calculating interest

Alan asks you to calculate the interest Rackets & Runners would have to pay on display racks costing £1749 if it took the hire purchase option with Hillhead Shopfittings over three years.

Pay slips

As well as paying for goods and services from suppliers, Rackets & Runners has to pay its staff. All employees have a legal right to expect remuneration (payment) in exchange for labour.

Rackets & Runners pays its employees weekly, directly into their bank accounts. It is important for staff to know how much they have been paid and how their net pay (pay after deductions like tax and National Insurance) has been reached. They each receive a pay slip giving them this information.

Financial and administrative support

PAY ADVICE

PAY & ALLOWANCES		DEDUCTIONS	
BASIC PAY	807.69	P.A.Y.E.	233.75
BONUS	378.78	NAT INS.	92.78
		PENSION	21.80
TOTAL PAYMENTS	1186.47	TOTAL DEDUCTIONS	348.33

RACKETS & RUNNERS
MR ANDREW LUCAS
EMPLOYEE NO: 000003
TAX CODE: 300L
DATE: 13/08/96

NAT. INS. NO: JN1234567A
NET PAY: 838.14

Labels:
- Employee's name
- Employee's number
- Employee's tax code (this shows how much personal allowance the employee can earn tax free)
- Voluntary deductions – such as superannuation (pension), trade union levy, savings club
- Statutory deductions – such as income tax (PAYE, Pay As You Earn) and National Insurance
- Gross pay – the total amount earned
- National Insurance number
- Net pay (sometimes called 'take home pay') – wages after deductions

Receipt documents

Whenever money changes hands between two people or organisations – whether it's by cash, cheque, credit or computer – a receipt is needed as proof of payment. Businesses use several types of receipt documents to show they have made or received a payment, including:

- receipts for purchases
- paying-in slips showing money paid into the bank
- bank statements showing money going in and out of an account.

Receipts

When Rackets & Runners receives payment from customers, it gives them a receipt. A receipt is proof of payment. It usually shows:

- the date and time that a customer paid for goods
- how much they spent
- where they spent it
- what they bought.

Rackets & Runners' shops have computerised tills, which print receipts automatically when a customer makes a purchase. When Rackets & Runners buys goods from suppliers it receives many different types of receipts; from handwritten notes, to printed, itemised records.

---

*foster***stationery***ltd* *receipt* 8234

UNIT 55 · ALBION INDUSTRIAL ESTATE · EDINBURGH · EH20 1LF

customer Rackets & Runners
date 8 December 1995
Payment of A/c No 46930   £75.20
Received with thanks L White

229

Financial and administrative support

Toolkit, page 74

A — Completing a receipt

The computerised till in one of the Rackets & Runners' shops has broken. A customer wants to buy a tennis racket for £39.99 and a pair of shorts for £19.99, and says he will pay by cash. It is 10.30am on 20 January 1996.
Write a receipt for the customer, to prove that he has paid for the goods.

Paying-in slips

Rackets & Runners pays its takings into the bank once a week, unless it takes over £750 in cash (too much cash on the premises is a security risk).

At close of business each day (when the shops shut), Gemma adds up:
- cash taken
- cheques received
- debit and credit card vouchers.

She then compares the total takings with the total recorded by the tills. If there is a large discrepancy (difference), Gemma investigates further and takes action if necessary.

A — Total takings

When Gemma was preparing the week's takings for banking, she counted £718.03 in cash and £409.29 in cheques. The cash was made up of the following denominations:

£160 in £20 notes
£230 in £10 notes
£155 in £5 notes
£97 in £1 notes
£46.50 in 50p pieces
£16.60 in 20p pieces
£3.80 in 10p pieces
£5.45 in 5p pieces
The remainder in 2p and 1p pieces (bronze)

How many of each denomination of note and coin make up this total? For example, £245 in £5 notes would be 49 X £5 notes.

Denomination: *a type of coin or note. The most common denominations used in the UK are 1p, 2p, 5p, 10p, 20p, 50p and £1 coins, and £5, £10, £20 and £50 notes.*

Once Gemma has counted the week's takings, she completes a bank paying-in slip. She fills in:
- details of the cheques she's paying in on the back of the slip
- details of the cash she's paying in on the back of the slip
- the number of cheques she's paying in on the front of the slip
- the total amount she's paying in by cheque
- the cash she's paying in, broken down into different denominations.

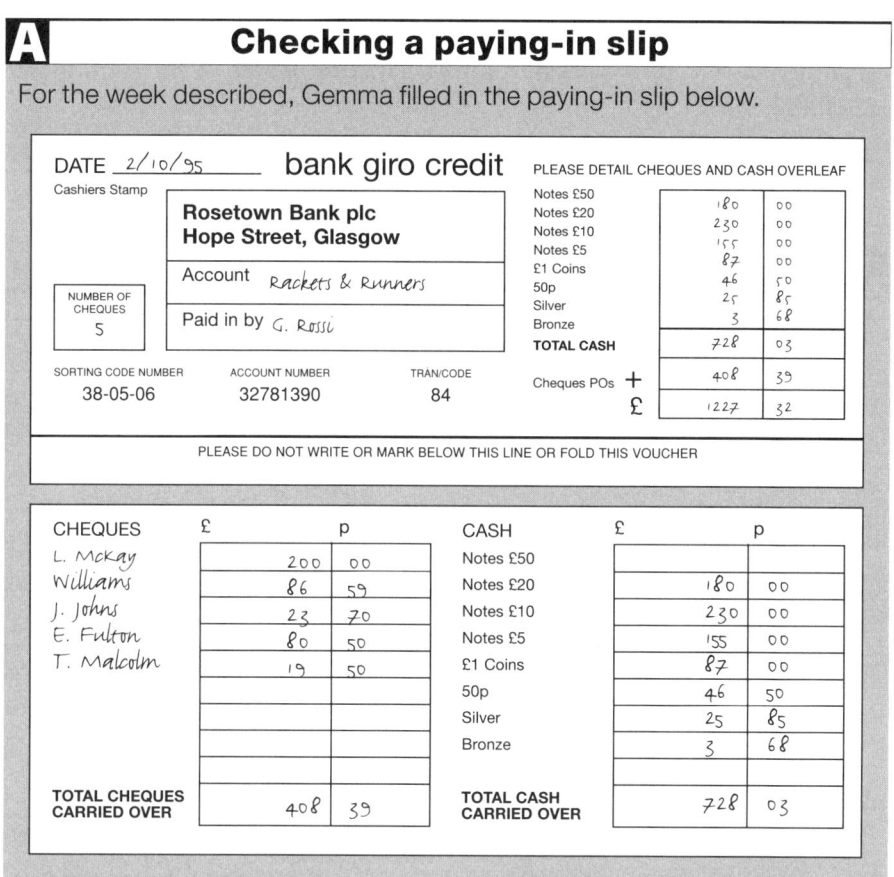

Financial and administrative support

A Checking a paying-in slip

For the week described, Gemma filled in the paying-in slip below.

bank giro credit

DATE 2/10/95
Cashiers Stamp

Rosetown Bank plc
Hope Street, Glasgow

Account: Rackets & Runners
Paid in by: G. Rossi

NUMBER OF CHEQUES: 5

SORTING CODE NUMBER: 38-05-06
ACCOUNT NUMBER: 32781390
TRAN/CODE: 84

PLEASE DETAIL CHEQUES AND CASH OVERLEAF

	£	p
Notes £50	180	00
Notes £20	230	00
Notes £10	155	00
Notes £5	87	00
£1 Coins	46	50
50p	25	85
Silver	3	68
Bronze		
TOTAL CASH	728	03
Cheques POs +	408	39
£	1227	32

PLEASE DO NOT WRITE OR MARK BELOW THIS LINE OR FOLD THIS VOUCHER

CHEQUES	£	p		CASH	£	p
L. McKay	200	00		Notes £50		
Williams	86	59		Notes £20	180	00
J. Johns	23	70		Notes £10	230	00
E. Fulton	80	50		Notes £5	155	00
T. Malcolm	19	50		£1 Coins	87	00
				50p	46	50
				Silver	25	85
				Bronze	3	68
TOTAL CHEQUES CARRIED OVER	408	39		TOTAL CASH CARRIED OVER	728	03

▶ Toolkit, page 73

Has Gemma filled in the paying-in slip correctly? Check that the amounts she has entered correspond with the cash she has counted.

Photocopy a blank paying-in slip from the Toolkit, and fill it in correctly so that Gemma can pay the money into the bank.

Bank statements

Every month, Rackets & Runners receives a bank statement showing money which has gone in and out of its account.

Gemma checks all bank statements carefully, to make sure that the company's payment records and receipts agree with the statement.

Rosetown Bank plc
Hope Street, Glasgow

Account: Rackets and Runners
81 Hope St
Glasgow
(No 4 Account)

Sheet 25

Statement Date

Account Number

Date	Details	Withdrawals	Deposits	Balance
2 Oct	Balance from sheet 24			871.28C
	Cheque 002742	22.41		848.87C
	Cheque 002739	18.22		830.65C
4 Oct	DD British Telecom	90.00		740.65C
8 Oct	SO Elite Insurance	78.00		662.65C
19 Oct	Cheque 002743	13.54		649.11C
28 Oct	Counter Credit 104431		382.87	1031.98C

The debit column shows money Rackets & Runners has spent, including cheques, standing orders, direct debits and cash withdrawn

The credit column shows money Rackets & Runners has received, including cash and cheques banked, and direct credits

A running balance is shown in the end column

The letter C against the balance figure shows that the account is in credit (in the black). A letter D would show that the account was overdrawn (in the red)

Financial and administrative support

Security and financial transactions

As part of his assignment while on work experience at Rackets & Runners, Ismail was expected to investigate the importance of security when carrying out financial transactions, and the security checks made on receipts and payments at the company. Before writing his report, he prepared a list of questions for Gemma to answer.

Recording financial information

Questions on security at Rackets and Runners

1. Can any staff order stock?
   Stock will be ordered by a member of staff on a Purchase Requisition which should be authorised by one of the partners before a purchase order is sent.

2. What do you do when you receive an invoice?
   The invoice is checked against the Purchase Order. If it is correct it is initialled and dated. We place it in an 'outstanding order' folder.

3. What happens to Goods Received Notes?
   The GRN is checked against the initialled invoice to make sure the goods delivered are correct.

4. If the GRN matches the invoice, what is the next stage?
   A cheque will be written to pay the supplier, and paperclipped to the invoice to await signature. The invoice will be stamped 'PAID' and date of payment and cheque number are written on invoice.

5. Who is authorised to sign cheques?
   Rackets and Runners cheques must be signed by any two partners. This should prevent fraud.

All businesses have to keep up-to-date records of financial transactions. Accurate financial information helps a business to:

- ensure security – by making it easier to trace errors and fraud
- monitor income and expenditure – by having up-to-date records of money earned and spent
- keep customers' accounts up to date – by ensuring that bills are paid and debts collected
- keep the business' accounts up to date – by providing monthly and quarterly financial records which are used to produce final accounts for the year
- monitor performance – by tracking spending against budgets on a weekly, monthly or quarterly basis.

It is important for businesses to keep up-to-date financial records

▶ Inland Revenue and Customs & Excise, page 216

Ismail work-shadowed Gemma as she entered copy invoices into Rackets & Runners sales day book, and suppliers' invoices into the purchases day book.

He watched the following invoice data being entered:

		SALES DAY BOOK			
	Invoice no	Customer	Sale (ex VAT)	VAT	Total
3 March	001576	L Holmes	28.00	4.90	32.90
3 March	001577	S Singh	162.41	28.42	190.83
3 March	001578	A McIntyre	390.00	68.25	458.25
3 March	001579	Spoiled invoice			
3 March	001580	B Ho	25.44	4.45	29.89
3 March	001581	K Menzie	197.00	34.47	231.47
3 March	001582	Z Smith	250.00	13.75	293.75
3 March	001583	Park Drive School	98.00	17.15	115.15
			1150.85	201.39	1352.24

Note that copy invoices run in numerical order.

Any spoiled invoices must be included in the sales day book to enable the numerical order to remain correct and to help prevent fraud.

A Purchases day book

Draw up a day book as shown below:

Enter the following invoices into the day book on 3 March:
- Invoice no 964731 from Nike for £320 total (VAT £47.66)
- Invoice no 7429 from City Sports Centre for £117.50 total (calculate the purchase excluding VAT and the VAT figure)
- Invoice no 003781 from Adidas for £470 (VAT £70).

Date	Invoice no	Supplier	Purchase (ex VAT)	VAT	Total

Total the columns and check that:
Purchases (ex VAT) + VAT = Total.

What is the difference in credit sales and credit purchases on 3 March?

What do you call the difference between cost price (purchase price) and selling price?

Financial and administrative support

Rackets & Runners keeps monthly and quarterly records of income and expenditure for its own use, so that it can monitor its financial position on an ongoing basis. Then at the end of the financial year, it prepares final accounts. As well as providing useful information for the company, these are used by:
- the Inland Revenue to assess how much tax Rackets & Runners has to pay for the year
- the Customs & Excise Office to assess how much VAT Rackets & Runners has to pay.

▶ Inland Revenue and Customs & Excise, page 216

There are two main types of final accounts – the trading and profit and loss account, and the balance sheet.

Trading and profit and loss accounts
Rackets & Runners trading and profit and loss account shows the profit (or loss) made by the business over the financial year.

Rackets and Runners
TRADING AND PROFIT AND LOSS ACCOUNT
FOR THE YEAR ENDING 30 NOVEMBER 1995

	£	£
Sales		280,000
less Cost of Sales		100,000
Gross Profit		180,000
Expenses		
Rent	10,000	
Heating and lighting	4,000	
Wages and salaries	83,000	
Stationery and telephone	1,000	
Insurances	8,000	
Sundry expenses	10,000	
		116,000
NET PROFIT		64,000

'Sales' refers to sales of stock, receipts from racket stringing and coaching

The figure for cost of sales is reached by calculating: opening stock (the value of stock at the start of the trading period), plus the cost of purchasing stock, less closing stock (the value of stock at the close of trading period)

Gross profit is profit before expenses have been deducted

Net profit is the amount of profit the business made after expenses have been deducted

Balance sheet
The balance sheet shows the value of what the business owns (its assets) and how much it owes to individuals and other businesses (its liabilities).

Rackets and Runners
BALANCE SHEET
AS AT 30 NOVEMBER 1995

Assets	£		£
Fixtures and fittings	15,000	Capital	60,000
Equipment	25,000	Liabilities	
Motor vans	10,000	Loan - R McKay	5,000
Stock	5,000	Creditors	1,000
Debtors	1,500		
Cash at Bank	9,000		
Cash in hand	500		
	66,000		66,000

Racket & Runners' balance sheet shows:
- a list of its assets
- a list of its liabilities
- its capital (what the partners invested in the business).

The assets side of the balance sheet should add up to the capital plus liabilities side. This is called the 'accounting equation' –
ASSETS = CAPITAL + LIABILITIES.
You can learn about this in more depth in an optional unit.

Budgets

A business' final accounts record what has already happened. But it is also important for businesses to plan ahead – forecast – if they are going to survive. Rackets & Runners tries to plan its monthly expenditure so that it will not exceed its monthly income. Businesses which do not have enough cash coming in to cover payment of debts and expenses are said to have 'cash flow problems'.

Every quarter, Gemma prepares a budget for Rackets & Runners using a spreadsheet package. She estimates expenditure on certain items, and enters the figures in a column headed 'Planned'. She then fills in the exact amount spent in a column headed 'Actual'. Any difference between planned and actual spending is then recorded in a column headed 'Variance'. If there is a large variance, she needs to investigate why.

A Producing a budget

Enter the following extract from a Rackets & Runners budget into a spreadsheet. Use the correct formulae to calculate variances. The first period is shown.

	Period One			Period Two			Period Three		
	Planned £	Actual £	Variance £	Planned £	Actual £	Variance £	Planned £	Actual £	Variance £
Stationery	200	250	+50	20	240		200	190	
Light and heat	1,000	900	–100	1,000	1,100		1,000	1,000	
Van expenses	750	600	–150	–	100		350	400	

Print one copy of your spreadsheet.

Amend your spreadsheet to include an extra column for each period. Head the column 'Total Variance to Date'. Work out the formula you need to use, and ask your tutor to check it is correct before entering it. Print one copy of your amended spreadsheet.

Rackets & Runners used to keep all its accounts manually. Now it has bought a computer, and uses accounting software and spreadsheet packages to maintain financial records.

Financial and administrative support

> ### A   Finding out about software
>
> Obtain software catalogues from computer retailers and identify any packages you consider useful for accounting purposes. Present your findings in the form of a table, like the one below.
>
> | Name of software | Cost | Features of software | Supplier |
> |---|---|---|---|
> | | | | |
> | | | | |
> | | | | |

Producing, evaluating and storing business documents

Rackets & Runners is a flourishing business with healthy profits – and this hasn't been achieved just by selling sports equipment.

Much of the success of a business is down to good communication:
- with customers – letting them know about new products and services, responding efficiently to enquiries and complaints
- with colleagues – making sure all employees are up to date with meetings, initiatives and progress, so they can work well together as a team
- with other businesses – responding to enquiries, keeping business customers and wholesalers up to date with progress.

To ensure good communication on a day-to-day basis, businesses use a range of routine business documents.

Business documents

Most businesses have their own:
- house style (way of setting out documents)
- logo.

These make it very clear where documents are from, and also show the company's image.

> ### A   Company logos
>
> [Logos shown: Rackets & Runners, Abbey National, Interflora, Oxfam Working for a Fairer World, C&A, RAC]
>
> Do you recognise these logos? What sort of image do they create? What business documents do you think they would appear on?
>
> Using your knowledge of Rackets & Runners, design a new logo for the company to print on all its business documents.

Financial and administrative support

Memos

Memoranda – or memos for short – are the most common documents which people in business use to communicate with their colleagues. Memos are sent to one or more people within an organisation. They are usually word processed on a computer in the company's house style, and printed on A4 paper.

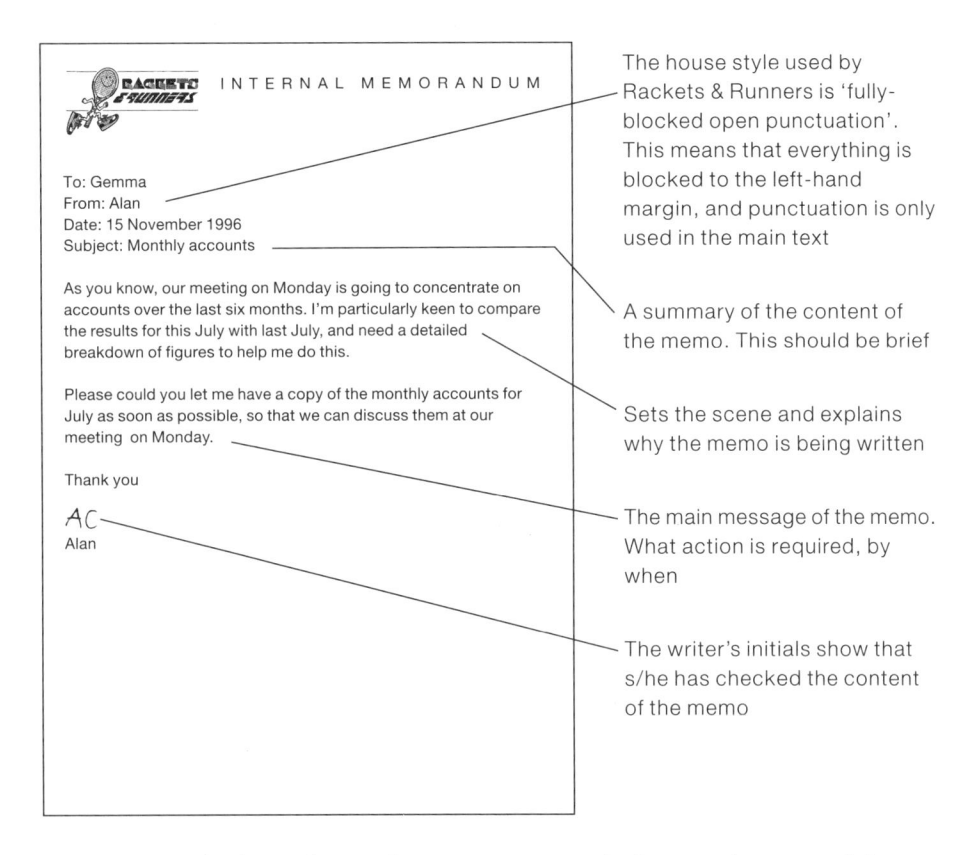

```
RACKETS
& RUNNERS         INTERNAL MEMORANDUM

To: Gemma
From: Alan
Date: 15 November 1996
Subject: Monthly accounts

As you know, our meeting on Monday is going to concentrate on
accounts over the last six months. I'm particularly keen to compare
the results for this July with last July, and need a detailed
breakdown of figures to help me do this.

Please could you let me have a copy of the monthly accounts for
July as soon as possible, so that we can discuss them at our
meeting on Monday.

Thank you

AC
Alan
```

- The house style used by Rackets & Runners is 'fully-blocked open punctuation'. This means that everything is blocked to the left-hand margin, and punctuation is only used in the main text
- A summary of the content of the memo. This should be brief
- Sets the scene and explains why the memo is being written
- The main message of the memo. What action is required, by when
- The writer's initials show that s/he has checked the content of the memo

A memo's style depends on who is writing it and what it is being used for. A memo from a Managing Director or Head of Department to a junior member of staff will have a different style to a memo from a junior member of staff to his or her manager.

▶ Memos, page 17

A   Writing a memo

Alan needs to find out from Ian which schools have regular tennis coaching, and how this service is marketed. Write a memo to Ian from Alan, using the correct house style.

Do you think a memo is a good way to communicate with staff? Do you think Rackets & Runners' memos are clear and easy to read?

Letters

Businesses usually communicate with their customers and other businesses by letter. The main reasons for writing a business letter are to:
- confirm a meeting
- answer an enquiry
- deal with a customer complaint.

Financial and administrative support

When Ian was talking to Foster Stationery about the design of the carrier bags, he wrote several letters, including the one below.

The house style used by Rackets & Runners is 'fully-blocked open punctuation'

The date on which the letter was written

The name of the person the letter is written to, and their address. This should always include a courtesy title (for example, Mr, Miss, Mrs, Ms, Dr, Rev)

Salutation. If possible, this should include the person's name (as here, 'Dear Mr Murphy'), or if not, 'Dear Sir'. Letters should never start with 'Dear Mr John Murphy', or 'Dear John Murphy'

Heading. This should be short, and instantly give the reader an idea of the letter's content

Complimentary close. If the letter is written to a named person, as here, this should be 'Yours sincerely'. If the letter begins 'Dear Sir' or 'Dear Madam', this should be 'Yours faithfully'

Signature. A letter must always be signed by the person who has written it

Designation. This is the writer's title or position

This indicates that something is enclosed with the letter

▶ Formal letters, page 15

RACKETS & RUNNERS 81 HOPE STREET · GLASGOW · G2 6AJ · TEL: 0141 221 3424

4 February 1996

Mr J Murphy
Foster Stationery Ltd
Unit 55
Albion Industrial Estate
Edinburgh EH20 1LF

Dear Mr Murphy

CARRIER BAG DESIGN

Thank you for sending me the carrier bag proofs. I like the design very much but would prefer a different colour.

Please can you change the colour of the bags from green to blue and make the logo silver. I presume this change of colour would not affect the overall price.

I enclose samples of the new colours and look forward to receiving a new proof.

Yours sincerely

Ian Jefferson

Ian Jefferson
Marketing Manager

Enc

Invitations and notices

A Writing a letter

A customer, Darren Atkins, has written to Rackets & Runners complaining about a faulty pair of trainers he bought and asking for a refund. Write a letter back to Darren apologising for the sub-standard goods and offering him a full refund. Think about the appearance of your letter – make sure you use the Rackets & Runners' house style. Check your use of language in the letter. Why do you think spelling and grammar are so important in business documents?

A new sports centre is opening in Glasgow, and Alan has received an invitation to the opening ceremony.

> ### Mr A. Connors
>
> Linford Christie will be opening the new Glasgow Recreation Centre on Thursday 14 March 1996. You are invited to a champagne buffet reception at 8 p.m.
>
> R · S · V · P
>
> GLASGOW RECREATION CENTRE
> 36 PALMERSTON HILL
> GLASGOW G59 4TU

An invitation is usually printed formally, and must always include:
- the time
- the place
- the address
- who people should reply to, where (RSVP).

An invitation is sent to one person, whose name is usually handwritten on it. If a business wants to invite everybody to a function, it can print notices or posters and display them in public places.

A Producing an invitiation

Rackets & Runners has decided to hold a Christmas promotional evening, with 20% off all goods. It wants to invite its regular customers to this special event, to be held on 12 December between 7 p.m. and 9 p.m. at the Hope Street branch.

Come up with two ideas for invitations and two ideas for posters advertising the event. Look at the appearance and wording of your ideas, choose the best invitation and the best poster, and produce finished designs.

Messages
When Ismail was working at Rackets & Runners, he was responsible for answering the telephone and leaving messages for other members of staff. Rackets & Runners has its own pre-printed message pads, and Ismail got plenty of practice filling them in during his time at the company!

Financial and administrative support

RACKETS & RUNNERS	To *Alan*
	From *Ismail*

Message

~~Tony Bissett~~ Russell phoned from Foster stationery to check the ~~pantone~~ pantone colour of the logo. Please phone back ASAP

Taken by *Ismail*

Date *11 Nov*   Time *10:40*

A — Leaving a message

Do you think Ismail's message to Alan is clear? How would you improve its appearance? How would you improve his use of language?

Mrs Jones, Rackets & Runners' accountant, has just phoned and wants to leave a message for Gemma. She needs to know which company the carrier bags are being ordered from and what the invoice number is. She is in a meeting all morning, but would like Gemma to phone her urgently after 2 p.m.

Photocopy a blank message sheet from the Toolkit, and leave a message for Gemma.

▶ Toolkit, page 75

Ways of processing business documents

All business documents must be clear and easy to read. Because of this, staff need to think carefully about how to produce different documents.

Staff at Rackets & Runners process business documents in several different ways:

- they write telephone messages **by hand**
- they **type** envelopes when sending letters and other documents to customers and suppliers
- they **word process** memos and letters, and print them out on a laser printer
- they use a **photocopier** if they need more than one copy of a document
- they get invitations, notices and posters professionally **printed** at a printers.

Financial and administrative support

> **RACKETS & RUNNERS**
>
> INTERNAL MEMORANDUM
>
> To: Gemma
> From: Alan
> Date: 15 November 1996
> Subject: Monthly accounts
>
> As you know, our meeting on Monday is going to concentrate on accounts over the last six months. I'm particularly keen to compare the results for this July with last July, and need a detailed breakdown of figures to help me do this.
>
> Please could you let me have a copy of the monthly accounts for July as soon as possible, so that we can discuss them at our meeting on Monday.
>
> Thank you
>
> AC
> Alan

> **RACKETS & RUNNERS**   81 HOPE STREET · GLASGOW · G2 6AJ · TEL: 0141 221 3424
>
> 4 February 1996
>
> Mr J Murphy
> Foster Stationery Ltd
> Unit 55
> Albion Industrial Estate
> Edinburgh EH20 1LF
>
> Dear Mr Murphy
>
> CARRIER BAG DESIGN
>
> Thank you for sending me the carrier bag proofs. I like the design very much but would prefer a different colour.
>
> Please can you change the colour of the bags from green to blue and make the logo silver. I presume this change of colour would not affect the overall price.
>
> I enclose samples of the new colours and look forward to receiving a new proof.
>
> Yours sincerely
>
> *Ian Jefferson*
>
> Ian Jefferson
> Marketing Manager
>
> Enc

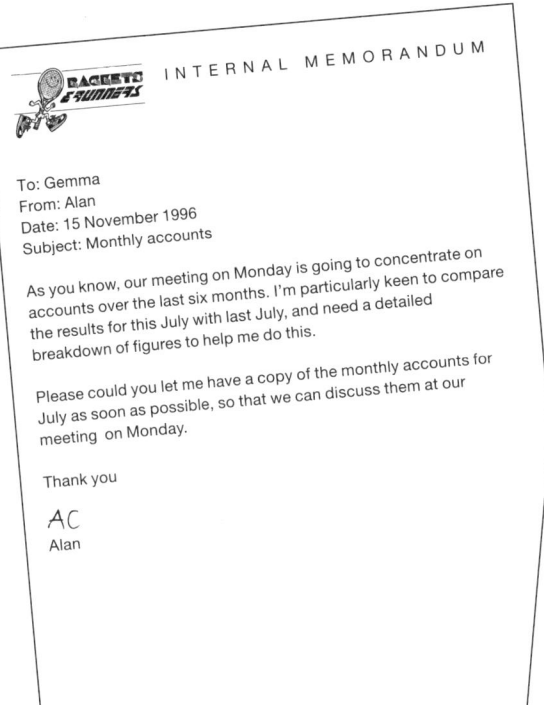

Alan explains the pros and cons of these different methods of processing documents:

'It makes sense to write phone messages by hand because it's quick and easy, although sometimes handwritten messages are really difficult to read! People spend longer writing a memo, and use a word processing package so the document is clear. The same goes for letters to customers and suppliers – we always word process letters to create a professional impression of the business. Another advantage of word processed documents is that they're all stored on our computer's hard disc, and it's easy to make changes or print out extra copies. If we want extra copies of a document for our own use within the business, we tend to use the photocopier as it's cheaper than the laser printer. Finally, if we really want to make a good impression with an invitation or notice we get it professionally printed, but this is very expensive and takes a long time to organise, and we try to avoid it whenever possible.'

A Which processing method?

Rackets & Runners has asked you to produce the following documents. How would you process them?
- a letter in response to a customer complaint
- one hundred copies of a poster advertising the January sale
- ten copies of a document on health and safety, to circulate to staff who work in the shops
- a phone message from a supplier
- a memo to staff about this year's Christmas party

Sending business documents

In the past, Rackets & Runners used to send all its correspondence to customers and suppliers by post, but now it relies more and more on faxing documents. Most businesses have fax machines, and Alan can contact his suppliers by fax at any time of the day or night, and know that the document will get there quickly.

Sometimes, Alan, Ian and Gemma use other delivery services. If they are sending valuable documents by post, they choose registered post or recorded delivery. These cost more than normal post, but mean that a record is kept of when the documents were sent and when they were received. Other delivery services they use include Parcel Force for posting parcels (part of Royal Mail), and motorbike courier services for fast delivery of packages to people in their area.

Both of Rackets & Runners' shops now have computers, which are linked together by a computer network. This means that staff in one shop can send messages and memos to staff in the other by electronic transmission (often known as electronic mail or e-mail). So if Gemma is working in one shop and wants to send a message to all staff about claiming expenses, all she has to do is type the message on the computer and send it by pressing a key. The message is then stored in the mailbox of the other shop's computer.

A Ways of sending documents

Alan has asked you to decide how he should send each of the following documents:
- a cheque to a supplier for £1200, in payment for stock
- a letter to a customer explaining why her order is late
- a letter to a wholesaler, confirming an order (this needs to be with them within the hour).

Write a memo to Alan advising him how to send each document. Explain your decision in terms of ease of sending the document, cost, and security of the document.

Financial and administrative support

Storing business documents

By now you will have realised that Rackets & Runners deals with a wide range of business documents. These all need to be stored carefully so that up-to-date information is easy to find.

Up to now, Rackets & Runners has kept records on paper, stored in filing cabinets. Alan, Gemma and Ian all have their own filing systems so that they can find documents easily. Between them, they file documents in four main ways:

- alphabetically (by name)
- numerically (by number)
- by subject
- chronologically (by date).

Ian keeps detailed records of all the schools which have coaching sessions. He has a file for each school, and stores them alphabetically by school name.

A Filing alphabetically

Ian has just been given the names of ten new schools which are interested in coaching. List them in strict alphabetical order.

St Anne's School
Westhaven Grammar School
Clark Primary School
Dowsing Junior School
Saint Joseph's Catholic School
Dane Court School
Clark Secondary School
Jedburgh High School
Handstead Secondary School
Stanford High School

(Note that 'Saint' and 'St' both become 'Saint', and if the words are identical you need to look at the next word.)

Gemma finds it easier to file all her suppliers by number. She then keeps a separate alphabetical index to identify the numerical files.

Alan deals with a variety of correspondence. He stores his files alphabetically by customer name, but then stores letters in each file chronologically. This means the most recent letters are always at the top of the file.

In Rackets & Runners' shops, filing is done by type of stock (by subject). For example, there are separate files set up for trainers, football boots, tracksuits and so on. Paperwork on each type of stock is stored in the relevant file. This makes it easy for Ian to check stock levels quickly, and to find out whether there have been any complaints about a product.

Now Rackets & Runners has a computer system, it is going to start storing information on computer. Ian is planning to set up a customer database, so that the partners can store and retrieve customer information alphabetically, by subject, by number or by date – which will please all of

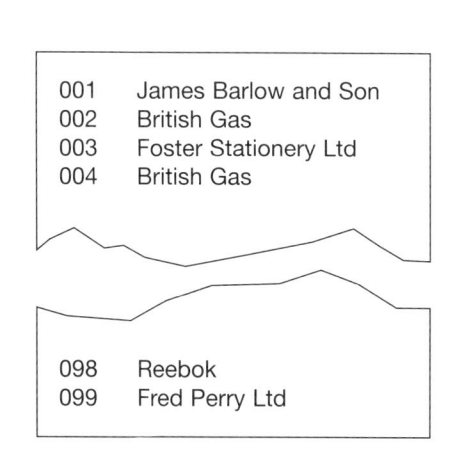

001	James Barlow and Son
002	British Gas
003	Foster Stationery Ltd
004	British Gas

| 098 | Reebok |
| 099 | Fred Perry Ltd |

them! He has already talked to Gemma and Alan about giving files names that are easy to remember, so that they will be able to find them quickly and not waste time and money searching the database.

The safety and security of documents is important whether they are stored on paper or on computer. Rackets & Runners locks its filing cabinets at night, and only the partners have keys. Ian is planning to back up computer records onto floppy disc twice a week, and to store the discs in a fire-proof safe. All staff will have their own password, and only Gemma, Ian and Alan will be able to look at some of the confidential information.

A Paper versus computer

What are the advantages and disadvantages of storing documents on paper and on computer? Make a chart listing the pros and cons of each, remembering to include:
- ease of storing information
- ease of finding and retrieving information
- cost
- safety of documents
- security of documents.

You have now seen all the business documents used by Rackets & Runners and how they are completed. Setting up a sports shop isn't as easy as it looks at first, but good financial and administrative procedures help Alan, Gemma and Ian to run their business as efficiently as possible.

Assignment

EXPLORING FINANCIAL DOCUMENTS

Setting the scene

For the following tasks, you need to carry out some research on your own to identify and collect examples of financial documents. Ask your parents if they have examples of the documents – they may deal with more documents than they realise! You could use examples from mail order catalogues, store credit cards, electricity or gas bills and so on. Remember to ask permission before taking anything from home, as some documents are confidential.

Task 1
Collect examples of the following purchase documents:
- order
- invoice
- credit note
- goods received note.

▶ Purchase documents, page 217

Paste them onto A4 paper and write an explanation of each document's purpose alongside.

Task 2
Collect examples of the following sales documents:
- order received
- delivery note
- credit note
- statement of account
- remittance advice.

▶ Sales documents, page 221

Paste them onto A4 paper and write an explanation of each document's purpose alongside.

Task 3
Collect examples of the following receipt documents:
- receipt
- cheque
- paying-in slip
- bank statement.

▶ Reciept documents, page 229

Paste them onto A4 paper and write an explanation of each document's purpose alongside.

▶ Payment documents, page 224

Task 4
Select four different payment methods and briefly describe when you would use each method of payment.

Opportunities to collect evidence
On completing these tasks, you will have the opportunity to meet the following requirements for Intermediate GNVQ Business.
Unit 4
Element 4.1 PCs 1, 2, 3, 4

Core skills
Communication
Elements 2.2, 2.4

▶ Core skills coverage grid, page 252

Financial and administrative support

245

Assignment

COMPLETING DOCUMENTS

Setting the scene

At the start of his work experience placement, Ismail asked Alan if he could have examples of blank sales and purchase documents to put into his GNVQ folder. Alan suggested that Ismail should use copies of documents which he completed during his work experience placement, as this would provide him with appropriate evidence for his portfolio.

Working in pairs, complete the sequence of documents Ismail dealt with during his placement. To complete all the documents in the chain, one of you should work in Ismail's position, and the other in the position of the accounts clerk at Foster Stationery Ltd.

Ismail's tasks for Rackets & Runners are marked (R).

Tasks for the accounts clerk at Foster Stationery are marked (F).

When you have completed Ismail's tasks, change roles with your partner and complete the accounts clerk's documents.

You may photocopy the blank documents on pages 66–75 for the tasks which follow. Remember your figures must be accurate and legible.

Task 1 (R)
Send a purchase order to Foster Stationery Ltd for five reams of headed notepaper.
- The order number is 588.
- The notepaper should be delivered to Rackets & Runners.
- This is a repeat order, and the reference number for the headed notepaper is HN 398.
- The unit price is £8.35 excluding VAT.
- You have been authorised by the partners to sign the purchase order on their behalf.

Task 2 (F)
Prepare a delivery note from Foster Stationery Ltd to be sent with the notepaper.
- The goods will be sent by Securicor.
- Invoice number 405223 will be sent on the date the goods are sent.

Work out the total cost of the order.

Task 3 (R)
When the order arrives at Rackets & Runners, you check the parcel and discover that one ream of paper has been damaged in one corner. You must make a note of this problem on the delivery note before returning it to Foster Stationery.

Task 4 (F)
Complete the invoice from Foster Stationery Ltd to Rackets & Runners.
- The account number is 46930.
- Terms are 'carriage paid'.

Task 5 (F)
Complete a credit note for the damaged notepaper and send it to Rackets & Runners.
- The credit note number s 4786.

Task 6 (F)
Prepare the monthly statement to send to Rackets & Runners.
- The opening outstanding balance was £64.29.
- Record the transactions made this month.
- Show clearly the closing balance owed by Rackets & Runners.

Task 7 (R)
Prepare the cheque to be sent to Foster Stationery Ltd in full settlement of the amount owing. Complete the remittance advice slip and attach it to the cheque.

Task 8 (R)
Ismail was sent by Gemma to buy teabags and sugar. She asked him to pay for the items and told him he would be reimbursed when he returned.
- The total cost of the purchases was £2.46.
- The petty cash voucher number was 67.

Task 9 (R)
The PE teacher at Lauderdale High School asks for a receipt for racket re-stringing.
- He pays by cash.
- The total cost is £45.
- The receipt number is 298.

Task 10 (R)
Ismail has been helping Gemma count cash and complete paying-in slips all week, and is now going to prepare one unsupervised. The following amounts are to be paid into the bank:

22 X £20 notes
47 X £10 notes
62 X £5 notes

102 X £1 coins
101 X 50p pieces
34 X 20p pieces

44 X 10p pieces
33 X 5p pieces
29 X 2p pieces
16 X 1p pieces

Cheques for: £19.95, £87.20, £14.99, £29.98 and £27.50.

Financial and administrative support

Task 11 (R)

On his last day of work experience, Ismail work shadowed Gemma preparing wage slips for the shops' employees. She suggested that he prepare a 'specimen' pay slip for his portfolio, inserting the following information and using the information sheet she provided to work out the missing information.

Employee name: Ismail Shar
Employee payroll number: 20377
Basic pay: £187.33
Overtime: £56.00
Tax code: ((see hard copy for what should be added here))
Income tax for the week:
National Insurance:
Take home pay for the week.

Information sheet

Personal taxation:	
Personal allowance p.a.	£3765
Income tax rates	
Lower rate	20%
on taxable income up to	£3900
Basic rate	24%
on taxable income up to	£25,500
Higher rate	40%
on taxable income over	£25,500
National Insurance:	
Employees	
below £61 per week	no payment
from £61 to £455 p.w.	2% of £61
	= 10% of the rest up to £455

Note: Personal allowances are for one year (52 weeks).

Task 12 (both)

Having found Ismail's take-home pay, draw a pie chart to show how Ismail's pay was distributed between:
- take home pay
- income tax
- National Insurance.

Task 13 (both)

When you have both completed all the tasks, discuss the experience. Make a note of any difficulties you had, and of how you dealt with them. Explain why different types of financial information must be recorded.

▶ Pie charts, pages 44 and 51

Opportunities to collect evidence
On completing these tasks, you will have the opportunity to meet the following requirements for Intermediate GNVQ Business.
Unit 4
Elements 4.2 PCs 1, 2, 3, 4, 5

Core skills
Application of Number
Element 2.1, 2.2, 2.3

Communication
Element 2.4

▶ Core skills coverage grid, page 252

Financial and administrative support

Assignment

ORGANISING A SALES CONFERENCE

Setting the scene
Rackets & Runners is a member of the National Sports Retailers' Consortium (NSRC). NSRC is holding a sales conference in the Cranmer Hotel in London in the new year. Jack Robertson, the south east manager of NSRC, is responsible for arranging the conference.

Alan and Gemma have agreed to help him this year, and they have been sent the following list of sports retailers who should be invited to attend.

Name of retailer	Town	Name of retailer	Town
A Johns	Glasgow	L Holford	Perth
S Philpott	Ayr	L Deeney	Londonderry
C Martin	Newcastle	R Farley	Oban
L Shemeld	Canterbury	R Dixon	Torquay
J Foster	London	C Derry	Southend
R Comfort	Belfast	K Bradley	Portsmouth
R Bennett	Oxford	M Harding	Exeter
K McIlvain	Glasgow	M Hogg	Wincanton
M Muller	Birmingham	J Mitchell	Tonbridge
J Laslett	Dover	L Hughes	Folkestone
C Crittenden	Liverpool	I Castle	Lingfield
C Garthwaite	Telford	J White	Prestwick
J Jones	Cardiff	J Fenwick	Dumbarton
M Bower	Carlisle	J Collins	Edinburgh
S Green	Plymouth	A Easson	Lincoln
L Orr	Looe	M Cannon	Winchester
D Thompson	Manchester	J Aire	Swansea
L Culmer	Brighton	A Eadie	Littlehampton
P Burnside	York	L Brough	Skegness

In order to ensure efficient planning, Gemma asks you to perform the following tasks.

Task 1
Write a memo to Jack Robertson at NSRC, explaining why it will be important to use the following documents when organising the sales conference:
- letters
- memos
- invitations
- notices
- messages.

▶ Memos, pages 17 and 237

249

Financial and administrative support

Task 2
Using the map of the UK below, prepare an index card for each of the conference delegates, indicating name, town and geographical region.

Task 3
Arrange cards in regions with Region A at the front. Then arrange retailers' names alphabetically within regions. Fasten your index cards with an elastic band.

Task 4
Use the map to *estimate* the distance each delegate will need to travel to the conference. What is the range of distances you estimated? How many do you think will need to travel more than 200 kilometres?

Use a distance grid from a map/atlas to find the actual distance each delegate will need to travel. For places not on the distance grid use a map with an appropriate scale to work out the distance. Calculate the mean distance travelled. Those travelling further than this mean distance will be regarded as 'travelling far', and will be given £50 towards travel. You assume this will involve about half the delegates. Find the ratio of those travelling far: those close to the conference. Is this what you would expect?

▶ Estimating measurements, page 38

▶ Ratios, pages 33 and 36

Task 5
Draft a letter by hand, from Gemma Rossi (Rackets & Runners) to the Cranmer Hotel, 3 Chester Avenue, London W2 4QR. The letter should inform the hotel that:
- the provisional booking made for the third weekend in January (Friday evening to Sunday after lunch) can now be confirmed
- 38 delegates will be attending, and 38 single rooms are required
- all meals will be taken in the hotel restaurant.

Task 6
Carefully check your handwritten letter and when you are happy with the content and layout, word process, spell-check, print preview and print one copy.

Task 7
NSRC would like to invite some sports personalities to a reception on the Saturday evening at 8pm in the hotel. Draft a suitable invitation. Include RSVP to Jack Robertson, NSRC, 4 Palace Street, Tunbridge Wells, Kent TN3 4KL.

Discuss your draft with your tutor. If it is acceptable, produce a sample invitation using IT with appropriate graphics and style.

Task 8
As a group, contact a local printer to cost the printing of 50 invitations. How quickly could they be prepared? Suggest alternative methods of producing the invitations, comparing costs and preparation times.

Task 9
The conference committee has decided to allocate a large area of wall space in the conference room to display members' promotional material. Design a colour poster to promote Rackets & Runners.

Task 10
Ian sends you a memo suggesting that a black and white poster would be cheaper to produce. Reply to his memo, justifying your use of colour.

Task 11
Evaluate all the documents you have prepared in this assignment, using the following as prompts:
- legible letters and figures
- accurate calculations
- correct grammar
- correct spelling
- house style
- cost of documents
- time to produce
- ease of editing
- storage of documents
- security of computer disks and hard copy.

▶ Memos, pages 17 and 237

Opportunities to collect evidence
On completing these tasks, you will have the opportunity to meet the following requirements for Intermediate GNVQ Business.
Unit 4
Element 4.3 PCs 1, 2, 3, 4, 5, 6

Core skills
Communication
Elements 2.1, 2.2, 2.3

Application of Number
Elements 2.1, 2.2, 2.3

Information Technology
Elements 2.1, 2.2, 2.3

▶ Core skills coverage grid, page 252

Core skills coverage grid

The following grid indicates opportunities for assessment of core skills from within assignments and can be used to help students with tracking. To claim achievement of these core skills students must perform in accordance with the Performance Criteria given in the specifications for each element.

Communication	Unit 1 1	Unit 1 2	Unit 1 3	Unit 2 1	Unit 2 2	Unit 2 3	Unit 2 4	Unit 3 1	Unit 3 2	Unit 3 3	Unit 3 4	Unit 4 1	Unit 4 2	Unit 4 3	Extra 3.4
2.1 Discussions															
one-to-one + known person	•	•		•											•
one-to-one + unknown person	•				•	•	•			•					•
group discussion + known person			•	•											•
group discussion + unknown person		•													
2.2 Written															
given format for known person									•	•					•
given format for unknown person			•												
usual format for known person		•		•		•			•					•	
usual format for unknown person	•				•		•			•				•	
2.3 Images in...															
written work for known people	•	•		•											
written work for unknown people	•	•		•	•					•					
one-to-one discussion with known person	•	•		•											
one-to-one discussion with unknown person	•		•	•											
group discussion + known people	•	•							•						
group discussion + unknown people				•											
2.4 Reading and responding...															
to text only	•	•		•				•		•		•			
to text with some images	•	•						•				•			
to images with some text	•	•													•
summarising orally	•														•
summarising in writing	•			•											
Information Technology															
2.1 Prepare information															
input text	•					•		•	•						•
save text	•					•		•	•						•
input numbers	•							•							•
save numbers	•							•							•
input graphics	•							•							
save graphics	•							•							
2.2 Process information															
process text	•					•		•	•					•	•
process numbers	•							•						•	•
process graphics	•							•							
process combined information	•							•							
2.3 Present information															
text on screen/printed/saved	•					•		•	•					•	•
numbers on screen/printed/saved	•							•							•
graphics on screen/printed/saved	•							•							
combined info on screen/printed/saved														•	
backup copies	•														•

252

Core skills coverage grid

	Unit 1			Unit 2				Unit 3				Unit 4			Extra
	1	2	3	1	2	3	4	1	2	3	4	1	2	3	3,4
2.4 Evaluate the use of IT															
explain reasons for using IT				•											
log of errors															
explain safe working practice															
Application of number															
2.1 Collect and record data															
money (state w or p)														• w	• w
measuring length (state w or p)														• w	• w
other measurements (state w or p)			•							•					• p
estimate distances									•					•	•
estimate size						•									
describe using fractions/decimals														•	• •
describe using percentages					•									•	• •
describe using ratios					•										•
describe using negative numbers															•
use measuring instruments													•		•
round															•
2.2 Tackle problems															
whole number work (+ − × ÷)									•				•		• •
using decimals									•				•		•
using fractions															•
using percentages													•		•
using ratios									•						•
using simple formulae														•	•
perimeter														• •	• •
area															•
volume															•
converting within															•
converting between															•
finding mode and range														• •	•
calculating the mean/median	•													• •	
2.3 Interpret and present data															
2-D drawing	•	•													•
2-D drawing of 3-D object		•													
use of 2-D drawing of 3-D object		•													
pictogram								•			•				
bar chart	•							•			•				•
pie chart						•		•			•		•	•	
line graphs								•			•				
explain/interpret the mean															•
explain/interpret the median															
explain/interpret the mode															•
explain/interpret the range						•									•
describe using probabilities															

Note: AoN collect and record data
w = from text/words   p = from people

Useful addresses

The following organisations may be able to help you with information and advice. However, remember that they are busy and don't overwhelm them with long lists of questions. Some may charge a small fee for carrying out research.

Advertising Standards Authority
Brook House
2–16 Torrington Place
London
WC1E 7HN

Advisory, Conciliation and Arbitration Service (ACAS)
Clifton House
83–117 Euston Road
London
NW1 2RB

Banking Information Service
Lombard Street
London
EC3V 9AT

British Safety Council
National Safety Centre
70 Chancellors Road
Hammersmith
London
W6 9RS

British Standards Institute
BSI Head Office
BSI Standards
389 Chiswick High Road
London
W4 4AL

Business in the Community
227a City Road
London
EC1V 1LX

Central Statistical Office
CSO Inquiry Service
Room 65c/3
Great George Street
London
SW1P 3AQ

Consumers' Association
14 Buckingham Street
London
WC2N 6DS

Consumers in the European Community Group
24 Tufton Street
London
SW1P 3RB

Crafts Council (The national organisation for promoting the contemporary crafts)
44a Pentonville Road
London
N1 9BY

Department for Education and Employment
Public Inquiry Office
Caxton House
Tothill Street
London
SW1H 9NA

Department for the Environment
2 Marsham Street
London
SW1P 3EB

Eurostat
HMSO Books (agency section)
HMSO Publications Centre
51 Nine Elms Lane
London
SW8 5DR

Federation of Small Businesses
140 Lower Marsh
London
SE1 7AE

Health and Safety Executive
Baynards House
1 Chepstow Place
London
W2 4TF

HMSO
St Crispins
Duke Street
Norwich
NR3 1PD

The Market Research Society
15 Northburgh Street
London
EC1V 0AH

Office of Fair Trading (OFT)
Field House
15–25 Breams Buildings
London
EC4A 1PR

The Prince's Trust
8 Bedford Row
London
WC1R 4BA

Skills and Enterprise Network
PO Box 12
West PDO
Leen Gate
Lenton
Nottingham
NG7 2GB

Small Firms Service
Department of Employment
Steel House
Tothill Street
London
SW1H 9HF

Trades Union Congress
Congress House
Great Russell Street
London
WC1B 3LS

Young Enterprise
Ewert Place
Summertown
Oxford
OX2 7BZ

You might also find it useful to contact local:
- employment offices
- branches of the Office of Fair Trading
- branches of the Health and Safety Executive.

Look for their details in your local telephone directory.

You may also find the following publications useful:
- *Labour Market Trends* (HMSO)
- *Annual Abstract of Statistics* (HMSO)
- *Monthly Abstract of Statistics* (HMSO)
- *Regional Trends* (HMSO)
- *Social Trends* (HMSO).

Look for copies in the reference section of your public library.

Answers

Unit 1
1. b extracts raw materials or crops
2. a adds a further stage of development to raw materials
3. d concentrates on providing services
4. a has declined in recent years
5. a has declined in recent years
6. b has increased in recent years
7. b is owned and controlled by the government
8. d is owned by individuals, rather than the government
9. d has unlimited liability
10. c is usually a legal arrangement between up to 20 people
11. a has owners who do not lose all their personal assets if the business goes bankrupt
12. c buys and sells shares on the stockmarket
13. c has shared ownership with an established, nationally recognised organisation
14. b is when all the employees share in the ownership and control of the business
15. a is owned and controlled by the government
16. c one of the main purposes of businesses
17. c is the percentage of total sales claimed by a business
18. b the owners don't lose their personal assets if the business gets into difficulty
19. c the owners do lose their personal assets if the business gets into difficulty
20. a a business needs a skilled and experienced workforce nearby
21. a often the reason for businesses being located where they are
22. a they may provide important supplies and services
23. a businesses need to be able to sell their goods and services to people who want them
24. b to distribute goods to customers and receive supplies easily
25. d finding out what customers want
26. c making sure the business' products are attractive and useful
27. d keeping customers informed

Unit 2
1. b two or three levels
2. d the people who work for a company
3. c a pyramid structure
4. d the customer service department
5. d the finance department
6. b maintaining employee records
7. b shift work
8. c contribute to the decision-making process
9. d it helps the product maintain standards
10. c her trade union representative
11. a provide protective clothing
12. c 2 months
13. b providing employees with holidays
14. b ACAS
15. c a supervisor
16. c an electrician
17. b a home help
18. c the Training and Enterprise Council

Unit 3
1. c *Social Trends*
2. d lifestyle
3. c an increase in interest rates
4. c age
5. b it is a good way to get publicity via television
6. d an advert in the local paper
7. d an increase in the cost of living
8. a low cost
9. b to encourage people to shop in the supermarket regularly
10. c tobacco
11. b honest
12. c Trades Description Act
13. a Sale of Goods Act
14. a Trading Standards Office
15. c information
16. b identify problems with products or services
17. c ethical constraints
18. d personal customer service

Appendix

Key legislation

The framework of the law

British law is a very large and complex system involving four countries and at least two very different legal systems. However, most of the law which you will need to know about will have come from an *Act of Parliament*, such as the Health and Safety at Work Act 1974.

An Act of Parliament will usually have been introduced by the government of the day and then debated, voted upon and possibly changed by both Houses of Parliament. During this stage it is called a Bill. It is only known as an Act once it has passed through Parliament and been given royal assent.

However, before the government takes proposed legislation to Parliament it will usually have gone through a period of consultation, starting with what is known as a *Green Paper*, a document published by the government in order to test opinion. Alternatively, the government may ask a committee or an individual to produce a report.

The next stage will probably be what is known as a *White Paper*, which is a statement of what the proposed legislation will be about. The White Paper can often be an important means of understanding the philosophy which may lie behind an Act of Parliament.

Not all Acts of Parliament are proposed by the government. Some are introduced by individual Members of Parliament who may be working on behalf of groups of interested organisations in order to change the law. These are called *Private Members' Bills*. This path will often be used for socially controversial legislation on which the government wishes to take a neutral stance, such as the abolition of capital punishment.

Acts of Parliament may contain powers which allow the government to introduce them a piece at a time. So just because an Act has been passed, you should not assume that everything in it is current law. This is particularly likely to happen where there are resource implications to introducing the whole Act at one time.

An Act of Parliament may include a clause which gives the senior Minister involved (usually called the Secretary of State) the power to introduce *Regulations* at a later date, which give more detailed law on specific areas covered by the Act. This is done by means of a *Statutory Instrument* which is placed before Parliament but is usually not debated.

With major pieces of legislation, *Guidance* may be introduced at a later stage. Whilst this does not have the force of law, it explains, clarifies and amplifies the law and defines what may be considered to be good practice and must therefore be considered very seriously by practitioners.

Because the structure of the law and service provision in Scotland is different from England and Wales, Scottish legislation must often be treated differently. Sometimes this is done within the main Act by explaining how it will be applied in Scotland, and defining specifically Scots terminology. On other occasions there will be a separate Act for Scotland.

In the case of Northern Ireland, legislation must be introduced by

Order in Council. This is because it had a separate legislature (the Northern Ireland Assembly) until 1972, when its powers were taken over by the Secretary of State for Northern Ireland. Although this power lies with the Secretary of State, there is a consultative process and, as a result, there is usually a time lag between the appearance of the main Act and its Northern Irish equivalent. The Order itself, once put before Parliament, cannot be amended, but simply accepted or rejected.

Health and safety at work

The **Health and Safety at Work Act 1974**, as amended by the Management of Health and Safety at Work Regulations 1992, aims to ensure health, safety and welfare in the workplace.

Under the Act, an employer must:
- provide a safe and healthy workplace for everyone on their premises, whether worker, client or visitor
- provide and maintain safe machinery and equipment
- ensure safe handling, use, storage and transportation of articles and substances
- provide information, instruction, training and supervision to employees on health and safety
- produce a safety policy and bring it to the notice of employees.

However, the Act also recognises that we all have some responsibility, both for ourselves and others. In line with this, employees:
- have a responsibility for the safety of themselves, colleagues, clients, and anyone else on the premises
- must co-operate with their employers to ensure that the Regulations are kept
- must not interfere with or damage equipment provided in the interests of safety (for example, fire extinguishers).

The Health and Safety at Work Act applies to the whole of the UK.

Non-discriminatory legislation

Discrimination on the grounds of sex, race, colour or national origin is illegal, whether through recruitment, conditions of work, promotion, training or dismissal.

The **Race Relations Act 1976** makes it illegal to discriminate in housing, education, employment, membership of public or private clubs, entertainment, or the provision of goods or services, on the grounds of race, colour, nationality or ethnic origin. The Act defines discrimination as being direct, indirect or victimisation. Under this Act, the Commission for Racial Equality (CRE) was established. The CRE publishes information, carries out research and can investigate the practices and procedures of organisations and pursue action to redress discriminatory practices.

The Act also gives local authorities a duty to ensure that they pay due regard to the need to eliminate unlawful discrimination and to promote good relations between people of different racial groups. Services must be provided in a non-discriminatory way. You may have seen job advertisements saying that because a particular group are poorly represented 'applications will be invited from...'. This is because employers are allowed to take positive action in order to encourage the participation of a particular group if they have been under-represented.

Appendix: Key legislation

The Race Relations Act does not apply to Northern Ireland, where the issues of discrimination have a very specific local character. Because of this, the **Fair Employment Act (NI) 1989** made it unlawful to discriminate in employment against, or arouse fear of, groups because of their colour, race, nationality, national origin or religious beliefs.

The **Sex Discrimination Act 1975** makes it illegal to discriminate or give favourable treatment on the grounds of sex or marital status, and covers both men and women. As with the Race Relations Act, it allows for positive action in order to address imbalance. It also permits gender to be used as a specific qualification for a job in certain circumstances, for example a woman working in a woman's refuge, where it is a Genuine Occupational Qualification. It can also permit the provision of women-only occupational courses in work areas where they may be seriously under-represented.

The Act also established the Equal Opportunities Commission, which provides advice and undertakes research on the promotion of equality of opportunity between the sexes. It applies in England, Wales and Scotland. Northern Ireland is covered by the **Sex Discrimination (NI) Order 1976**.

The **Equal Pay Act 1970 (amended 1988)** requires that women must be paid equally with men if:

- they do the same job
- their jobs are rated as equivalent (in terms of pay structures and job grades)
- their work is of equal value.

Under the Act, it is also illegal for an employer to treat women less fairly than men in terms of holidays, pensions and sick pay. These issues are covered in Northern Ireland by the **Equal Pay Act (NI) 1970 (amended 1988)**.

Whilst both the Sex Discrimination and Equal Pay Acts may be considered landmark legislation for women's rights, the statistical evidence suggests that discrimination continues in employment (where women are much more likely to accept part-time work), pay and education.

Customer and consumer legislation

Customers and consumers who buy goods and services are protected by a range of laws. These give consumers rights and state standards they can expect, including goods and services which:

- match their description (if the label says 100% cotton, the garment should be 100% cotton)
- are not faulty
- are not dangerous (unsafe)
- are fit for use.

Laws have been developed to ensure good quality in products and to deal with disputes between suppliers and consumers. There are three main Acts covering these areas.

- **The Sale of Goods Act 1979** – which states that goods must:
  – match the description given of them
  – be fit to be sold
  – be fit for the purpose for which they are bought (be able to be used in the way expected).

- **The Consumer Protection Act 1987** – which states that it is a criminal offence for a trader to sell unsafe goods. A consumer who is injured by an unsafe product is able to sue the manufacturer of the product for compensation.
- **The Trades Descriptions Act 1968** – which made manufacturers, retailers and advertising agencies responsible for the truth in the way they describe goods and services in advertisements and labels.

By law, consumers who are sold faulty goods are entitled to:
- a good replacement, or
- a free repair and a replacement while the repair is being done, or
- a refund.

Civil law deals with disputes between individuals. When a consumer and a supplier make an oral or written agreement, it is called a **contract of sale**. If the terms of the contract are broken by either side – for example, if the buyer does not pay for items or the seller does not deliver goods or they are faulty – legal action can be taken.

Index

Note: entries followed by the symbol* indicate a cross-reference button

ability to buy 106-7
ACAS (Advisory Conciliation and Arbitration Service) 158, 160*
    accessibility, and customer service 202
account number 225
accounts 146*, 232
    balance sheet 234-5
    statements of 146*, 198*, 222-3, 224*
    trading and profit and loss account 234
    see also bank statements
action plans 5, 7
activities vii
Acts of Parliament 256
addresses
    formal letters 15
    useful 254
administration, changes in 147
administration department, provides office support 146-7
administrative assistants 138
advertisements 110, 142, 149, 187-8
    cost 193-4, 205
    design 191-2, 205
    placing of 192-3, 205
    see also job advertisements
advertising 110*, 190
    and consumer demand 107
    free 148
    misleading 189
    targeting of 181
advertising campaigns 185
Advertising Standards Authority 189
advice notes 219
after-sales service 111, 147
age, and buying habits 181
alphabetical filing 243
AL's mobile phones
    departmental structure 144-9
    job roles 136-9
    organisational structure 139-42
    working arrangements 149-52
annual sales turnover 81
area 39-40
articles of association 85
assessment
    outcome flow chart 6-7
    preparing portfolios 6
    unit tests 8
assets 234-5
assignments viii
    alternative approaches 5
    plan, monitor, evaluate 5-6
    see also research; work (study), management of
audio/video recordings 4

automation, production lines 152
balance owing 223
bank sort code 225
bank statements 231, 247
Banking Automated Clearing Services (BACS) 227-8
bar charts 44, 60, 81*, 114*, 185*
    choice of scale 45
    composite 47-9
    drawing and reading 46-7
Barnaby's new department store, case study 97-9
batch production 145
body language 9
brainstorming 9, 14, 124
British Standards Institution (BSI) 100
budgets 235
business activities, to improve market position 109-11
business communications 198-9, 206*, 236
business contacts 4
business documents 215, 236-40
    storage of 243-4
    ways of processing 240-1
    ways of sending 242
business environment 77, 130*
    affecting businesses 100-1
business language, command of 6
business links 77, 93
business location 77, 93, 130*
    important factors 94-9
business objectives 153-4
business organisations 129*
    local 2, 90, 129
    maintaining ethical standards 196
    operation of 92-3
    ownership of 83-8, 162*
    purposes/types of 77, 78-92, 93*, 111*
    small, medium and large 81-3
    structures and working arrangements 135, 136-52
business ownership, types of 93, 173*
business terms, personal glossary of 4, 6
business trends 93
businesses
    defining their markets 101-3
    purchases made by 217
buttons, cross-reference viii
buying, on credit 228
capital employed 81
capital (industrial) goods 108
careers officers 165
'carriage paid' 220, 247
case studies viii
choice of business location 97-9
    communication 199
    complaints procedures 200
    customer care 197-8

    customer service 201
    industrial decline 113
    market share 102
    privatisation 90
promotional campaign 190-4
questionnaires 195
secretarial work 162
self-employment 164
    service industries 113
    Sunday opening 13
technology and employment 112
working condition 126-7
    see also AL's mobile phones; Comp-U-Clic case study; Linda Penn's business (case study); San Clu hotel
cash 226
cash flow problems 235
casual employment 125
CD-ROMs, for information 2
census of employment 115
centralised working 147
chain of command 140, 141
Chamber of Commerce Report 128-9
Chambers of Commerce 166
charitable organisations 91, 173
charts 20, 59, 122*
    see also bar charts; pie charts
checking, cheques and cards 226
    checkout displays 186
cheque guarantee cards 225-6
cheques 225-6, 247
    cheque number 225
    cheque stub 225
children, as consumers 181
    chronological filing 243
circles, area/circumference of 40
Civic Centre, information from 2
civil law 259
clauses 22-3
co-operative retail and wholesale societies 87
co-operatives 87
college courses 94
colons 23
Commission of the European Communities 165 Commission for Racial Equality (CRE) 257
communication 9-24, 126
    see also business communication
community work
    see voluntary employment
Comp-U-Clic case study 129*
    advertising 110
    Chamber of Commerce Report 128-9A
    market share 102-3, 108
    markets, products and customers 108
    Mud Monsters (shareware) 105
    operation of 92-3, 129
    the payroll 125, 131*

    a small business 81, 82
    Steve's budget 111
Companies House 82, 85
company logos 236
competition 95, 152
    and privatisation 90
competitions 188, 190
    design of 194
complaints procedures 147, 160, 196*, 206*
computer services department 147
computers
    backing up information 244
    computer networks 242
    for work presentation 4
conservationists 101
consumables 107
consumer demand 107*, 184
    and customer demand 107, 108*, 179*
    trends in 146*, 182-3, 185, 204*
consumer goods 79, 108
Consumer Protection Act (1987) 100, 189, 200, 259
consumers 107
    buying habits of 180-2
    effects on sales of goods and services 179-82
    importance of 177, 178-86, 204*
    individual 108
    see also customers
consumers and customers, what do you know 204A
contract of sale 259
contracts (of employment) 151, 154, 170
    termination of see dismissal
conversion 37
    factors 41
    graphs 42
    tables 41-2
copy invoices 233
core hours 150
core skills 1, 4, 6, 7, 13
core skills coverage grid 252-3
cost of living 184
costs, and consumer demand 184
couriers 148, 242
credit cards 227
credit control 146*, 216-17, 228
    see also budgets
credit notes 221, 224*, 247
crossed cheques 225
cultural factors, and employment 124
customer charters 198
customer comments cards 195, 201*
customer databases 243
customer information 198
customer loyalty 200
customer satisfaction 201-2
customer service 89-90, 147*, 177, 197-8

260

Index

getting it right 89
improvements to 177, 200-2, 208*
provision of 195-200
see also customers, needs and wants
customer service department 147
customer services assistant 142
customers 101-3, 107
access to 95
complaints see complaints procedures
external and internal 198
importance of 177, 178-86, 204*
needs and wants 90*, 105-9, 107*, 144*, 179*, 184, 185, 195-7
and products 107-8
satisfied 90
Customs and Excise see HM Customs and Excise
cylinder, volume of 40
databases 59
deadlines 4
debit cards 227
decentralised working 147
decimal places, rounding of 27-9
decision-making process 140, 142
deductions 154
statutory 229
see also pay slips
'Deed of Partnership' 84
delegation 142
delivery notes 219*, 222, 224*, 246
demand 179-80
causes of change in 184-5
defined 103
extension/contraction of 106
and marketing 103-9
denominations (coins, notes) 230
Department of the Environment 101
Department of Trade and Industry 101
departments, within organisations 144-9, 170
design(s) 109, 131
new, development of 144
desk research 109
diagrams/illustrations/photographs 4
dismissal 149
direct credit 228
direct debit 227
direct mail 110, 188
disagreements, resolution of 159-61, 172*
discipline 157
see also legal representation
discrimination 159
discussions
listening during 9-10
preparation for 9
your contribution 10
dismissal 149*, 157
disposable income 184
distribution department 148
dividends 85, 87
documents
completion of 246-8A
for organising a sales conference 249, 251

paper v computer 244
safety and security of 244
Dodd Engineering, a medium-sized business 81
durables 107
E & EO (errors and omissions excepted) 220
e-mail (electronic mail) 242
earnings 184
see also pay
Economic Development Units 2
economic factors, and employment 124
economically active people 115
effective demand 106
efficiency
improved 112
and technology 152
EFTPOS (Electronic Funds Transfer at Point of Sale) 227
emergency procedures 138-9
employees 81
full-time and part-time 151
skilled and unskilled 125
employer/employee co-operation 153, 172*
employers, private and public sector 163
employment 77, 114
analysis of information 112-27
by industrial sector 80, 114, 122
census of 115
decline in 119
full-time and part-time 125
information sources 165, 173*
investigation of 111-12
primary sector 78
secondary sector 79
and technology 112
tertiary sector 79
trends in 80*, 81, 111-12, 113-23
types of 125, 131, 135, 162-4, 162-9
employment agencies, local 165
employment booklet 171-2A
employment opportunities 164-7, 173*
employment rights 154
employment statistics, Ile de France and West Midlands 121
environmental care 202
environmental considerations 130
environmental influences, and the business environment 100-1
Environment, the, Department of 101
equal opportunities 136*, 156*, 171, 172*
Equal Opportunities Commission 258
Equal Pay Act 1970 (amended 1988) 156, 258
Equal Pay Act (NI) 1970 (amended 1988) 258
error/fault log 63
European Court of Justice 158, 160*
European Union incentives 96
fact files 127
Ile de France 120
West Midlands 119

Fair Employment Act (NI) 258
fashion, and demand 179, 182
faulty goods 259
fax machines 242
Federation of Self-Employed 166
field research 109
filing, of documents 243-4
final warnings 157
finance department 146
financial documents, exploration of 245A
financial records 216
financial transactions
and documents 215, 216-36
and security 232-6
'5-barred gate' tallying 57
fixed-term contracts 151
flat structures 142-3, 170
flexible working (flexitime) 149-50
flip charts 11
float 226
forecasting 235
formats, outline and pre-set 13
fractions 29-30, 32, 33
decimal 30
franchises 86-7, 164
gender
and buying habits 181
and employment 115, 116, 117, 118
geographical locational factors see locational factors
GNVQ business, general skills for 1-8, 168*
goods 108
goods received note see delivery note
goods and services, sales affected by consumers 179-82
government grants 124
government incentives 96
government subsidy 90
grammar 16, 238
and punctuation 22-4
Granada Group PLC 82
case study 102
a large business 81
grants see incentives
graphic design companies 192
graphs 20*, 59, 103*, 117*, 122*
and charts, drawing of 4*, 44-54
conversion 42
produced by computer 60-1
showing demand 106
Green Papers 256
gross profit 88
Guidance (to legislation) 256
Hatton Garden, London, and competition 95
headed paper 16
health and safety 110*, 147*, 149*, 155-6, 172*
Health and Safety at Work Act (1974) 100, 155*, 200, 257
hierarchical structures 139-41, 170
historical factors, and employment 124
HM Customs and Excise 216, 232*
assessing VAT 234

house style 236, 237, 238
human resources department 136*, 148-9
human resources manager 136-7, 142, 149, 153, 171
Ile de France 120, 121
images, use and placement of 4*, 24
Imperial System 36, 37
incentives 95*, 96, 124*
see also subsidies
income, and demand 179, 182, 184
income tax 228, 248
through PAYE 154
industrial factors, and employment 124
industrial sectors 111*, 117*, 129*
developments in 78-81, 162*
employment in 80, 114, 122
see also primary, secondary and tertiary sectors industrial
services 108
Industrial Tribunals 158, 160*
industries
primary 78
secondary 79
information
card index 8
collection 3-4
identifying needs 5
presentation 4
see also graphs; images; presentations; reports
information sources 2, 3, 163, 164, 165, 173, 204
identification and use of 5
information technology (IT)
errors and faults 63
growth of 126
safety and security 63
use of 59-62
see also computers
Inland Revenue 216, 232*
assessing tax 234
see also income tax
'inside an organisation' 170-1A
insurance, by employers 147
interest 227
calculation of 228
invitations 238-9, 251
production of 239
invoice number 220, 246
invoices 220, 222, 224*, 233, 247
processing 146
job advertisements 128, 131
national newspapers 163
Job Centres 2, 142, 165
job gains 111
job losses 81
primary sector 78
reasons for 111
secondary sector 79
job opportunities see employment opportunities
job production 145
job roles 135, 136-9, 140-1, 171*
'just the job' 172-3A
kitemarks 100
labour force, France and UK 122

261

Index

labour supply 94
large businesses 81, 82
leaflets 186
legal positions 161
legal representation 158
legislation 106*, 130, 161*, 172*, 189*, 200*, 256-9
    and the business environment 100
    customer and consumer 100, 189, 200, 206, 258-9
    health and safety at work 100*, 155, 200, 257
    non-discriminatory 156, 257-8
    and promotional materials 189
letterheads 16
letters (formal) 15-16, 198*, 237-8, 251
liabilities 234-5
liability, limited and unlimited 84
librarians, for information 2
'lifelong learning' 169
lifestyle, and buying habits 181
limited liability 84
Linda Penn's business (case study) 84
    aromatherapy resources 95
    calculating the profit 89
    a co-operative? 87
    franchise? 87
    market share 89
    partnership? 84
    private limited company? 85
living habits, changes in 183
loans 96
local government incentives 96
locational factors 94-9, 124
logistics companies 148
long-term trends 183
McDonald's
    communication 199
    complaints procedure 200
    customer care 197-8
    customer comments cards 195, 201
    customer service 201
    purchasing 146
magazines 2
    and advertising 187, 193-4
managing director 136, 142
Mander Centre see Wolverhampton
manufacturers, meeting consumer demand 180 'In the market' 130-1A
market share 81*, 89*, 102-3, 108*
    marketing 181
    and demand 103-9
marketing communications 109, 110, 130*
marketing department see sales and marketing department
marketing research 103*, 109, 146*, 182, 195
marketing research companies, independent research 200-1
marketing staff 146
markets 77, 101-3, 130*
mass/flow production 145
matched funding 96

matrix structures 143, 144, 170
mean 56-7, 81*, 105*, 114*
mean, mode and range 20*, 56-8
measure 36-8
    conversion of 42
    estimation of 38, 250*
medium-sized businesses 81, 82
meetings 18, 19
memo forms (headed) 17
    house style 237
memoranda (memos) 17, 137, 161*, 198*, 237
    in assignments 204*, 208*, 249*, 251*
memorandum of association 85
message pads, pre-printed 239-40
messages 239-40
Metric System 36-7, 40*
mind maps 14
minutes, of meetings 18
misconduct 157
mnemonics, use of 8
mode 57
money, rounding of 27, 29
money management 214
Mud Monsters (case study) 105
National Insurance (NI) 125, 154, 228, 248
national insurance number 229
nationalised (state-owned) industries 83
natural resources 94, 124*
negative numbers 43
net profit 88
newspapers 2
    advertising 187, 193-4
    national and local 165
noise pollution 100
non-routine tasks 138, 171*
Northern Ireland, legislation in 256-7, 258
notes
    linear and patterned 13-14
    for meetings 19
notices 238-9
number and information technology, application of 25-58, 209-11
    numerical files 243
occupational skills 168-9, 174
opportunity cost 107
oral communication 198, 199, 206
order number 218, 219
Orders in Council (Northern Ireland) 256-7
order(s) received 218*, 221
organisational charts 140, 142, 143, 144*, 170, 171
organisational structure 139-43, 170*
outstanding balance 223
overhead projector 12
overhead transparencies 11
overheads 84, 93, 98
paid employment 162, 165, 172
paper
    headed 16
    sizes of 38
Parcel Force 242
partnerships 84, 164, 216

passwords 63, 244
pay, gross and net 228, 229
pay slips (pay advice) 146*, 154*, 228-9, 248
PAYE (Pay As You Earn) 229
paying-in slips 230-1, 247
payment documents 245*
    and methods 224-9
peer group pressure 181
pension schemes 154-5
percentages 20*, 29-36, 82*, 105*, 117*, 122*, 185*
    describing situations 31-3
    VAT and discount 30-1
perimeter 39-40
personnel manager see human resources manager petty cash 146*, 224-5
petty cash vouchers 225, 247
photocopiers 240, 241
phrases 22-3
pictograms (pictographs) 44, 49-50
π, use of 39
pie charts 44, 103*, 173*, 248*
    drawing 53-4
    reading 51
    use of 54
    working out the angles 51-3
point-of-sale promotions 186
political factors, and employment 124
pollution 100-1
portfolios 6
postal services 242
posters 186, 187, 251
presentations 4*, 131, 171*, 205*, 208*, 211
    get your message across 12
    preparations 11-12, 130*
pressure groups 101
price 103, 106
    pricing and demand 180
primary sector 78, 80
printing, professional 240, 241, 251
private limited companies (Ltd) 85
Private Members Bills 256
private pension plans 154
private sector 83, 162, 173
privatisation 83, 90
probability 55, 173*
producer goods 79
production 103*, 110
production department 145
production lines 145
    automation of 152
production manager 153
production operatives 137-8
productivity 152
products 77, 93
    and customers 107-8
    exchange of 197
    information 198, 199
professional updating 169
profit 88-9
    gross and net 234
progress monitoring 6, 7
promotional materials 110*, 177, 186-95

    constraints on 189, 205*
    evaluating success of 194-5
    planning, design and production 152*, 190-5, 205
promotions 103*, 110, 146*, 205
    evaluation of 195
    new 205
    type of 186-9, 205*
protractors, use of 53
public corporations 83
public influence 101, 130
public limited companies (PLC) 85-6, 136*
public sector 83, 90*, 162, 173
public services 83, 90
publicity 189
punctuation and grammar
    colon or semi-colon 23-4
    phrase or clause 22-3
    sentences 22
purchase documents 217-21, 245*
    purchase invoices 220
purchase orders 218-19, 220, 246
purchasing department, responsibilities 145-6
quality assurance 145*, 152
quality control 145
questionnaires 2*, 20-1, 82*, 195*, 208*
Race Relations Act (1976) 156*, 257-8
Rackets & Runners, use of business documents 214-44
radio advertising 187
radio/television programmes 2
range 58, 81*
ratios 33-6, 250*
    use of 35-6
    writing 33-4
raw materials 110
receipt documents 229-31, 245*
receipts 229-30, 247
reception area, improvement of 208-11
recession, and consumer demand 184
recruitment 137*, 142, 149
    and non-discrimination 156
recruitment officer 142
redeployment 112
redundancy 112
reference number, formal letters 15
refunds 147, 197
regional development agencies 96
regional differences, and marketing 182 registered charities 91
Regulations 256
remittance advice slip 222-3, 247
    remuneration 154-5
    see also pay slips
reports 4*, 19-20, 127, 129*, 130*, 208*, 210-11
    drafts 20
    statistical 20, 208
    visual material for 61, 62
research 1-3, 5*, 80*, 129
    for discussions 9
    research in action 131A
    see also marketing research

Index

research and development (R&D) department 144
research diaries 3, 4
resource folders 3, 4
responsibilities and rights, employer/employee 135, 148*, 153-8, 171 retirement, early 112
rounding 25-9, 114*
    decimal places 27-9
    money 27, 29
    short cuts for 26
routine tasks 138, 171*
safety 63
    equipment 155-6
    notices 198, 199
    standards see legislation
Sale of Goods Act (1979) 189, 200, 258
sales
    and after-sales service 103*, 111, 147*
    literature 110
    staff 146
sales conference, organisation of 249-51
sales documents 221-4, 245*
    completion of 223-4
    sales invoices 220*, 222
    and the sales (purchase) day book 233
sales and marketing department 141, 144*, 146
sales representatives 111
San Clu Hotel 170
    organisational structure 142-3
    shift working 150
scattergrams 14
scrapbooks 3
secondary sector 78-9, 80
security 149
    and financial transactions 232-6
    for IT work 63
self-employment 125, 135, 164, 172
    considerations 166
semi-colons 23-4
sentences 22
service industries 79
services, customer and industrial 108
Sex Discrimination Act (1975) 157*, 160*, 258
Sex Discrimination (NI) Order (1976) 258
shape 39-40
shareholders
    private limited companies 85
    public limited companies 85-6
shift work 150
shipyard closures, effects of 113
short-term trends 183
Shrewsbury, a location option 98
sickness 149
skills
for GNVQ Business 1-8, 168*
    identification, improvement and development 167-8
    'Your Skills' 174
sleeping partners 84
small businesses 81, 82, 164

software
    for accounting 236
    shareware (Mud Monsters) 105
    spreadsheets 59-61, 235
    word processing packages 241
sole traders 83-4
span of control 140, 141
special needs 196, 197
special offers 186
spelling 16, 238
spidergrams 14
sponsorship 110, 188, 190
spray charts 14
spreadsheets 59-61, 235
staff development 155
staff welfare 149
staffing ratio 170
standards authorities 189
state-owned organisations 88
statements of accounts 146*, 198*, 222-3, 224*
Statutory Instruments 256
stock market, and share performance 86
subject filing 243
subsidies 90
Sunday opening 13
superannuation 149
supervisor 137
supply and demand 180
support staff 138-9
surveys
    chocolate bars and fizzy drinks 104
    see also questionnaires
take home pay 248
talks see presentations
tally charts 57, 58
target advertising 191
target groups 191
target marketing 181
tax code 229
tax point 220
taxation
provides income for public services 90
see also income tax; Inland Revenue
team working 135, 143-4, 170*
technology 152, 170
    and change 169
    and employment 112, 152*
    increase in 111
    new, consumer demand for 185
    see also information technology (IT)
tele-sales 110
telephones, use of 10-11, 198*
temperature, using negative numbers 43 terms 220
tertiary sector 79, 80, 107*, 112*
    employment growth 113
    Ile de France 122
The Thomson Local Directory 163, 164
tills, computerised 229
totals, and composite bar charts 48-9
Trade and Industry, Department of 101
Trade Union Reform and Employment Act (1993) 154

trade unions, role of 159, 160
Trades Description Act (1968) 189, 200, 259
Trading Standards Office 189
Trading Standards Officer 189
traditional industries, decline in 112
training 112, 149, 155, 169
Training and Enterprise Councils (TECs) 83, 166
training schemes 117
transferable skills 168
transport services 95-6, 97, 98, 119, 130
    Ile de France 120
    West Midlands 119
transportation network 148
travel agency
    improvements 207-8
    setting up 206-7
The Traveller's Survival Kit 165
unemployment 112, 114, 118
    and demand 179
    Ile de France 120
    West Midlands 119
unit tests, approaches to 8
unlimited liability 84
value for money 181
VAT 234
    and discount 30-1
verbal warnings 157
visual material 11
vocabulary 16
volume 39-40
voluntary employment 163, 167, 172, 173
voluntary organisations 163
wage slips see pay slips
wages
    low 79
    see also remuneration
'watchdogs' 88, 90
West Midlands
    employment statistics 121
    fact file 119
    see also Wolverhampton
White Papers 256
Wolverhampton 122*
    analysis of employment 117
    employment statistics 115-17
    a location option 97-8, 99
word processing 20, 240
word processing packages 241
work (study)
    evaluation 5, 7
    management of 4-5
workbases (working environments) 151
worker (producer) co-operatives 87
workers see employees
workforce 114
    flexible 169
working arrangements 149-51, 170*
    reasons for change 151-2, 170*
working conditions 126-7
working from home 151
Working Holidays 165
written material 12, 206
    formal letters 15-16

making notes 13-15
memoranda (memos) 17
minutes of meetings 18
notes of meetings 19
punctuation and grammar 22-4
questionnaires 20-1
    reports 19-20
written warnings 157
Youth Training (YT) 125

Acknowledgements

Illustrations and other printed matter

The authors and publishers are grateful to the following for permission to reproduce copyright material. If any acknowledgement has been omitted, the omission will be rectified at the earliest opportunity.

Table 1.1 on page 80 and Table 1.3 on page 114 are taken from *The Monthly Digest* magazine published by HMSO. Crown copyright material is reproduced by permission of the controller of HMSO

The illustration on page 83 contains corporate logos which are reproduced by kind permission of British Airways plc, British Steel plc, British Telecommunications plc, Network SouthCentral Ltd and the Post Office.

The illustration on page 86 (bottom) contains corporate logos which are reproduced by kind permission of the Communications Department, MacDonald's Restaurants Ltd; the British School of Motoring; Tie Rack plc; Pizza Hut (UK) Ltd.

The Mander Centre plan on page 99 appears by kind permission of Graham Evans, Centre Manager.

The advert on page 110 appears by kind permission of The Coca-Cola Company ('Coca-Cola', 'Coke' and 'Sprite' are registered trade marks of The Coca-Cola Company. 'Obey Your Thirst' is a trade mark of The Coca-Cola Company. This image is reproduced with kind permission from The Coca-Cola Company.)

The kitemarks which appear in the artwork on page 100 are © The British Standards Institution.

Tables 1.6 to 1.10 are partially based on information in *Portrait of the Regions*, published by Eurostat.

Tables 1.4, 1.5 and 1.9 are partially based on information in the Annual Abstract of Statistics, Social Trends, published by HMSO. Crown copyright material is reproduced by permission of the Controller of HMSO.

The illustration on page 193 is reproduced from the Wimbledon, Mitcham and Morden Guardian: individual advertisements appear by permission of Railtrack South West, Ionics (UK) Limited, Gallup Market Research, Avro plc, Balmoral Group Ltd, Merton, Sutton & Wandsworth Health and Home from Hospital Ltd

The Visa card design and Delta card design on page 227 are reproduced by permission of Visa International.

The illustration on page 236 contains corporate logos which are reproduced by kind permission of Abbey National plc, Interflora (the Interflora roundel is owned by FTD Incorporated and Interflora [FTDA] British Unit Ltd, Sleaford Lincolnshire is a registered user), Oxfam, C&A and the Royal Automobile Club.

Photographs

Allsport: page 188
Graham Evans, Centre Manager, The Mander Centre: page 97
Len Cross: pages 6, 51, 164, 165, 223
Federation of Bakers: page 34
Robert Greshoff: page 76 (right)
Image Bank: pages 35, 98, 145, 176 (top left), 200
Images Photo Library: page 78, 81 (reproduced by permission of Granada), 86, 152
John Lewis plc: page 134 (bottom left)
MacDonald's plc: pages 176 (top right), 197, 201
Andrew Ross Photography: pages 3, 9, 10, 12, 134 (centre right and bottom right), 136 (all), 137, 138, 147, 176 (bottom left, bottom right), 186, 214 (all), 216, 241
Stockphotos: page 76 (left and centre)
David Thomas: pages 125, 127 (lower)